TURKEY'S ENGAGEMENT WITH GLOBAL
WOMEN'S HUMAN RIGHTS

Gender in a Global/Local World

Series Editors: Jane Parpart, Pauline Gardiner Barber
and Marianne H. Marchand

Gender in a Global/Local World critically explores the uneven and often contradictory ways in which global processes and local identities come together. Much has been and is being written about globalization and responses to it but rarely from a critical, historical, gendered perspective. Yet, these processes are profoundly gendered albeit in different ways in particular contexts and times. The changes in social, cultural, economic and political institutions and practices alter the conditions under which women and men make and remake their lives. New spaces have been created – economic, political, social – and previously silent voices are being heard. North-South dichotomies are being undermined as increasing numbers of people and communities are exposed to international processes through migration, travel, and communication, even as marginalization and poverty intensify for many in all parts of the world. The series features monographs and collections which explore the tensions in a 'global/local world', and includes contributions from all disciplines in recognition that no single approach can capture these complex processes.

Also in the series

Un(thinking) Citizenship
Feminist Debates in Contemporary South Africa
Edited by Amanda Gouws
ISBN 0 7546 3878 2

Vulnerable Bodies
Gender, the UN and the Global Refugee Crisis
Erin K. Baines
ISBN 0 7546 3734 4

Fashioning Inequality
The Multinational Company and Gendered
Employment in a Globalizing World
Juanita Elias
ISBN 0 7546 3698 4

Setting the Agenda for Global Peace
Conflict and Consensus Building
Anna C. Snyder
ISBN 0 7546 1933 8

Turkey's Engagement with Global Women's Human Rights

NÜKET KARDAM

Monterey Institute of International Studies, USA

Routledge
Taylor & Francis Group
LONDON AND NEW YORK

First published 2005 by Ashgate Publishing

Reissued 2018 by Routledge
2 Park Square, Milton Park, Abingdon, Oxon OX14 4RN
605 Third Avenue, New York, NY 10017

First issued in paperback 2021

Routledge is an imprint of the Taylor & Francis Group, an informa business

© Nüket Kardam 2005

A Library of Congress record exists under LC control number: 2004028586

Notice:
Product or corporate names may be trademarks or registered trademarks, and are used only for identification and explanation without intent to infringe.

Publisher's Note
The publisher has gone to great lengths to ensure the quality of this reprint but points out that some imperfections in the original copies may be apparent.

Disclaimer
The publisher has made every effort to trace copyright holders and welcomes correspondence from those they have been unable to contact.

ISBN 13: 978-0-815-39869-1 (hbk)
ISBN 13: 978-1-351-14388-2 (ebk)
ISBN 13: 978-1-138-35784-6 (pbk)

DOI: 10.4324/9781351143882

Contents

Series Editors' Preface   *vii*
List of Abbreviations   *ix*
Acknowledgements   *xi*

Introduction   1

1   The Emergence of a Global Women's Human Rights Regime and
Turkey's Involvement   7

2   Gender Norms in Turkey: Construction and Contestation   30

3   Institutionalization of Women's Human Rights   56

4   Empowerment Through Training   82

5   Violence Against Women   108

6   Women's Participation in Local Governance   136

Conclusions   163

Bibliography   *172*
Index   *186*

Series Editors' Preface

This series critically engages debates on globalization through focusing upon gendered processes and identities at the intersections of global and local sites. *Turkey's Engagement with Global Women's Human Rights*, by Nüket Kardam, continues the series' preoccupation with the global/national/local nexus by exploring the intersection between global women's human rights norms and the Turkish context. Much has been written about the rise of women's networks around the world and their influence in shaping global women's human rights norms. Indeed, the terms 'gender', 'gender mainstreaming', 'women's empowerment' or 'women's human rights' litter development discourse. Kardam first asks whether these developments signify a new international regime or a system of global governance in the area of women's human rights and gender equality. The evidence suggests that a gender equality regime has indeed emerged, albeit with weak monitoring systems and ongoing debates over meanings. However, we still do not know enough about the impact of this regime in local contexts and how meaningful it has been for women around the world.

Kardam explores this question in Turkish society, a particularly interesting case because of its history of modernization and its division between secular and Islamist women's groups and ideologies. Using a constructivist approach, she explores the intersection between global women's human rights norms and the complex and fragmented local gender regimes in Turkey. The Western and Islamic world views, value systems and gender identities at first glance appear radically different. In the Western value system, women's individual rights are upheld in a secular democracy as individual citizens, while in the Islamic viewpoint, women and men derive their rights from God, and as members of a community (*umma*), they have separate but complementary responsibilities and rights. This would seem to be an either/or situation – a true dichotomy. However, Kardam discovers a much more fluid and interactive reality on the ground. These supposed dualisms are not locked in implacable opposition, but rather are engaged in a dynamic exchange. Indeed, they are breaking down and the opportunity for increased dialogue among women is visible. Secularist and Islamist women in Turkey have begun to learn from each other and started adopting each other's strategies and terms.

Kardam's research thus throws doubt on the uncritical acceptance of supposedly inevitable dualisms between secularism/Westernism and Islam, and suggests that the now often cited *Clash of Civilizations* by Samuel Huntington needs to be fundamentally challenged before it becomes a self-fulfilling prophecy. Indeed many of the social tensions, but also opportunities, for dialogue are to be found within civilizations rather than between them. The task of finding solutions to these supposed dualisms and oppositions involves, therefore, acknowledging the critical importance of examining global change in local as well as global contexts.

List of Abbreviations

AÇEV	Mother and Child Education Foundation
AKDER	Ayrımcılığa Karşı Kadın Hakları Derneği
AKP	Justice and Development Party
ANAP	Anavatan Partisi (Motherland Party)
ÇATOM	Multipurpose Community Centers
CDF	Comprehensive Development Framework
CEDAW	The Convention on the Elimination of Discrimination Against Women
CHP	Cumhuriyet Halk Partisi (Republican People's Party)
CSW	The Commission on the Status of Women
DGWSP	The Directorate General of Women's Status and Problems
DPT	Devlet Planlama Teşkilatı/ State Planning Organization
DYP	Dogruyol Partisi (True Path Party)
ECLAC	Economic Commission on Latin America and the Caribbean
ECOSOC	UN Economic and Social Council
EU	European Union
GAP	Güneydoğu Anadolu Projesi (Southeast Anatolia Project)
GNA	Grand National Assembly
ICC	International Criminal Court
ICRW	International Center for Research on Women
ILO	International Labor Organization
INSTRAW	International Research and Training Institute for the Advancement of Women
IULA-EMME	International Union of Local Administrations – Eastern Mediterranean and the Middle East
IWHC	International Women's Health Coalition
KA-DER	Association to Support Women Candidates in Politics
KA-MER	Kadın Merkezi (The Women's Center)
KASAUM	Women's Center at Ankara University
KEDV	The Foundation to Support Women's Economic Work
LACAP	Project for Leader Women
NGOs	Non-governmental organizations
NWM	National Women's Machinery
OAS	The Organization of American States
PfA	Platform for Action
RP	Welfare Party
SEWA	Self Employed Women's Association
SHCEK	Department of Social Services and the Protection of Children

SHP	Sosyal Demokrat Halkçı Parti (The Social Democratic Populist Party)
SSP	Self-Education Process
UN	United Nations
UNDAW	UN Division for the Advancement of Women
UNDP	The United Nations Development Programme
UNICEF	The United Nations Children's Fund
UNIFEM	UN Development Fund for Women
WALD	World Academy of Local Governance and Democracy
WEDO	Women's Environment and Development Organization
WID	Women in Development
WWHR	Women's Human Rights/New Ways

Acknowledgements

This book is both a personal and professional quest to understand Turkey and women in Turkey. As a woman born and raised in Turkey but living and working in the United States, this book fulfills wishes close to my heart. As a researcher and academic, I began with a focus on the global level, on international regimes and organizations, and how international development organizations responded to women's issues. When I was doing my dissertation research in the 1980s, there was very limited attention by international donors to women. In the last two decades, however, a 'global gender equality regime' has emerged and women's human rights have become an integral part of the international development discourse. But the question remains as to how this 'global discourse' is really received, changed or rejected at local levels. This question, as well as the desire to understand Turkey better prompted me to write this book.

I think that I am particularly fortunate because I can view Turkey from both inside and outside, so to speak. My background in international development studies, and many years spent outside of Turkey allow me a 'bird's eye view' that I would not have had otherwise. At the same time, having a home, family and friends in Turkey and spending several months of the year there means I can still be part of society and keep up with the momentous changes that are occurring. I did not know when I started this research that Turkey would become singularly important, a Muslim country on the verge of starting membership talks with the European Union, with a high level of economic growth and a stable democracy. At this juncture, Turkey's engagement with women's human rights acquires a special kind of urgency as that engagement demonstrates how Turkey will resolve or reshape the so-called dualisms between Islam and the West, between the private and the public, between individual and collective identities, and between individual rights and state control, and most visibly, between a secular and a religious state.

Such a book could not have been written without the involvement of many people and organizations, to whom I would like to express my gratitude. The initial research was supported by a Fulbright research grant, under the auspices of the Middle East Technical University in Ankara and a Mark Faculty Development grant administered by the Monterey Institute of International Studies, my home institution. I then served as a consultant to the UNDP office in Turkey on Gender and Governance. Later, Women for Women's Human Rights-New Ways based in Istanbul asked me to conduct an evaluation on their Women's Human Rights Education Program offered in Community Centers across Turkey in partnership with the Social Services Administration. This proved to be an invaluable experience. I also worked closely with another women's organization, Uçan Süpürge (Flying Broom) based in Ankara. All these institutions and my friends and colleagues who worked in them were tremendously helpful. I would also like to thank the Department of International Relations at Marmara University in Istanbul, to the World Academy for Local Democracy (WALD) in Istanbul, where I had the opportunity to present my research at conferences. I owe a great deal to my friends at all these organizations.

There are many individuals who have offered support, shared their own understanding and research with me, read and commented on draft chapters. There are three people who I owe special thanks to: Donald Crone, Büşra Ersanlı and Yannis Toussulis for being who they are. Other wonderful friends and colleagues I would like to mention here include Selma Acuner, Yıldız Ecevit, Yakın Ertürk, Halime Güner, Nur Mardin, Nur Otaran, and Ulviye Yalım-Fischer. My graduate assistant, Hülya Özönen did an excellent job of locating research materials, discussing the chapters with me and copy-editing. Filiz Kardam, the co-author of Chapter 4, and I have worked together since 1999 on various aspects of women's rights issues in Turkey. Filiz Kardam would like to thank Mother Child Education Foundation (ACEV), Ka-Mer and the Contemporary Women and Youth Foundation. We would both like to express our gratitude to the many women who took the time to talk to us throughout this project and answer our questions. I would like to thank Jane Parpart, who worked with me throughout the process as an Ashgate Gender in a Global/Local World series editor, as well as all other editors at Ashgate Publishers for their encouragement and patience. Finally, I owe the greatest gratitude to my family, my husband Donald Crone and to my children Maya Crone and Timur Kardam Crone. All shortcomings, of course, remain mine.

Introduction

Much has been written about the rise of women's networks around the world and their influence in shaping global women's human rights norms. These norms are now embodied international and regional conventions such as the Convention on the Elimination of Discrimination Against Women (CEDAW), the European Convention for the Protection of Human Rights and Fundamental Freedoms, the Inter-American Convention on the Prevention, Punishment, and Eradication of Violence against Women. Development assistance organizations incorporate such norms into their programs and projects in varying degrees. The governments that have ratified these conventions are obliged to abide by their stipulations, including setting up national mechanisms for the advancement of women. A new discourse has emerged so that international development organizations, governments and non-governmental organizations (NGOs) all use such terms as 'gender', 'gender mainstreaming', 'women's empowerment' or 'women's human rights' that were not so common before the 1990s. The United Nations Development Programme (UNDP) has spearheaded the development and dissemination of knowledge in this area; its 1995 Human Development Report focused on women's empowerment and gender equality (UNDP, 1995). A transnational network of multilateral and bilateral development agencies, NGOs, and women's organizations continue to define, debate and refine the terms of this discourse.

I begin by asking whether these developments signify a new international regime or a system of global governance in the area of women's human rights and gender equality.[1] Are there global principles and norms, legal instruments and monitoring mechanisms in place? Have states subscribed to this regime as demonstrated by their behavior? Is there now a 'shared understanding' on women's human rights among actors? The answers reveal that a gender equality regime has indeed emerged, despite weak monitoring systems and ongoing debates on meanings. What we still do not know much about is what difference this regime has made in local contexts, and how meaningful it is for the women around the world who are supposed to be benefiting from it. Meaningful here refers to the extent to which the norms developed at the international level are debated, challenged, refined, and applied in national and local contexts. We know that global conventions, platforms of action, or resolutions are sometimes purposefully kept vague and ambivalent in order to elicit agreement. But the interpretation and translation of what they mean and how they can be applied is left to others who often have had very little to do with the wording of such documents.

Unfortunately, there is still not much research on the engagement of societies with global women's human rights norms. I do not here mean the formal responses of governments alone. We do have knowledge through the work of the

United Nations that monitors governments' responses to CEDAW and the work of researchers on how specific governments have responded and how their national women's machineries fared.[2] But this usually does not move us beyond the level of political and bureaucratic responses, to the complexities of ongoing debates on the meanings and interpretation of gender equality and women's human rights. At the expense of oversimplification, I would argue that most of the answers we have so far either lament the political obstacles to implementing gender equality norms, or point to the barrier of cultural, religious or traditional values that discriminate against women.

In this book, a constructivist perspective is adopted to examine Turkey's engagement with global women's human rights norms because such a perspective allows us to examine how social norms are constructed, and how gender identities and norms are shaped, contested and negotiated within different institutions globally and locally.[3] Constructivism questions state interests, not just accepting them as preferences shaped by particular beliefs or knowledge but asking where they came from. The social construction of norms is examined and not accepted a priori. Every culture, institution, society or historical period constitutes and interprets sexual difference in a certain way. If that is the case, we should go beyond classifying all resistance to gender equality as stemming from culture, tradition or religion. Instead, we should examine where these norms come from and what types of power relations underlie them.

Turkey presents a significant and complicated case in which to explore these questions. Although it has embraced Western modernity, which has provided much of the discourse about human rights and women's human rights, Turkey still has complex and deeply entrenched traditional norms and practices that are at the heart of gender roles and relations. It is a secular democracy, but the party in power, the Justice and Development Party (AK Party) has Islamist roots. Yet, this is the party that has brought Turkey closest to potential membership in the European Union. Turkey's experience is also closely watched by other countries with significant Moslem populations.

Turkey subscribes to the principles of universal rights, equality and individual freedoms within which women's human rights are included. These values are embodied in the Copenhagen Criteria and in CEDAW, which promote women's equality with men in every sphere of life. How are these values understood in Turkey with its competing social and political norms, which are often perceived as potentially mutually exclusive? Are the values of human rights, equality and individual freedoms sacrificed when other priorities take over, such as protecting secularism or promoting national unity? How do individual rights and freedoms live comfortably with women's identities which are firmly anchored in the family and community? Individual rights and freedoms may be compromised when the definition of 'masculinity' includes the protection of family honor – meaning ensuring the chastity of the female members of the family. If ensuring chastity entails regulation and control of female sexual behavior, does not this contradict women's human rights? What is important to understand is *how* Turkey has chosen to engage with women's human rights norms. How is this engagement changing various groups and institutions within society? What are the new ways in which they interact with each other and with global institutions and norms?

This book examines this intersection between global women's human rights norms and the complex and fragmented local gender regimes that exist in Turkey. In today's world, a central debate has emerged on whether Islamic and Western civilizations and value systems stand in opposition to each other or whether there is the possibility of synthesis and of commonality. In this larger debate, gender relations and women's human rights assume an extraordinary importance, as signifiers of seemingly two opposing civilizations and world views.[4] The Western and Islamic world views, value systems and gender identities appear at first glance as radically different. In the Western world view, several values stand out as the most important ones: belief in human progress through greater rationality, belief in technological advancement, secular democracy and individual freedom. When we turn to Islamic values, the ones that are upheld include relatedness, honor, and social harmony. These differences have extremely important implications for gender relations and women's human rights. In the Western value system, women's individual rights are upheld in a secular democracy as individual citizens, while in the Islamic viewpoint, women and men derive their rights from God, and as members of a community (umma), they have separate but complementary responsibilities and rights. The mistake that is often made is to assume that these world views are in complete opposition to each other. The solutions offered are either a more widespread adoption of Western values *or* that of Islamic values. Such solutions reflect political positions, ignoring complex realities. In the Turkish case, there are and have always been ways in which Western and Islamic values systems have engaged with each other. Therefore, it is imperative that we first understand the historical context within which gender identities developed, interacting with Western norms starting from the Ottoman Empire in the nineteenth century and during the establishment of a secular Republic of Turkey. The dynamics of this engagement then and today needs to be explored in order to gain insights into the Turkish engagement with global women's human rights norms. Such an exploration may reveal that often assumed dualisms such as Western/secular versus Islamic values, individual versus collective identities, private versus public spheres, or top-down state control versus bottom-up participation do not correspond to the complex realities of Turkey today.

The recent legal reforms related to women's human rights are based on a view of women as individuals in their own right. Yet, values of relatedness, honor, and social harmony based on a notion of collective identity rather than individual liberty are still very much part of Turkish society and constitute the values of the majority of the Justice and Development Party's supporters. According to some observers, the most successful grassroots organization and political campaign was undertaken by Welfare Party (Refah Partisi) women in the mid-1990s, whose activities were legitimized and justified within Islamic values. But as they became politicized, they also became more aware of their individual rights as women. University students in hijab (Islamic dress) have filed lawsuits against their universities and schools (for not having been allowed to study) long before the

Strasbourg-based European Court of Human Rights brought international human rights norms to bear on their search for justice. The Justice and Development party proclaims Islamic values; yet, the government has included in its program the implementation of CEDAW principles in combating violence against women, women's poverty and economic exploitation, among others. The minister of foreign affairs, Abdullah Gül, who attended the Organization of the Islamic Conferences (OIC) meeting in May 2003, declared that the Islamic countries of the world must work to embrace and act with a renewed vision, adding that freedoms, basic rights and gender equality were among the vital issues to be addressed.[5] This is not to say that AK party government does not frequently find itself in a quandary of contradictions. Most recently, the government proposed a legislative bill to make adultery punishable by law, justified on the basis of protecting the family institution *and* greater gender equality! The strong negative responses from both the EU representatives, and Turkish women's rights advocates most likely led to the withdrawing of this bill. The complexity of the Turkish engagement and the need to enter into this query, with a fresh pair of glasses, withholding any prejudgments and avoiding a perspective of 'either/or', should be obvious from the few examples above.

Undoubtedly, the preparations to join the European Union have encouraged greater attention to gender equality in Turkey. The Council of Europe and the EU have both undertaken to abide by CEDAW and the Beijing Platform for Action principles. The fulfillment of the Copenhagen Criteria is a condition of membership and these criteria stipulate equal treatment of women and men in all spheres of life. As the country prepares for membership in the EU, changes are being made towards greater democratization and implementation of human rights. The new Civil Code acknowledged the equality of women and men in marriage, and stipulated equal division of property upon divorce. The new Penal Code is deemed to be revolutionary; it no longer provides lighter sentences for 'honor crimes' under the rubric of 'provocation'. It lifts the lighter sentences for rapists who marry their victims, but the recent legal reforms cannot only be attributed to external pressure from the EU. Before Turkey became a formal candidate to the EU, women's advocacy groups had already started drafting a new Civil Code in collaboration with the Directorate of Women's Status and Problems, the National Women's Machinery (NWM). This process accelerated after 1999, when Turkey became a formal candidate to the EU, but gender issues, especially violence against women and women's human rights, had been on the national agenda during the whole 1990s. For example, the women's human rights education programs implemented across the country are not Turkish responses to external incentives, but the result of women's NGOs and government agencies working together.[6] To be sure, the global attention to women's human rights and European Union's criteria for membership created a window of opportunity where the traditional gap between the Turkish state and society began to narrow. Women's human rights is an issue area that constitutes a important example of this greater openness and fluidity, and of an increasingly effective advocacy by women's civil society organizations to influence government policy. For example, one of the directors of the NWM was a former NGO leader active in the women's movement. Multiple identities were assumed by women who switched between being academics, bureaucrats, NGO leaders, or activists at one time or another. Turkish women's NGO representatives participated in government delegations at global forums and influenced norm development at those forums. In short, a diverse Turkish women's movement has arisen and became quite influential in agenda setting, policy-making (including legal reforms) and implementation processes. They have also engaged with transnational and regional networks and solicited their support for policy advocacy.

The Outline of the Book

Chapter 1 addresses the emergence of a global gender equality regime. What are the norms, rules, and monitoring mechanisms? Can we ascertain from state behavior that such a regime has emerged? Assuming that regimes can also be defined as new discourses, can we speak about a women's human rights regime? The evidence shows that such a regime has emerged. To what extent is Turkey engaged with this regime? In Chapter 2, I examine the Turkish historical, political and social contexts up until the 1990s to see how gender identities have been shaped in interaction with Western values and norms. Chapter 3 delves further into the limits and possibilities of international women's human rights norms as mechanisms for fundamental improvements on women's lives. It examines the extent of state accountability for gender equality, and the state and women's groups engagement with each other against the background of a global gender equality regime, and donor support to advance women's rights.

In the second half of the book, I continue to explore the above questions in terms of case studies, as I reflect on how three of the most important 'areas for action' to achieve gender equality and promote women's human rights – empowerment through education, eradicating violence against women, and their participation in local governance – fared in Turkey. This means examining, in all three areas, the global norms, their interpretation and implementation, the stakeholders (international organizations and donors of development assistance, government institutions, civil society organizations and groups) that are involved and their interests and values. These three issue areas are selected for two reasons. First, they represent vital areas in which women are discriminated against in Turkey.[7] Second, I have first hand experience in these areas based on field research, consultancies and program evaluations. Chapter 4 on women's empowerment education is co-authored with Filiz Kardam. She conducted field research on several of the organizations focused in this chapter. We have shared our ideas on women's empowerment education for several years and finally decided that it would be best to merge them in this chapter.

Throughout the book, the following questions are explored.[8] Have global material and discursive changes become opportunities for the introduction of new definitions, new interpretations for Turkish women as active agents? How can we identify and analyze global women's human rights, and opposing or complementary gender norms and identities in different historical and institutional contexts in Turkey? How do competing gender norms in institutions such as marriage, legal systems, politics and religion interact? How do gender relations or gender regime in one set of institutions affect the gender relations and regimes in other sets of institutions? Are there greater instances of dissonance, or opportunities for mutual understanding and change? Are there new avenues for the empowerment of women through defining and redefining gender norms in local contexts and through local activism?

Notes

[1] In this book, gender equality and women's human rights are used interchangeably because CEDAW is a document that deals with women's human rights in order to achieve equality between women and men, defined as non-discrimination on the basis of sex in all areas of life.

[2] UN Division for the Advancement of Women (UNDAW) tracks and analyzes information on government responses to international obligations regarding gender equality.

[3] See Chapter 2 for a more in-depth discussion of social constructivism and its application to the Turkish case.

[4] As defined by Bourdieu, 2001, a world view is a socially constructed system of cognitive and motivational structures.

[5] Milliyet, 29 May 2003.

[6] See Chapter 4 on empowerment programs for women.

[7] These three issues continue to be crucial for gender equality in Turkey. The female adult literacy rate is 88.4% in Turkey and it goes down to 67.8% in rural areas (UNICEF, 2003). There are different reports on the level of violence against women. A recent report by Amnesty International estimated that at least one third of Turkish women are victims of domestic violence in which they are 'hit, raped, and in some cases, killed or forced to commit suicide'. (BBC News, 'Spotlight on Turkish women's rights', 23 September 2004). Participation in local governance by women is very low. According to the 1999 local election results, 0.6% of elected municipality directors are women, and 1.6% of municipality council members are women. Ka-Der Brochure)

[8] These questions are also posed in Bayes and Kelly, 2000; Sassen, 1998.

Chapter 1

The Emergence of a Global Women's Human Rights Regime and Turkey's Involvement

Introduction

It is necessary to first assess whether a global gender equality regime exists and how it was established before exploring Turkey's engagement with it. How this regime was formed, and the extent of its implementation has important implications for Turkey's response to it. International regimes are important because they embody mutually accepted norms. Thus, a regime constitutes a high level of acceptance by states that is close to international law. Gender issues have recently emerged as a global concern but scholars to date have not asked whether there is a global gender equality regime and if so, how it is identifiable, how it has arisen and is being implemented. Since the early 1980s, there has been an unprecedented rise in the importance accorded to gender equality issues in international forums. There is now a growing international understanding that gender equality is a prerequisite to the achievement of human and sustainable development. Over the past quarter century, the UN has convened five world conferences on women's issues, 1975 in Mexico City, 1980 in Copenhagen, 1985 in Nairobi, 1995 in Beijing and 2000 in New York. Each has marked a different stage of a process that has raised gender equality to the center of the global agenda. These conferences have highlighted that women lag behind in virtually all aspects of life (such as education, health, literacy, access to income, and labor markets) and established Platforms of Action for promoting gender equality.[1] These conferences have also provided a platform for women's NGOs and global women's networks to lobby for a gender perspective to be included in development policies and strategies. They have generated cross-cutting coalitions from all classes and economic groups from North and South with an unprecedented and indisputable effect on changing awareness and programs for women in many countries (Chen, 1996). In the two decades between Mexico City and Beijing, the way women are viewed in the development struggle has changed. Gender equality is embodied in an international legal instrument, the Convention on the Elimination of Discrimination Against Women (CEDAW), which entered into force in 1981 and has been ratified by 178 countries – over 90 per cent of UN member states.[2] States have further established national women's machineries on gender issues (bureaucracies, departments, policies and programs) and some have changed laws and policies to follow up on global commitments. All of these developments point to the emergence of a regime.

The concept of regimes has been used to analyze global problems such as international financial exchanges, security and climate change (Krasner, 1983; Haas, 1990; Young, 1989 and 1991; Hansenclever et al, 1996). There is a wide literature on the factors that lead to regime formation, that affect regime maintenance and how regimes can be utilized to address global problems in the future.[3] Furthermore, the tensions and contradictions among normative principles in international life and how states are embedded in dense networks of transnational and international relations that shape their perceptions and their preferences are being explored by scholars. But surprisingly, even though there is an extensive literature on global women's networks and the role of the UN as an ally, gender issues have not systematically been explored from the perspective of international regimes. Thus, this chapter addresses the following questions: a) Does a gender equality regime exist and how is it identifiable? b) If so, what factors have led to its formation? c) How is it maintained? What are its strengths and weakness in terms of implementation? d) Is Turkey a party to this regime and has it complied with its stipulations?[4]

Does a Gender Equality Regime Exist? How is it Identifiable?

I suggest that one could examine the rise and maintenance of a gender equality regime in terms of both its legal instruments and compliance mechanisms, and its underlying normative principles, that is, the tensions and contradictions of gender equality as a normative principle that has begun to shape perceptions and preferences of states. Virtually all discussions of international regimes proceed from the 'consensus definition' first proposed by Stephen Krasner. According to Krasner, regimes are:

> implicit or explicit principles, norms, rules and decision-making procedures around which actors' expectations converge in a given area of international relations. Principles are beliefs of fact, causation and rectitude. Norms are standards of behavior defined in terms of rights and obligations. Rules are specific prescriptions or proscriptions for action. Decision-making procedures are prevailing practices for making and implementing collective choice. (Krasner, 1983, p. 2)

This definition is not without its critics. One of the criticisms involves the precise meaning of and relationship among the four regime components. What distinguishes principles, norms, or rules of a regime from each other? The other problem arises from the phrase 'around which actors' expectations converge' which is considered too vague to provide explicit criteria when regimes exist or when they do not. How can we know when a regime exists in a given issue area or when it does not? The three distinct positions on how regimes can be identified have emerged over time and these argue that regimes are best identified on the basis of formal, behavioral and cognitive criteria, respectively (Hansenclever et al, 1996). These three criteria are examined below to see if a gender equality regime can be identified.

The Formal Approach: Principles, Norms, Rules and Decision-Making Mechanisms

Keohane has proposed that regimes are agreements in purely formal terms, or explicit rules agreed upon by more than one state and embodied in treaties or other documents. Regimes arise when states recognize these agreements as having continuing validity. A set of rules need not be 'effective' to qualify as a regime but it must be recognized as continuing to exist (Hasenclever et al, 1996, pp. 180-83). Turning to gender equality issues, one can identify an international gender equality regime in the form of explicit rules that are agreed upon by states and embodied in treaties and other documents such as platforms of action. The *rules* are the legal instruments created to formalize and implement the principles and norms of an international regime. Rules are derived from principles and norms and are usually codified into international law; we can observe efforts to implement and enforce them. The 'rules' of international regimes such as those found in 'Conventions' and 'Covenants' are legally binding once adopted and ratified by the appropriate decision-making body of a state. There are a number of conventions regarding women's status that deal with the human rights of women, but the definitive legal instrument on gender equality is the Convention on the Elimination of Discrimination against Women (CEDAW). After being adopted unanimously by the General Assembly of the UN on 18 December 1979, it came into force in September 1981 after ratification by the twentieth state party. By September 2004, 178 states had ratified it. The other conventions include the Convention for the Suppression of the Traffic in Persons and the Exploitation of the Prostitution of Others; the Convention on the Nationality of Married Women; and the Convention on Consent to Marriage, Minimum Age for Marriage and Registration of Marriages. The International Labor Organization (ILO) predates the UN in setting standards for the specific protection of women in the workforce, concerning such matters as maternity protection (1919), night work (1919), employment in underground mines (1935), the Convention Concerning Equal Renumeration of Men and Women Workers for Work of Equal Value, and the Convention on the Prohibition of Discrimination in Employment and Occupation and Workers with Family Responsibilities (ILO, 1994). These conventions remain in effect among ratifying states, but their purpose in protecting women's legal rights equally with those of men is incorporated into CEDAW, which is also described as an international bill of rights for women. Sex discrimination is also prohibited in the regional human rights conventions, such as the European Convention for the Protection of Human Rights and Fundamental Freedoms, and the African Charter on Human and People's Rights. Finally, the Inter-American Convention on the Prevention, Punishment, and Eradication of Violence against Women (1994) is the first of its kind to define violence against women as a violation of women's human rights and identify the duties of states to address this endemic social problem. It defined violence against women as 'any act or conduct based on gender which causes death or physical, sexual, or psychological harm or suffering to women, whether in the public or private sphere'.[5]

These rules rest on a set of principles and norms and are accompanied by decision-making procedures, or monitoring mechanisms which oversee compliance. The basic *principles* that underpin the gender equality regime are the prohibition of all forms of discrimination against women, and the active promotion of equality between the sexes through women's empowerment. The active promotion of gender equality through women's empowerment goes beyond promotion of equality between genders towards an explicit recognition of unequal power relations between women and men. As Cook notes:

> In contrast to previous human rights treaties, the Women's Convention frames the legal norm of prohibition of all forms of discrimination against women as distinct from sexual nondiscrimination. That is, it develops the legal norm from a sex-neutral norm that requires equal treatment of men and women, usually measured by how men are treated, to recognize the fact that the particular nature of discrimination against women and their distinctive characteristics are worthy of a legal response. (Cook, 1997, p. 188)

For purposes of legal application and enforcement, CEDAW contains a legal definition of 'discrimination against women' in Article 1 of the Convention:

> The term 'discrimination against women' shall mean any distinction, exclusion, or restriction made on the basis of sex which has the effect of impairing or nullifying the recognition, enjoyment or exercise by women, irrespective of their marital status, on a basis of equality of men and women, of human rights and fundamental freedoms in the political, economic, social, cultural, civil or any other field. (Cook, 1997, p. 189)

How do we determine what constitutes 'discrimination against women'? Cook provides these two questions:

> Do the laws, policies, practices or other measures at issue make any distinction, exclusion or restriction on the basis of sex? If they do make such a distinction, exclusion or restriction, do they have the effect or purpose of impairing or nullifying the recognition, enjoyment or exercise by women, irrespective of their marital status, on a basis of equality of men and women, of human rights and fundamental freedoms? (Cook, 1997, p. 189)

The *norms* of a regime, on the other hand, define the rights and obligations of actors by establishing standards to overcome discrimination. The Nairobi Forward Looking Strategies and the 1995 Beijing Declaration and the Platform for Action both define the rights and obligations of governments and of international and regional organizations based on the principles of equality and non-discrimination. The Nairobi document was ground-breaking in the sense that it contained measures for achieving equality at the national level. Governments were to set their own priorities based on their development policies and resource capabilities. The Beijing Platform for Action aimed to accelerate the implementation of the Nairobi document and identified twelve critical areas for action: women and poverty; education and the training of women; women and health; violence against women; women and armed conflict; women and the economy; women in power and decision-making; institutional mechanisms for the advancement of women; human rights of women; women and the media; women and the environment; and the girl child. The documents that were adopted at these conferences establish the following norms for international organizations: increased development assistance for women by donor agencies, and strengthening and monitoring a whole range of actions on behalf of women. Obligations of governments are defined as the identification and elimination of obstacles to gender inequality in constitutional, legal, political and bureaucratic realms by means of political and legal reforms. These documents urged governments to translate the Platform for Action into national strategies with time-bound targets and benchmarks for monitoring.

Some key changes in norm development have taken place since 2000. On 31 October 2000, the UN Security Council unanimously adopted Resolution 1325, which develops an agenda for women, peace and security. It calls for the prosecution of crimes against women, increased protection of women and girls during war, the appointment of more women to UN peacekeeping operations and field missions and an increase in women's participation in decision-making processes at the regional, national and international level. This resolution outlines the actions to be taken by the Secretary General, the Security Council, UN departments and member states to 'mainstream gender' into peace and security policies and practices. SC 1325 is highly significant because it is the first time the Security Council has devoted an entire session to debating women's experiences in conflict and post-conflict situations. In 2002, the UN General Assembly adopted resolution 57/179 on 'Working towards the elimination of crimes against women committed in the name of honor'. Violence continues to be viewed as a violation of human rights, which compels states to engage in international law in dealing with issues of violence. The Rome Statute of the International Criminal Court (ICC) includes rape, sexual slavery, enforced prostitution, forced pregnancy in the definition of crimes against humanity and war crimes.[6]

Regimes would be incomplete without rules and decision-making procedures that reflect their norms and principles. By *decision-making procedures* are meant those supervisory and monitoring mechanisms that are established to formulate and enforce the rules. These include a variety of commissions, courts, expert groups whose jobs are to monitor compliance and sometimes apply sanctions. The Commission on CEDAW is entrusted with the responsibility to monitor compliance by ratifying state parties. Various other UN bodies act in a monitoring capacity. The Commission on the Status of Women (CSW) and its secretariat, UN Division for the Advancement of Women (UNDAW) monitor the implementation of measures for the advancement of women and review progress made at all levels, global, regional, sectoral and national. The UN Subcommission on the Prevention of Discrimination and Protection of Minorities also addresses the violations of women's rights within several procedures. These include the Working Group on Contemporary Forms of Slavery, which developed a Plan of Action for governments on child prostitution and child pornography and a Plan for the Prevention of the Traffic in Persons and the Exploitation of the Prostitution of Others (Cook, 1997, p. 207). Finally, the implementation of ILO Conventions related to women's rights are supervised by the ILO Committee of Experts on the Application of Conventions and Recommendations. Also reports are provided by the specialized agencies of the UN on the implementation of CEDAW in areas falling within the scope of their activities.

As the evidence shows, a gender equality regime can be identified by its formal components: principles, norms, legal instruments and monitoring mechanisms. The next approach to regime identification questions whether formal components of a regime are sufficient to identify a regime and instead focuses on the behavior of states.

The Behavioral Approach: The Compliance of States

According to some regime analysts, the best way to identify regime is by examining the actual behavior of states. In other words, only state behavior demonstrates that particular injunctions are accepted in a given issue area, and that an international regime exists. As Mark Zacher observes:

> Occurrences of major or long-term noncompliance, particularly involving participation of or support by major actors in the system, bring into question the efficacy of regime injunctions. We must doubt the effectiveness of behavioral guidelines if glaring violations are allowed to persist or if states tend to violate norms and rules on those few occasions when they would benefit from doing so. (Zacher in Hansenclever et al, 1996, p. 181)

Does state behavior demonstrate that an international gender equality regime exists? 180 states have ratified CEDAW binding themselves to do nothing in contravention of its terms. Furthermore, in a landmark decision for women, the General Assembly, acting without a vote, adopted Optional Protocol to CEDAW on 6 October 1999, and called on all states to become party to the new instrument as soon as possible. By ratifying the Optional Protocol, a state recognizes the competence of the Committee on CEDAW to receive and consider complaints from individuals or groups within its jurisdiction. As of October 2004, 76 states have become signatories to the Optional Protocol.

What is the extent of compliance with CEDAW? State parties to CEDAW are obligated under Article 18 of the Convention to report to the Committee on CEDAW within one year of ratification or accession, and subsequently every four years. These reports include measures that states have taken to eliminate discrimination against women and to indicate factors and difficulties they have encountered in fulfilling their treaty obligations. The Committee examines these reports in public meetings in which governmental representatives are present to answer questions raised by the members. To what extent have states fulfilled their obligations? By the end of the UN Decade for Women in 1985, 127 member states had reported the creation of a national machinery to deal with women's advancement and participation in development.[7] As of 2004, 165 countries have established national machineries.[8]

In accordance with the recommendations of the Platform for Action, steps to improve the status of women were taken on several levels including public policy change, legal and legislative change, institutional change, programmatic change and change in generation and dissemination of knowledge and data disaggregated by sex.[9] Many countries have made progress over past decades towards ensuring gender equality in their legal frameworks. To cite a few examples, Japan has enacted an 'Equal Employment Opportunity Law', seeking equal treatment of women and men in the workplace. Tunisian family law now prohibits marriage without consent and polygamy and establishes equal rights for men and women to seek divorce (UNDP, 1995). In successful cases the National Women's Machineries have begun to move out of social and welfare sectors into central decision-making locations such as Ministries of Planning and Finance as in the Philippines, Zambia and Namibia. Bolivia set up a subsecretariat for gender issues as part of the Ministry of Human Development and opened the Office of Battered Women, which runs a shelter. The Bahamas, Barbados, Belize and Malaysia have criminalized domestic violence, and a number of others have similar laws under consideration. Some countries in Latin America have created women-only police stations to facilitate the reporting of domestic abuse. Other recent government initiatives against gender-based violence have been undertaken in Canada, Chile, Australia, Brazil, Colombia, Ecuador and Turkey. At the same time, reform and training projects have been carried out in the United States, Zimbabwe, Costa Rica, Malaysia, Azerbaijan, and Turkey to sensitize the judiciary and the police to issues of rape and violence against women (Kardam, 1997, Keck and Sikkink, 1998). In short, it seems that states are at the very least demonstrating acceptance of this regime by their behavior.

The Cognitive Approach: A New Shared Discourse?

According to Kratochwil and Ruggie, international regimes can be identified by 'intersubjective meaning' and 'shared understandings' rather than overt behavior of states. They argue that the consensus definition of Krasner makes such an approach mandatory:

> International regimes are commonly defined as social institutions around which expectations converge in international issue-areas. The emphasis on convergent expectations as the constitutive basis of regimes gives regimes an inescapable intersubjective quality. It follows that we *know* regimes by their principled and shared understandings of desirable and acceptable forms of social behavior. (In Hasenclever et al, 1996, pp. 181-82)

Focusing on gender equality, the gender regime has brought about a new understanding and consensus, with some regional differences, that is, a view of women as full and equal partners with equal rights to resources and opportunities. This understanding fits in with the three foundational normative elements that international social life is now organized: bureaucracies, markets and human equality (Finnemore, 1996). A similar transformation began to take place in development thinking with the shift from an earlier belief that development served to advance women to a new consensus that development was not possible without the full participation and empowerment of women. The UN conference in Nairobi in 1985 broke new ground by declaring all issues to be women's issues. Women should be included in every sphere of human activity from employment, health, education and social services to industry, science, communications and the environment. A fundamental shift occurred in Beijing in 1995 with the recognition to shift the focus from women to the concept of gender, recognizing that the structure of society, and all relations between men and women had to be reevaluated. Only through such a fundamental restructuring of society and its institutions could women be fully empowered to be equal to men. This change represented a strong affirmation that women's rights were human rights and that gender equality was an issue of universal concern. The discourse on gender equality has also emphasized how women would contribute to larger goals such as the attainment of development, democratization, universal human rights or population reduction. It is now broadly accepted that gender discrimination has deleterious effects on the development agenda as a whole and on a range of other development indicators: and that gender is central to all aspects of a Comprehensive Development Framework (World Bank, 1999).

After the collapse of the Soviet Union, there has been a new focus on human rights and democratization around the world. Global women's networks have used this window of opportunity to coalesce around the issue of gender- based violence where there is little disagreement, and insert it into the human rights framework. As a result, violence against women has been hailed as a global concern and a new focus on violence in the private sphere forced a reconceptualization of the boundaries between public and private. Violence against women is carried out by the state as when rape is used systematically as an instrument of war, or when prison guards are particularly abusive towards female prisoners, but it is also carried out by private individuals which states condone and implicitly support by lack of action. Important discursive change has occurred at both national and international levels, as reflected in the positions governments took condemning violence against women at the UN conferences at Nairobi, Vienna and Beijing. CEDAW entitles women to equal enjoyment with men not only of civil and political rights, but also of economic, social and cultural rights. It is fair to say that gender equality claims have taken greater root in the area of political and legal rights than economic rights.

At the same time, as Finnemore (1996) points out, tensions and contradictions among normative principles in international life will continue to persist as competing values and understandings of what is good, desirable and appropriate form the basis of what politics is about. In this sense, the rise of the gender equality regime is a story of debate, contestation and dissent in norm development. The 1975 Mexico conference revealed a major division among women's organizations when the conference disintegrated into a heated debate from Western countries who stressed discrimination, and women from the developing world who wanted to focus on the more pressing issues of development and justice that affected both men and women. The solution to bridge that gap was the debate over 'women and development'. Its demands included more income and credit opportunities for women, change in laws about property rights and inheritance, access to education and training etc. As women's human rights were placed on the global agenda, economic rights have found less support in a neo-liberal environment. Global economic institutions such as the World Bank still search for 'business reasons for gender equity', and has been much more comfortable with providing resources for women's education, family planning and micro-credit, all justifiable in ultimately serving market-based economic growth and efficiency norms.

Another venue of contestation occurred between conservative forces who reacted to the challenge to traditional gender power arrangements, and local and global feminist activists. As Sally Baden and Anne Marie Goetz suggest (1997):

> Conservative opposition to the concept of gender during the Beijing process expressed a second-wind reaction after the failure to prevent agreement at the International Conference on Population and Development in Cairo on a broad definition of women's reproductive health rights. Other factors explaining the conservative fixation on gender may include the perceived greater influence and presence of feminist NGOs, the greater visibility of lesbians in NGOs, and the inclusion, for the first time in the UN series of Conferences on Women, of very open language on sexual and reproductive rights.[10]

Debates continue on how principle of gender equality complements and/or contradicts other principles (such as the superiority of men over women, or the principle of efficiency of markets over state intervention for the purpose of positive discrimination and empowerment of disadvantaged groups) embodied in religions, traditions and customs, and in political philosophies and practices (such as capitalism or socialism) on the appropriate role of markets and states.

Regardless of contestations, what matters is that gender equality has become an international political issue. All political issues embody contestations over values. Even though there are many differences, there is also a broad consensus that gender equality and women's access to resources, voice and rights as the World Bank puts it, has to be reckoned with (2001). In conclusion, the evidence above points to the existence of a gender equality regime that can be identified by a) its formal components: principles, norms, legal instruments and monitoring mechanisms; b) the behavior (and compliance) of states who are party to this regime; and c) a cognitive framework – an emerging intersubjective consensus at the global level that women's rights are an integral aspect of human rights.

If a Gender Equality Regime Exists, What Factors Account for its Formation?

The formation of this regime is mainly due to three factors: a) the leadership of a global women's movement and its associated non-governmental organizations that exercised 'structural' and 'intellectual' leadership in the codification of gender equality norms and promoting a collective understanding of these norms,[11] in alliance with b) the UN system which provided the forums for agenda setting, negotiation and norm development,[12] accompanied by c) funding and other types of support of the Canadian and some European governments and their bilateral aid agencies, and Western liberal foundations. These agents took advantage of the window of opportunity provided by the collapse of the Soviet Union and its aftermath, when the world focused on democratization and human rights to bring attention to women's human rights and gender-based violence (Joachim, 1999).

Leadership and Policy Advocacy of Women's Networks

Women's global networks and their activities constitute an important case study illustrating the leadership of non-state actors in regime formation. Starting as early as 1975, the idea for the 1975 International Women's Year came from a women's NGO which had consultative status with the UN, the Women's International Democratic Federation, and was taken up by two official women representatives to the UN Commission on the Status of Women (Chen, 1996, p. 140). Many observers have noted that the impetus to include women's issues in UN conferences came from the informal women in development (WID) network, particularly from supporters in non-governmental development organizations (Maguire, 1984). Leaders of these groups often have their roots in women's organizations or research centers. Other groups were founded by women who previously worked within mainstream NGOs on issues such as population, environment, technology, energy, and who felt that their perspectives were ignored by the dominant male leadership. These groups have been influential in many recent international conferences.

Overall, as Chen observes, tens of thousands of women have been mobilized around the world who represented every hue in the ideological rainbow: secular, religious, radical, conservative, grassroots, and elite. They were local, national, regional, and international and their goals were to bring women together to share information, resources, strategies and to create alternative spaces for them to practice organizing, lobbying and legislating issues at all levels (Chen, 1996, p. 141). Chen's arguments are supported by others such as Razavi who comments:

> At the recent global conferences, one could not help but notice the growth of an astute and regionally diverse cadre of advocates skilled in navigating the murky waters of global and regional policy and in moving through circuitous corridors of influence. (Razavi, 1999, p. 24)

But this has, in no small measure, been due to the pressure that individual activists, women's groups and specialized feminist NGOs have brought to bear on the powers-that-be – even under difficult circumstances in authoritarian and exclusionary regimes.

Global women's networks shaped the international gender equality regime by policy advocacy. Advocacy requires developing specific skills and strategies: compiling 'expert' information to support one's political claims or desired policy changes; framing one's points of view in ways that are comprehensible to policy-makers; understanding and accepting to work within the establishment in order to change it. Advocacy involves both (information) knowing how to argue your case, and having concrete information to back your arguments and make your case a strong one, as well as (political know-how) knowing how to lobby, form alliances and influence decision-makers. Young characterizes effective leaders as 'entrepreneurs' or 'brokers' who use negotiation skill and ingenuity, rather than power to present issues and to come up with new institutional options.

Chen summarizes the strategies used by the women's movement to shape international policy agendas as the following:

1. Mounting global campaigns – lobbying at the national, regional and international levels, petition drives, gathering evidence, etc.
2. Building coalitions and consensus – holding multiple strategic planning meetings from women's NGOs around the world at the local, national, regional, and international levels.
3. Preparing policy documents – drafting of resolutions, treaties, protocols, conventions and platform documents.
4. Influencing official delegations – publishing reports, holding briefings, lobbying, and nominating women to be members of official delegations.
5. Bridging NGO and official delegations through mechanisms of the women's caucus – a daily time at all policy-making meetings for NGOs to strategize and to hold dialogues with official delegates and policy makers. (Chen, 1996, p. 151)

Advocacy was a specialized skill perfected by feminist international NGOs based mostly in the North. NGOs in other regions began to perfect this skill by attending more and more international conferences and learning the process, and by receiving training in policy advocacy funded by international foundations. Alvarez (2000) argues that the very notion of policy advocacy was foreign to most Latin American activists who became involved at the outset of the Beijing process. But they were aided by UN openness to their participation, feminist allies inside UN agencies, and Western foundations who supported their attendance in world conferences, as well as their training in the skills of policy advocacy.

There is now ample evidence that global women's networks indeed collected information to make their cases, lobbied state delegations, influenced the wording of global documents to shape the international gender equality regime. Keck and Sikkink (1988) point out the influence of women's NGOs at the Beijing conference. While the initial program document for the Beijing conference was full of bracketed language indicating areas of disagreement, the women's networks monitored the status of bracketed issues, suggested language to government delegations so that they had real input into the final document. In some cases government delegations incorporated language suggested by NGOs directly and in others governments consulted with NGOs to shape their positions on issues (Keck and Sikkink, 1988, p. 188). Moreover, by working with members of official delegations and rallying public opinion, NGOs have helped to craft much of the language that has been adapted in many of these forums.[13]

Gender networks have been effective in linking gender issues to the broader social goals of development, human rights, population control and the protection of the environment. The major conferences where consensus formation occurred are the UN Conference on Environment and Development in Rio in 1992, the UN Human Rights Conference in Vienna in 1993, and the UN Conference on Population and Development in Cairo in 1994. In each of these conferences respectively, women's contributions to sustainable development, women's human rights, and women's health and reproductive rights were deemed priority issues central to the goals of these conferences. For example at the Rio conference, the women's NGOs collaborated with another social movement, the environmental movement.

Much of the success was the result of the strong organization at the preparatory phase where WEDO (Women's Environment and Development Organization) introduced a public forum called the 'Women's Caucus' which provided a bridge between the official and parallel NGO deliberations. In Cairo, WEDO set up its daily caucus, briefing NGOs, official delegates and the media. The result was possibly the most feminist document to emerge from any UN conference, as Tinker (1999) suggests. Principle 4 builds on previous UN conferences and it declares: 'Advancing gender equality and equity, the empowerment of women, the elimination of all kinds of violence against women, and ensuring women's ability to control their own fertility are cornerstones of population and development-related programmes' (Tinker, 1999, p. 100). Other principles declare women's rights to health and education to be prerequisites for all population programs.

The Declaration on the Elimination of Violence against Women, adopted by the UN General Assembly and the Programme of Action at the end of the 1993 World Conference on Human Rights in Vienna, identified gender violence and all forms of sexual harassment and exploitation, including those resulting from cultural prejudice and international trafficking, as incompatible with the dignity and worth of the human person, and called for their elimination. Thus, violence against women, including domestic, societal and war-related violence, was brought into the public arena and was defined as a human rights issue (Joachim, 1999). This was the direct result of lobbying by the women's rights networks who demanded that the UN address women's human rights at every level of its proceedings and recognize gender violence as a human rights violation. The final document explicitly recognized gender-based violence, including rape and sexual slavery as human rights issues. Governments at the Vienna conference urged the UN General Assembly to adopt a draft declaration on violence against women. One of the more specific accomplishments of the women's rights network was the appointment of a Special Rapporteur on Violence against Women, endorsed by the Vienna conference (Keck and Sikkink, 1988). According to Keck and Sikkink (1998), violence against women acquired special prominence as a result of two previously separate transnational networks around human rights and women's rights converging and mutually transforming each other. They argue that the network built around violence against women drew on the human rights networks that were open to the issues related to women's human rights; and violence against women resonated across significant cultural and experiential barriers.

International Donors: A Helping Hand

These accomplishments were very clearly aided by United Nations agencies. As Cook puts it:

> The greatest accomplishment of the UN system regarding human rights law relating to women have been to define discrimination against women, to identify normative standards for the elimination of discrimination against women that state parties to the Women's Convention must pursue in both the public and private sectors of their national life, and to provide mechanisms by which discriminatory practices may be identified and remedied. (Cook, 1997, p. 186)

The United Nations conferences and forums, in turn, were largely responsible for the development of both a global women's movement and the more formal governmental and non-governmental infrastructure that could begin to serve as the basis of an international gender equality regime (Stephenson, 1995). According to Keck and Sikkink (1998), the emergence of international women's networks was more intertwined with the UN system than other networks such as human rights or environmental networks. In fact, the chronologies of the international women's movement are largely a collection of UN meetings: Mexico, Copenhagen, Nairobi, Vienna, Cairo, Beijing. Many researchers have pointed out how UN conferences have served as locations to build and connect the emerging international network. The conferences served as the forums to create more networks but they certainly legitimized the issues and brought together unprecedented number of women from around the world. For example, the NGO meeting at the Nairobi conference spawned many new regional networks, including the Latin American Committee for the Defense of Women's Rights, the Asia-Pacific Forum on Women, Law and Development, and Women, Law and Development in Africa. These conferences also became the venues where feminist activists learned how to lobby and how to influence the content of documents discussed by government representatives.

Referring specifically to the Latin American activists' involvement in the Beijing process, Alvarez (2000) discusses the deliberate efforts of feminist allies working within UN agencies such as the UN Development Fund for Women

(UNIFEM), and the women's unit of the UN Economic Commission on Latin America and the Caribbean (ECLAC) to encourage feminist NGOs to participate more fully in the official preparatory process and also, the considerable amounts of targeted bilateral and multilateral agency and foundation funding that enabled some local NGOs to do so. She further points out that UNIFEM and other UN agencies took the initiative to rally NGOs and assumed the challenge of putting pressure on governments to be receptive to NGO proposals (Alvarez, 2000, p. 42).

International organizations have an important role in shaping, defining and diffusing norms (Barrett and Finnemore, 1999). International organizations have established units or departments and appointed gender experts/advisors to mainstream gender equality in their respective operations.[14] Gender issues are included in central policy statements, guidelines , and procedures of major donor agencies. In successful cases, gender advisors have been 'mainstreamed' in operational departments of donor agencies. Some donor agencies are attempting to bring gender analysis into the policy processes of economic reform and programme aid. Donor agencies' efforts have had an impact on state responses, as many projects and programs on gender issues are funded by multilateral and bilateral donors. A number of them have functioned as arenas for the development of gender-based social and causal knowledge, as well as for the negotiation of norms and the adaptation of declarations and treaties. The UN Commission on the Status of Women (CSW) established by the UN Economic and Social Council (ECOSOC) in 1946 based on the UN Charter is the primary UN body responsible for advancing the status of women. One of the most important achievements of the CSW is the drafting of the specialized conventions dealing with women culminating in 1979 when the General Assembly adopted CEDAW. The Mexico City Conference led to the establishment of the International Research and Training Institute for the Advancement of Women (INSTRAW) and UNIFEM to provide the institutional and financial framework for research, training and operational activities. The UN Division for the Advancement of Women (UNDAW) was established to monitor and implement the Programs of Action that emerged from the UN conferences. Regional organizations such as the European Union (EU) and the Organization of American States (OAS) have allowed women to become diplomatic or political agents as members of women's commissions or as staff in bureaucracies. It is, however, also fair to say that it has taken many international agencies, including for example, the UN Development Programme and the World Bank, until the 1990s to begin to seriously integrate gender issues into their operations. I have argued elsewhere that international organizations have responded to gender issues in specific ways depending on their 'position' within the international development regime, the fit of gender issues into their goals and procedures, as well as the extent of internal policy advocacy (Kardam, 1991).

A number of key foundations set aside funds specifically for women's issues. The Ford Foundation's board of trustees set aside reserve funds that field offices could claim for funding on women's issues, leading to significant Ford funding on the issue of violence against women in the late 1980s (Keck and Sikkink, 1988, p. 182; Kardam, 1991). Also major US and Western European foundation grants on women's rights increased in the late 1980s and 1990s. Keck and Sikkink (1998) point out that foundations and Northern American and European governments were key supporters of the organizing efforts that turned women's groups into a powerful presence at the Vienna Conference on Human Rights, as well as the Cairo Population Conference and the Beijing Women's Conference. According to Alvarez (2000), Latin American activists gained substantial funding from the Ford Foundation to mount a region-wide advocacy training project.

As the East-West conflict has subsided, and the Soviet Union dissolved, new central concepts that guide countries have emerged such as democratization, participation by civil society, good governance and respect for human rights. Human rights are no longer divided as starkly as civil and political rights, on the one hand, and economic, social and cultural rights on the other. As human development has become a core concept and human dignity is at the center of human development, it is impossible to overlook human rights, including women's human rights.

While the Cold War had only a few years ago hampered the agenda-setting efforts of women's organizations, its thaw now provided opportunities for these groups. According to Joachim, it freed up agenda space:

> In the absence of East-West conflict, issues that UN policymakers had once considered important began to appear meaningless. Looking for new issues to fill the vacuum, UN policymakers decided to hold a series of specialized conferences in the early 1990s, starting with the UN Conference on Environment and Development in Rio de Janeiro in 1992, followed by the World Human Rights Conference in Vienna in 1993 and the International Conference on Population and Development in Cairo in 1994. (Joachim, 1999, p. 151)

The UN also became more accessible to NGOs at the end of the Cold War as the standards of accreditation were relaxed, so that consultative status was now granted to regional and grassroots NGOs. Previously relegated to the visitor balconies and corridors, these NGOs were allowed in the negotiation floors. When these 'windows of opportunities' were presented, the global women's networks took advantage of them and succeeded in incorporating gender issues centrally to each of the above-mentioned UN conferences' agendas. In conclusion, this regime would not have been formed without the rise of global women's networks. These networks learned to influence global agendas through UN conferences and with the help of allies within the UN system. They also enjoyed substantial support from Western foundations and European and Canadian bilateral donor agencies in their work. Finally, the new structure of the world system afforded windows of opportunity to these networks who successfully took advantage of them.

Regime Maintenance

Formation of a regime is one thing, its maintenance is another. The 'translation' of international norms to national and local levels still remains elusive and there are many gaps when it comes to implementation between global norms and local responses.[15] States have much less incentive to actually 'do' something about gender equality by allocating budgets, staff, targets and deadlines, in other words 'put their money where their mouth is'. Laws are not implemented because the courts and the police have not made any changes in their behavior; women themselves are not necessarily aware of their legal rights or the new bureaucracies for gender are powerless and lack feasible budgets to put national plans into action. Some of the reasons for these gaps are explored below.

Government elites and bureaucracies are frequently hostile to mainstreaming efforts, which are seen as externally imposed political agendas bringing few benefits. Why do they attend international forums, sign platforms of action and conventions then? States have an incentive to sign and ratify conventions and treaties if it makes them look good on international forums and contributes to their 'international image' as elites see it, and if it is perceived as relatively costless. A certain level of international pressure and the desire to avoid embarrassment at an international arena may prompt state representatives to go along with decisions taken at international conferences. Having accepted a set of international norms, states would undermine their long-term existence if they acted independently of this set of norms, so they tend to comply. This is because states need to maintain their reputation as fulfillers of commitments they have undertaken. In other words, by collaboration they are sending a signal to the international community. This is called 'reputational effects' of international regimes by Keohane:

> International regimes help assess others' reputations by providing standards of behavior against which performance can be measured, by linking these standards to specific issues, and by providing forums, often through international organizations, in which these evaluations can be made. (Keohane, 1984, p. 102)

Thus, one could argue that the existence of international norms, at the very least, have made it awkward for states to keep their bureaucratic procedures and laws at variance with such norms and renders them vulnerable to both domestic and international criticism from women's networks and international organizations. World conferences also speeded up the ratification of CEDAW, and prodded states to change practices. But the embarrassment factor does not necessarily provide the incentive for concrete steps towards implementation.

States may cooperate on gender issues on the basis of humanitarianism, i.e. discrimination against half of humanity is morally wrong. For example, there is evidence that the formation of the international refugee regime is partly due to consensus on humanitarian principles by the international community (Skran, 1995). In the same way, women's advocates have generally claimed that discrimination against women is a violation of human rights and goes against humanitarian principles. But not all are willing to make substantive changes that reduce male privileges. To what extent can international organizations influence the behavior of states? What are the limits of their ability to enforce compliance? According to Young (1989), the lack of well entrenched and properly financed supranational organizations in international society ensures that international regimes must rely heavily on the ability and willingness of individual members to elicit compliance with key provisions within their own jurisdictions. As Cook (1997) suggests, UN instruments and institutions for the protection and promotion of human rights offer women an opportunity for recognition that the wrongs done to them are violations of their rights, but the UN system cannot guarantee their rights or offer women the security that their rights will be safeguarded.

The proposal that states make changes regarding women's roles and status creates deeper problems than just those of monitoring and verification. Issue areas which propose changes in the relationship between the state and its subjects are especially sensitive because they challenge a state's sovereignty. As Krasner (1983) points out, prevailing international norms and practices still place few inhibitions on a state's discretionary control over its subjects. Even though there are international commissions and courts that individuals can complain to, this can only be done after all national options are exhausted and if the state in question is a party to those commissions or 'optional protocols'.

Young suggests that for effective regime maintenance, clear-cut and effective monitoring and compliance mechanisms should be available.[16] Most observers agree that enforcement of CEDAW has not been adequate. The reports that governments submit to the Committee on the Elimination of Discrimination against Women do not always comply with CEDAW guidelines. They are sometimes quite short, sometimes overdue, and rarely self-critical. CEDAW, like other human rights treaty commissions, has adopted the practice of 'constructive dialogue' in the examination of reports by state parties since it is able to apply only the sanction of public scrutiny. These reports are discussed in public sessions and the representatives of the state that introduced the report respond to questions from the committee. As Tomasevski points out:

> A particular manifestation of this avoidance of collective pronouncements is the fact that CEDAW has never formally denounced a state party to be in violation of the Convention, even though the members have clearly felt that some states have failed to carry out their obligations. (Tomasevski, 1993, p. 119).

It is obvious that members of the CEDAW committee prefer to keep the dialogue going even with states that violate their obligations rather than to exclude them completely since one form of influence is to continue dialogue. It is also worth noting that the Committee on CEDAW is not the only committee that monitors advances on gender equality. The Human Rights Committee and other committees monitoring human rights instruments cover issues of concern to women in their reviews. But as Hijab argues, this may be as much part of the problem as it is part of the solution:

There is a great deal of duplication and overlap in what the different committees have to say about women's human rights. States – and individuals – have limited capacity and resources to monitor and implement. There is room for a more integrated approach to monitoring progress and supporting technical assistance to avoid waste of time and resources... There is not yet a circle linking the instruments and mechanisms on gender equality and women's rights – CEDAW and its monitoring Committee – to technical assistance to promote these rights, as there is in the case of the rights of the child. (Hijab, 1999, pp. 7-8)

A recent successful example of monitoring comes from UNICEF's experience in the area of children's rights, which constitutes an interesting example even though it is not centrally related to gender equity. UNICEF is directly involved in the monitoring and implementation of the Convention on the Rights of the Child; it works closely with the Committee on the Rights of the Child, which receives reports from states parties to the Convention. These reports then are fed into UNICEF's national plans of action at the country level, and into its technical assistance programs. In this way, its country programs become vehicles to promote and monitor the convention.

Furthermore, women's networks that work at the global level do not necessarily have influence at local levels. Also, national women's organizations may stretch themselves very thin as they strive to participate in global forums, and at the same time work in their own communities. The conferences stimulated global awareness and networking, but there was still considerable distance between the new resolutions and changing actual practices (Keck and Sikkink, 1998, p. 188).

Goetz's research (1995) shows that weaker bureaucracies have been more eager to take on gender-related goals, showing that international norms may have had a stronger influence on them. Yet, Goetz also points out that international donor agencies' support of gender equality and women's machineries and programs have proved to be a double-edged sword. On the one hand, they have lent strength and resources to gender issues, but on the other hand, the danger that the legitimacy of gender issues can be undermined as a 'foreign import' has remained. In short, donor funding has been pivotal in supporting gender equality in many countries, but such funding may relieve governments of responsibility and shape development activities toward donor priorities. As will be discussed in detail later, this remains mostly true in the Turkish case as well.

Under what conditions do states become more accountable to gender equality? Alvarez (1990) argues that in transitional regimes, gender-specific demands stand a greater chance of being met if women's mobilization is seen as necessary to consolidate the regime, to solidify its legitimacy and to achieve larger developmental goals. Research shows that in countries undergoing a period of transition, some political space to promote women's issues is likely to present itself. States may also see it in their self-interest to respond to civil society pressure for the purpose of maintaining their legitimacy. This is true in both developing and developed countries. Sawer (1995) discusses how women's machinery in Australia and Canada were assisted by a political opportunity structure which included both reforming governments eager to expand the policy agenda and the economic prosperity of the 1970s. She points out that 'social liberalism' in Australia and New Zealand has been an appropriate ideology for gender concerns, with its emphasis on the state as a vehicle for social justice. In the Turkish case, the establishment of a national women's machinery (NWM) was a top-down initiative undertaken by a female cabinet minister, the Minister of Labor and Social Welfare. But in the particular political and social context of Turkey, its introduction led to a polarization of Islamist and secularist views on women's issues, much national debate in the media, ending in the establishment of two separate bureaucracies, one for women, and the other for the family. The former then became an innovative bureaucracy in its collaborative style with women's groups, and in its efforts to produce and disseminate knowledge on gender issues, and in political advocacy.

As regime norms are translated into domestic law in participating states, this promotes compliance with regime obligations and can also strengthen the compatibility between the international and domestic constituencies. Even in Western industrialized countries like Canada, Australia, and New Zealand, Sawer (1995) argues that international pressure has been used by femocrats to press home policy change at the domestic level. Jehan (1995) discusses how women's groups supported by international networks of donors and NGOs, have begun to shape the national policy agenda in Bangladesh and Tanzania. Many feminists believe that the documents from conferences such as the Vienna and Beijing documents and the UN declarations and conventions give them leverage with their governments. They have begun to engage in accountability politics, demanding that their governments uphold the positions they supported. CEDAW, with all its shortcomings, does at least encourage compliance. Once a state has ratified a convention, it is expected to change its domestic laws to conform to its principles, and domestic and international groups have been able to use the ratification of CEDAW to reinforce changes in laws and behavior at the national level (Jaquette, 1995). Latin American rights advocates now more regularly invoke international human rights law to press for local compliance with new global gender equity norms, and they appeal to UN and OAS conventions in promoting women's rights locally (Alvarez, 2000).

Turkey's Involvement

In the mid-1980s, Turkey had returned to 'democracy' after a military coup, and had initiated economic liberalization policies. It seems that the actors involved were Turkish diplomats and members of the Ministry of Foreign Affairs, mostly for 'reputational effects' (Acuner, 2002a). In Turkey's case, to show the world that it abides by democratic ideals, one of which includes gender equality, at relatively little cost may have been an important factor, especially since Turkey, since its inception in 1923, has proclaimed gender equality as a strong symbol of its Westernization process. Turkey ratified CEDAW, with reservations, in 1985. This action was taken by diplomats in the Ministry of Foreign Affairs, who, as Acar puts it:

> thought this to be the 'proper' line of conduct to be followed by a state, where, since the establishment of the Republic by Mustafa Kemal Atatürk in 1923, official state ideology had loudly articulated a discourse on women's equality with men and their right to be free from sex-based discrimination. Consequently, Turkey's involvement with CEDAW originated on the initiative of the Turkish Foreign Affairs Ministry, the members of which regarded the women's Convention to be compatible with the Turkish state's long standing commitment to gender equality on the basis of the Republic's secular and modernist orientation. (Acar, 2000, p. 205)

As mentioned above, signing and ratifying CEDAW does not automatically guarantee compliance. Following ratification, a public petition campaign to encourage compliance with CEDAW was organized by the women's movement in 1987. Turkey's National Women's Machinery (called the General Directorate on the Status and Problems of Women) was established in 1990. It is housed in the same building and competes for resources with another bureaucratic unit established on the basis of a competing Islamist discourse on women, that of the family, called the Family Research Organization. This Directorate, like many similar ones around the world, has a minimal budget, and its activities have been mostly supported by donors. It still does not have a permanent legal status, does not have a permanent budget and continues to function without an organizational law, which is before the Parliament.

The governments that ratify the Convention are also asked to submit periodic reports to the CEDAW Committee at which government representatives are requested to answer questions by the Committee. These reports examine the legal system (including the Constitution, Civil Code, Criminal Code, Labor Law and the Turkish Citizenship Law), especially searching for articles in the law that are in violation of CEDAW and discuss the changes made to bring them in accordance with the principles of the convention. The first report was submitted in 1990. Turkey submitted its second and third periodic report (CEDAW/C/TUR/2-3) to the Committee on the Elimination of Discrimination against Women at its 318th and 319th meetings on 17 January 1997. This combined report (1994 and 1997) was lauded by the CEDAW Committee for its comprehensiveness and openness in dealing with issues. This report was prepared under the auspices of the NWM, with the collaboration of a group of academics, bureaucrats, NGO representatives and members of political parties. Similarly, the third and fourth combined periodic CEDAW reports (scheduled for review by the Committee in January 2005) were prepared in a collaborative manner. The fourth and fifth combined periodic report of Turkey (2002 and 2003) indicates that, state commitment to the principles of CEDAW and the Beijing Platform for Action (PfA) have remained intact. Changes in governments did not result in a deviation from compliance with this commitment.

The period since 1997 is marked by milestone legal reforms that eliminate fundamental discriminatory provisions against women, as well as other initiatives that contribute towards expanding the boundaries of equality and human rights of women. In 1997, compulsory basic education has been increased from five to eight years; in 1998, the law on domestic violence (Protection of the Family Law) was adopted; in 1999, the reservations to CEDAW were lifted; in 2002, after five years of long and hard work, the new Civil Code was adopted; in 2001, the parliament ratified the Optional Protocol to CEDAW; and within this enabling legislative environment, observance of CEDAW principles in combating violence against women, women's poverty and economic exploitation, among others, have been included in the program of the recently formed 58th Government by the Justice and Development Party. The new Civil Code represents a significant step forward in bringing Turkish laws in line with CEDAW. It abolishes the supremacy of men in marriage, establishes full equality of men and women in the family, and removes the final say over the choice of domicile and children from men. It sets the equal division of property acquired during marriage as a default property regime, assigning an economic value to women's hitherto invisible labor. It changes the legal minimum age for women's marriage from 15 to 18. In the last two decades, several other legal reforms have been implemented that made further progress towards overcoming sexual discrimination. Article 159 of the Civil Code was annulled by the Constitutional Court which had stated that women needed their husbands' consent to work outside the home. Article 438 of the Criminal Code was repealed which had provided for a reduction of one-third for rape if the victim was a sex worker. These legal reforms clearly represent responsiveness to and compliance with CEDAW by removing discriminatory clauses in legislation.

As part of the efforts to qualify for EU membership, the government revised the Constitution to incorporate gender equality, falling short, however of accepting the need for positive discrimination for women. This was in spite of strong advocacy by women's groups, and support from the Republican People's Party (CHP) in the National Parliament. The head of the CEDAW Committee, a Turkish scholar, stated publicly that Turkey had to abide by Article 4 of CEDAW which states that 'adoption of temporary special measures to accelerate equality between men and women shall not be considered discrimination as defined in the Convention, and such measures may be discontinued when the objectives of equality of opportunity and treatment are achieved. A new Penal Code was passed by the National Parliament in September 2004, which makes unprecedented changes in improving women's human rights. Accordingly, provocation will no longer be a defense in honor killings. It will also see that rape in marriage and sexual harassment are treated as crimes. However, virginity tests have not been explicitly banned, although the rights to carry them out are limited. The steps that Turkey has taken to fulfill the Copenhagen Criteria has now led to the European Union ruling on 6 October 2004 that the country has made enough progress in improving its human rights record and reforming its economy and judiciary to merit negotiations towards membership.

These are all momentous changes, and if we stopped our investigation here, we might conclude that the Turkish government is in the process of complying with global women's human rights norms, as a member of the gender equality regime, especially within the context of application to the European Union. But we would know very little about the richness and vigor of debates on competing gender norms that are going on, or how women themselves are trying to live with the messiness of individual rights legally accorded to them in a world where collective identities, relatedness and social harmony count more than women's individual achievement. As one woman recounted in a movie made by Binnur Karaevli, a Turkish female film director, she had two identities, one for the home, and one when she entered the doors of the American school that she went to in Turkey. One emphasized her identity as a member of the family, as a woman whose role was perceived as a future wife and mother, while the other taught her to be 'an individual', focused on achievement and personal freedom.[17] Turkey, indeed, has enacted significant legal reforms towards gender equality. What does this signify, to a woman in a village in the poor and conflict-ridden Southeast, to a woman living in the shantytown of a big city, having recently migrated or forced to move from her village, to a female bank executive living in a posh district of Istanbul, to female college students from small towns of Anatolia living in dorms away from their families and to their male relatives and friends, to those that claim to be 'Islamist' or 'secularist'? What are Turkey's unique circumstances, its political, economic and social context, its relationship with the European Union, and Western powers in general that have shaped its particular responses to the global women's human rights norms and its initiatives for change? How are international women's human rights norms understood, redefined and contested within political institutions, and in society? These questions will be explored in the coming chapters.

Notes

[1] See Chapter 1 in World Bank, 2001, for extensive statistics and other information on gender inequality.
[2] www.un.org/womenwatch/daw/cedaw.
[3] See, for example, De Nevers, 1999, for an overview of this literature.
[4] The following discussion of the factors that contribute to the emergence of a gender equality regime draw from Kardam, 2002.
[5] The Convention was adopted by acclamation at the 24th regular session of the General Assembly of the OAS on 9 June 1994, in Brazil.
[6] See United Nations, Economic and Social Council, Commission on Human Rights, 'Integration of the Human Rights of Women and the Gender Perspective: Violence against Women', e/CN.4/2004/66, December 2003.
[7] As listed in the Directory of National Focal Points for the Advancement of Women, quoted in Women 2000, No. 3, 1987, p. 3.
[8] As listed in the Directory of National Machineries for the Advancement of Women, DAW, March 2004.
[9] The UN Division for the Advancement of Women tracks these changes and analyzes reports submitted by states that have ratified CEDAW.
[10] Baden and Goetz, 1997, p. 45.

[11] 'Structural leaders' are those who can skillfully convert power based on material resources bargaining leverage and 'intellectual leaders' who can use the power of ideas to shape the way in which participants in institutional bargaining understand the issues at stake and to orient their thinking about options available. See Oran Young, 1991, p. 288.

[12] See, for example, Breitmeir, "International Organizations and the Creation of Environmental Regimes", in Oran Young, ed., 1997 and Barrett and Finnemore, 1999, for the role of international organizations in agenda setting, norm development and informational functions.

[13] For one analysis of these conferences, see Hartman, 1997.

[14] See for example Nüket Kardam, 1991; Shirin Rai, (ed.), 2003; Miller and Razavi, (eds.), 1998.

[15] See UNDAW analysis of state reports to CEDAW.

[16] Young, 1989.

[17] Searching for Paradise, directed and produced by Binnur Karaevli, 2003.

Chapter 2

Gender Norms in Turkey: Construction and Contestation

Gender and the Constructivist Perspective[1]

Formation of a regime is one thing, its maintenance quite another. The 'translation' of international norms to national and local levels remains elusive, and there are many gaps between global norms and local responses when it comes to implementation. As discussed earlier, the gender regime was, on the whole, not an initiative of states. It was supported and promoted by global non-governmental actors, international governmental organizations, and some Western industrialized states through their bilateral aid agencies. Even though there are strong national women's movements who use CEDAW to strengthen their positions and to hold their governments accountable, states are often reluctant to 'do' something if it means providing budgets, staff, and targets. Gender-sensitive laws may not be implemented if the judges, the police and the court system are guided by a different set of norms. Furthermore, women are not necessarily informed about their rights even if laws are passed and even if they are, they may be powerless in the face of competing social norms of gender that promote women's inferiority to men. If, in fact, the gender equality regime is mainly seen as an externally imposed political agenda, and if CEDAW lacks the clear-cut and effective monitoring and compliance mechanisms what difference can it make in national and local contexts?[2] If it is going to make a difference, this requires the interpretation of vague and general norms and principles so that they can be put into practice. It also requires an understanding and open debate on competing gender norms and identities, and competing notions of gender equality advocated or promoted by different institutions such as the legal system, the bureaucracy, the market, religious establishment or kinship and family systems. Otherwise, there is the danger that states will keep going through the motions of 'doing something' however little, to placate global monitoring committees and to receive donor assistance.

The constructivist approach is more helpful than the neo-liberal theory of international regimes in undertaking such an investigation. The neo-liberal theories yield insights into the identification of the regime, explanations of its formation, and the limits of external incentives for compliance. They do not examine how gender norms and identities are socially constructed, defined, contested, interpreted in different socio-political and institutional contexts. As Ruggie (1998) maintains, the neo-liberal theories lack a methodology to understand how social norms are constructed. Constructivism, on the other hand, questions state interests, not just accepting them as preferences shaped by particular beliefs or knowledge. Instead it asks where they come from in the first place. The social construction of norms are examined and not accepted as *a priori*. Many feminist scholars, along the same lines, define gender as an analytical category, like race, class and ethnicity, whose meaning is socially constructed. To adopt gender as an analytical category means to focus on the social and cultural construction of sexual difference. Every culture, institution, society, historical epoch constitutes and interprets sexual difference in a certain way. If that is the case, we need to go beyond classifying all resistance to gender equality as stemming from 'traditional and cultural norms' and examine where those norms come from, what types of power relations underlie them. For example, Tripp, in a case study on Uganda, notes that those defending harmful practices to women in the name of preserving their religious, ethnic, or other cultural identity are also often seeking to protect certain political and/or economic interests:

> (They) have a vested interest in maintaining the status quo and a set of power relations tied to certain practices. This is not to say that cultural preservation and identity concerns are not real, but rather that they are often tied to a broader political and economic context that affects their sustainability. (Tripp, 2002, p. 414)

A constructivist framework allows for a theoretical conceptualization of activism or 'struggle'. Feminist struggle locates power in social structures and seeks to fight this power. But feminists also emphasize power as an aspect of agency: women are not powerless and can be empowered through struggle. According to Prügl, understanding the dual character of power, its constraining and enabling effects, is a crucial element of constructivism (Prügl, 1996: p.16). Constructivist view goes hand in hand with the new term 'global governance'. This term signifies the proliferation of non-state actors and their growing importance and power as a distinctive feature of contemporary world affairs. However, it is more than that. For Rosenau, mobilizing support from the bottom up involves increasing the skills and capacities of individuals and altering the horizons of identification in patterns of global life. Elsewhere, Rosenau discusses systems of rule at all levels of human activity – from the family to the international organization – in which pursuit of goals through the exercise of control has transnational repercussions (Rosenau, 1995: p. 14).

For constructivists, success of regimes is found not just in external incentives but also in constitutive rules. These rules do not 'explain' in the positivist sense, but underlie everything else. These structures reproduce only through the practices of knowledgeable agents. Structures and agents cannot exist without each other. Actors draw on the rules which make up structures in their everyday routines, and in doing so they reproduce these rules. They also have the capacity to understand what they are doing and why they are doing it which allows them to reflexively monitor the social practices they engage in (Giddens, 1984; Wendt, 1987). Ruggie pointed out that both realism and liberalism rest on a positivist epistemology whose view of international relations is framed in utilitarian terms. He calls them neo-utilitarian approaches: 'an atomistic universe of self-regarding units whose identity is assumed given and fixed, and who are responsive largely if not solely to material interests' (Ruggie, 1998, p.3). Yet, understanding 'intersubjective meanings' necessitates a relational epistemology, where interpretation is required. According to Ruggie, social constructivism views international politics on the basis of a more relational ontology than the atomistic framing of neo-utilitarianism:

> In addition, it attributes to ideational factors, including culture, norms, and ideas, social efficacy over and above any functional utility they may have, including a role in shaping the way in which actors define their identity and interests in the first place. Finally, it allows for agency, – actors doing things – reflective acts of social creation, albeit within structured constraints. (Ruggie, 1998, p. 4)

Gender norms permeate all levels of society from the domestic to the international and global. Social interaction enacts gendered scripts; social institutions fix gendered norms; social communication involves gendered rules. Combining gender with a constructivist perspective in international relations thus yields a research agenda that can focus on, for example, contested norms such as human rights, or investigate how the concept of human rights may be based on a Western notion of self, and how the public/private distinction has prevented domestic violence from being defined as a violation of human rights. Such a research agenda might examine how gender identities are shaped, contested and negotiated within different institutions, globally and locally, and taking into account both structure and agency. By employing a constructivist perspective, feminist scholars have examined how global material changes may become opportunities for the introduction of new definitions and new interpretations for women's movements as active agents. A constructive perspective involves both structure and agency. For example, Sandra Whitworth has studied the ILO and demonstrated the shift from protectionism to equality regarding women's work conditions. She documented the role of agents and interests involved in the change, as well as the role of prevailing ideas and material conditions facilitating the change (Whitworth, 1994).

The social constructivist position would yield important insights into the relationships between global, national, and local contexts for women's human rights. The Turkish case is fascinating because Turkey represents an amalgam of Islamic and Western value systems with different, overlapping, sometimes complementary and other times conflicting gender norms operative in different institutions: markets, bureaucracies, legal systems, clans (asiret) or religious institutions (including sufi tarikats).[3] The opposing norms may particularly be relevant in a country like Turkey where different traditions and world views live side by side, but also where global processes disrupt and change local institutions. According to some feminist social scientists, such dissonance may open up space and opportunity, especially if accompanied by material conditions that provide an opening (Bayes and Kelly, 2001; Sassen, 1998). Because all of these institutions are interrelated in a society, changes in the gender relations or gender regime in one set of institutions can affect the gender relations or regimes in other sets of institutions.

A constructivist approach allows the examination of contested norms, their interaction with each other, and the power relations that legitimize those norms. For example, An-Naim (1995) encourages women's rights advocates to engage in both secular and religious discourses. Otherwise, the dichotomy between the so-called religious and secular discourse in Islamic societies continues with little communication or dialogue between them and 'global gender equality' remains a vague and little understood concept. Yet, it should be possible to take on gender norms in the religious discourse and debate and renegotiate them on their own terms, rather than dismissing them outright. This is being done by scholars and activists who are rereading the Quran by 'unreading patriarchal interpretations', and renegotiating Islamic gender norms in their own context, and facing Islamic politicians and scholars on their own turf (Barlas, 2002; Wadud, 1999). As An-Naim (1995) suggests, advocates of the human rights of women must begin by ridding themselves of their own inhibitions and educating themselves in the concepts and techniques of Islamic discourse and fully engage themselves in religious as well as secular discourse. Translation of global gender equality norms to local contexts in Islamic countries, including Turkey, will take an engagement with competing norms established by different institutions, along with an attempt to begin to integrate and synthesize them to create 'workable' gender equality norms applicable in real life situations.

Women's Human Rights: Global or Western Norms?

The concept of rights continues to be an area of contestation. For example, critical legal studies of human rights examine the gendered aspects of international law, exploring the liberal origins of the concept of rights and its biases. Especially, the public/private distinction, which is basic to liberal theory, serves to differentiate women's rights from human rights (Cook, 1997; Deutz, 1993). The term 'global norms' should be used with the caveat that they have, in fact, emerged from the Western enlightenment process but have spread across the globe, supported by powerful countries of Europe and North America. CEDAW and the Beijing Platform, as most would agree, endorse Enlightenment principles of universal rights, equality and individual freedoms. The feminist movements in the West drew on these principles of liberalism to argue for equality between women and men. Yet, this principle of equality is itself not devoid of flaws, especially of keeping the public/private distinction that relegated women to the private sphere, while simultaneously advocating 'equality'. Thus, women's movements claimed that Enlightenment principles of universal rights, equality and individual freedom mask the masculine norm as the subject of liberal contract theory and neglects the social conditions that make the universalist principles meaningful (Molyneux and

Razavi, 2002, p. 5). Liberal feminists have argued that despite legal equality, the continued separation of public/private spheres in modern states, and the relegation of women in the private sphere legitimizes discrimination against women. They have claimed that Western liberal concepts of modernity, democracy and equality hide an unequal relationship between women and men by maintaining the public/private distinction, a distinction that has been part of the Western history since the early Greeks. In terms of women's rights and gender equality, men as the dominant group have defined women's work as housework and child rearing and relegated it to the 'private' sphere, while maintaining control over the 'public' sphere of political power, law, and general public life (Ehlstain, 1974).

The ideal of equality is based on liberal political thought which claimed individual liberties and non-interference by the state on an individual's 'private' life. At the same time, there is no questioning of the dominance of men in the private sphere, and thus the continuation of patriarchal norms in the family. Once public and private are defined in opposition to each other, and women placed in the private sphere, then it is easy to see how men are then the 'citizens' who claim the public sphere to themselves, and women are excluded from public life and denied civil and political rights. The women's movements in the West have been fighting this patriarchal understanding of women's place in society. They claim that 'equality' and 'equality of opportunity' have meant that laws and institutions have been designed by men and where women are allowed to compete in institutions defined and designed by men. Given that the public/private distinction was an integral part of the liberal framework and Western nation-states, it is not surprising that the private domain continued to reflect gender-based discrimination. In fact, many laws also reflected an underlying gender discrimination that defined women as 'inferior and under the tutelage of their male relatives' until quite recently. It is very instructive, as Berktay (2004, pp. 19-22) points out, to examine the progress in women's rights in England, the home of liberal thought. In 1832, in the height of liberalism, women were prohibited from voting; English women did not have equal rights of custody of children until 1973. Berktay adds that while women acquired equal rights in divorce after the Second World War, up to 1970, English husbands had the right to ask for retribution from men who committed adultery with their wives! This view reflects how women were considered to be 'owned' by husbands. In short, one might conclude that even though the Western principle of equality incorporates equality between races, citizens, classes and the sexes as the ideal of democracy, this does not mean that the ideal of equality is achieved in reality, but that Western history has evolved in reference to this principle. In short, liberal feminism has remained loyal to the broad philosophical tenets of liberalism, while uncovering its androcentric nature. At the same time, it still turns to the state to create the conditions for the exercise of rights, and therefore, to the strand of liberalism that focused on social justice and state intervention, to solve the problem of gender injustice. It seems that the global norms embodied in CEDAW are based on these tenets of liberalism that rely on state intervention on behalf of protection of rights and social justice for women.

Liberalism includes two modern trends, only one of which emphasizes an interventionist role for the state (Molyneux and Razavi, 2002). These are:

1. The conservative, neo-liberal approach emphasizing political and civil rights and the *protection* of the individual from state interference to produce or consume freely.
2. The more liberal, social justice oriented approach emphasizing social and economic rights, and the *obligations* of the state to protect individual rights, and provide resources for the development of individual capabilities.

These two strands have led to two distinct approaches in practice that have been defended and advocated in separate podiums. The first one focuses on freedom of choice and market-led economics with relatively little state intervention. It is advocated by international institutions such as the World Bank and the International Monetary Fund. This paradigm is primarily concerned with growth of economic output by means of free enterprise, and with rights only secondarily, and to the extent that they encourage the growth of free enterprise and discourage government authoritarianism and corruption. The US affinity with this position is evidenced by the government's continued refusal to sign and ratify CEDAW, on the grounds that removing discrimination against women and holding the government accountable for its implementation would conflict with the principles of freedom of choice and of minimal state intervention. The other strand of liberalism, concerned with human rights, democratization and state responsibility for the promotion of social justice, including gender justice, tends to be supported more in Europe (especially Northern Europe), Canada, and by the United Nations agencies. The focus is on promoting state accountability in creating the conditions for human development and gender justice. Even though some claim that democracy and market-led economic development market are complementary, it is not at all clear how the two may be reconciled in theory or in practice. Whether liberalism can accommodate social rights and to what extent it can is still an open question (Molyneux and Razavi, 2002).

What is clear, however, is that markets do not necessarily deal with justice and equality. Global social movements such as the women's movement, environmental movement or the human rights movement, regardless of its weaknesses, still turn to the state for the implementation of a just legal framework. Thus, for the application of women's human rights and gender justice, CEDAW relies on states to make sure that human capabilities are developed and to create an enabling policy environment for the application of women's social and economic rights. In other words, we are hoping for a liberalism but one with a 'human face' that provides the conditions for the development of minimum capabilities so that the competition is fair. No other entity but the state is potentially in a position to do that. But then the question that still needs an answer is: 'Why and under what conditions should or would a state make gender justice a priority?' History tells us that states only do so when it is politically necessary and viable. Even then, announcing gender justice as a 'priority' and implementing it are, of course, two different things.

We know that neo-liberal policies have not led to gender justice. On the contrary, they have worsened the situation of women in many countries including in the former Soviet Union and in Latin America (Heinen and Portet, 2002; Schild, 2002; Subrahmanian, 2002). The solutions have not been couched in terms of the need for greater equality, but in terms of temporary 'social safety nets' that would lift people who are adversely affected by neo-liberal policies out of poverty. Universal entitlements, such as a state pension in Poland, have disappeared in favor of targeted assistance for the very poor. Many social benefits that used to be universal rights are now only those in the formal labor market, which indirectly places women at a disadvantage revealing what has been identified as a male bias in social policy. In Chile, privatized social security systems have exacerbated inequalities as funded pension plans have a built-in gender bias, given that women's labor lives are shorter and generally interrupted by raising children.

What type of state then would act on behalf of women's rights? According to Alvarez (1990) for example, the transition from authoritarian to democratic systems provides space for women's movements in the application of women's human rights norms. The evidence indicates that in the short term, this has been the case. Yet, new regimes have also tended to co-opt and institutionalize women's movements, including some reform movements that have supported women's rights, as they themselves became have become progressively more authoritarian, for example in the cases of Peru, Uganda, or Iran (Paidar, 2002; Blondet, 2002, Tripp, 2002). Women's movements have also been manipulated by political actors competing for power, for example in the competition among secular and Islamist elites such as in Malaysia or in Turkey (Mohamad, 2002, Kardam and Ertürk, 1999). While secular/Westernized elites have sided with 'global norms', Islamist elites have turned to arguments relying on their particular interpretation of gender relations in Islam.

In fact, much of the opposition from states against CEDAW and its universal norms have come from a position of 'multiculturalism', emphasizing the importance of cultures, traditions and religions in defining women's rights. But as Moller Okin argued, multiculturalism has subordinated women's individual rights to masculine privilege enshrined in group rights that are legitimized by 'culture', 'tradition' and religion (in Molyneux and Razavi, 2002, p. 13). It seems that for women's human rights, neither of these positions (siding with global or cultural norms) are helpful because, once they are placed in opposition to each other, they become fixed and unchangeable, with little chance of accommodation of differences. Gender justice gets trapped in these dualisms that are perpetuated by constituencies on each side. International donor organizations that develop and perpetuate global norms are not always sensitive to local practices, moral implications or complexities. That is why their approach is perceived as an imperialist, neo-colonial one promoting thinly disguised Western norms. Obviously, a naïve insistence on the application of global norms and state intervention on behalf of gender justice will have limited usefulness without a clear understanding of the cultural, historical and political contexts. On the other hand, multicultural arguments may end up defending local power structures. Local elites may use culture arguments to continue their own domination over women, claiming that their customs and traditions are not subject to change, and beyond external scrutiny.

In Turkey's case, such dualisms go back to the 'Tanzimat Reforms' of the Ottoman Empire implemented in the second half of the 19th century, when the Sultans began to adopt Western norms and practices. 'Modern' gender norms and identities during the Tanzimat period, and much more forcefully after the Republic of Turkey emerged, were constructed and defined in opposition to Islamic gender identities and values.

A New Country and New Identity for Women: Women as Symbols of Secularism

The West has, to a large extent, determined the very definition of modernity and became its guiding force on a global scale, on the basis of ideas stemming from the Enlightenment tradition and the industrial revolution. Meanwhile, societies of the Orient were successively forced to define their culture and history in reference to the Western model. As Göle (1999) puts it, the Turkish case represents a voluntary, at the same time perceived as 'unavoidable', commitment to establish a cultural liaison with the West. In fact, Turkish modernization is a good example of the adoption of Western values, including the primacy of reason, rules of logic, scientific knowledge based on positivism, and the separation of religion and state. As such, the history of Turkey reflects the opposition between the Islamist and Westernist viewpoints as two distinct projects for society.

Göle (1999) notes that if we see modernization in Turkey, at the expense of oversimplification, as the history of two conflicting cultural models and two movements, the Westernist and the Islamist, then it is also clear that the position of women is the determining factor in these conflicts framing the existing dualities, such as Islam/the West, traditional/modern, equality/difference, and private/public (Göle, p. 30). Gender justice, as discussed above, came to be trapped in the dualism between the West and Islam. The Westernist and Islamist perspectives on gender issues and on gender equality continue to shape the debates in Turkey today. However, these debates have become much more sophisticated, and there are growing contradictions and overlaps. The principle of gender equality has come to be equated with Westernist perspectives as in other Islamic countries. Since Westernist and Islamist perspectives have mostly been seen as mutually exclusive and in opposition to each other, placing gender equality firmly within the Westernist perspective tends to limit a dialogue on equality. Struggling for women's rights came to be understood as struggling for democracy, modernity and Westernization and cutting to the heart of the Islamic social organization.

The new Turkish Republic chose to adopt the Western principle of equality between women and men together with the social organization it represented, instead of the Islamic one based on 'mahremiyet' (privacy), relatedness, and hierarchical relations. The new Civil Code, adopted from Swiss civil law, established relatively egalitarian relationships between the sexes and outlawed the Sharia, which had hitherto regulated the relationship between men and women.[4] Polygamy was outlawed, divorce laws were made equal, Western-style dress was promoted and many elite women were encouraged to get an education, acquire a profession and serve their nation as equals to their men.

Why did Mustafa Kemal Atatürk, the founder of the Turkish Republic, promote the principle of gender equality? Was it because he was interested in endorsing Enlightenment principles of universal rights, equality and individual freedoms? These liberal principles in the West had still not been applied to women in many countries and feminist movements were struggling to achieve legal reforms that put the principle of equality into practice. Göle (1999) argues that the equality principle served some important purposes: it was put to the service of secularism as the main symbol of Westernization, and of building a unified nation-state. In short, the Kemalist state was more interested in the principles of secularism, in building a new nation-state based on rationalist, positivist values, than in democracy and individual freedoms. The state granted women certain rights, such as the right to political participation, to divorce, and to monogamy (banning polygamy), in order to define its own norms in opposition to Islamic norms of gender identity. But it was still an authoritarian, one-party state, and other rights such as women's right to work, to travel outside the country were still tied to husbands' permission. Women's rights were related to and subordinated to the exercise of secularism and a tool in eradicating the effectiveness of religion. The leading indicator of the principle of secularism was the importance accorded to women's rights in a Muslim country. Secularism and preservation of national unity against threats of ethnic separatism, communism, or Islamic revivalism have continued to be seen as primary values, serving as justifications for the violation of individual rights and freedoms. This is why women's rights in Turkey have to be understood within the context of these primary values.

For the new Republic of Turkey, individual rights and freedoms, whether for women or men, were not a priority. The priority was to build a strong, unified, and secular state. In fact, in 1923, when women appealed to the authorities for permission to found a Republican Women's Party, they were refused. It was argued that a woman's party could detract attention away from the Republican People's Party, soon to be founded (Tekeli, 1989). Similarly in 1935, when the Turkish Women's Federation collaborated with feminists from around the world to host a Congress of Feminism in Turkey and issued a declaration against the rising Nazi threat, the modernizing elite was not pleased. The federation was closed. This closure was based on the claim that there were no meaningful demands women could make on the state since the state had already given women their rights (Arat, 1997, p. 101).

The reasons cited for the lack of independent women's movements in the Third World, which are generally related to the nature of Third World states and societies, hold true in the case of Turkey as well (Çağatay and Soysal, 1990). It is suggested that Third World states favor nationalist ideologies which reject class, gender, and ethnic divisions and instead espouse some version of unity or a classless society where everyone works for the common good. Studies from many parts of the developing world show that newly independent Third World states have co-opted emerging women's movements for the above reasons and as a means of dismantling the old order (Molyneux, 1981). Turkey is no different in this case. It is clear that from its establishment in the 1920s up to the 1960s, the Turkish state controlled the gender discourse, and the rules over what women could and could not do. This hegemony formed an important basis of the newly formed Turkish state's power.

Alvarez suggests that the rules over women's status and behavior form part of the structural and ideological grid upon which state power is based (Alvarez, 1990). This has been true in the Turkish case. In Mustafa Kemal's Turkey in the 1920s, the new rules over women's dress (the lifting of the veil) was, in some ways, about who had the right and ability (religious or secular elites) to make the rules (Kardam and Ertürk, 1999). Linked to this, and even more fundamentally important is that the woman question became a core issue in the 'change of civilizations' or the Modernization and Westernization project that the new Turkish Republic undertook in the 1920s. Along with the rise of political Islam, the veil, or the 'scarf or turban' has come back to the Turkish national agenda since the 1990s and the military again as the defender of secularism played the central role in banning it from public spaces. and this time the stark dualisms of the 1920s no longer hold. Yet, ironically it is the same military that provided space for Islamic groups to gain power and popularity in the 1980s to fill the space formerly occupied by leftist political organizations. The issue of Islamic dress is a very complex one. It can no longer be seen solely as a show of Islamic identity: it signifies political, religious, modern, and individual inclinations of the wearer, and cannot simply be explained as one side of a stark dualism between Western and Islamic values.[5]

Returning to the 1920s, it is important to note that while women's roles were defined by men in their project of modernization, at least a critical number of women did benefit from these changes and supported them earnestly. They later constituted the core group of women called 'Kemalist feminists' or 'secular feminists' who vigorously opposed the rise of Islam, and the increased number of women who wear a headscarf/turban in public spaces in the 1980s and 1990s.[6] During the early years of the Republic, as Arat points out, the educated Turkish women saw themselves as agents of modernization, admiring Atatürk, and expressing readiness to do their part:

> Women assumed their new roles with a vengeance. Theirs was a nationalist mission, conscious of being women in the public realm and in line with the prevailing populist ethics. Hamide Topçuoğlu, a vanguard woman professional, recalled that being a professional 'was not to earn one's living'. It was to be of use, to fulfill a service, to show success. Atatürk liberated woman by making her responsible. The purpose of the professional work expected of women was service to the modernizing mission. They

worked in service to the modernizing state, nation. Women internalized this expectation and were proud to carry it out. (Arat, 1997, p. 100)

The Kemalist understanding of equality was based on an assumption of sameness between men and women that could be artificially created in the public realm. But this led to a denial of differences in the public domain and a continuation of patriarchal/hierarchical principles in the private domain. As Arat (1997) puts it, this particular understanding of equality was transformed into a hierarchical relationship between men and women when their differences had to be acknowledged in the private domain. Arat quotes a popular journey of the day:

> In the land of the Turks, male-female distinction does not exist anymore. Distinctions between masculinity and femininity are not those that the nation pays attention to, labors over. They belong to the private existence of a man, what is it to us? What we need are people, regardless of whether they are men or women, who uphold national values, national techniques. (Arat, 1997, p. 102)

Denying differences while legitimizing equality on the basis of sameness led to significant cognitive dissonance. While the state encouraged increasing the involvement by a group of elite women in public life, it sent a different message to an increasingly large number of 'other' women who were expected to contribute to the modernization process by becoming housewives by bringing 'order' and 'rationality' to the private realm by going to 'evening girls' art schools' (akşam kız sanat okulları) where they learned to cook, sew, run a household as a 'modern housewife'. In short, the Kemalist principles of gender equality produced a group of elite women who had the opportunity to receive education and practice their professions, while the majority lived in smaller towns and village, mostly unaffected by these changes.

This schism is also one that exists in the works of Western modernization scholars in the 1950s and 1960s, who on the one hand, advocated women's equality and women becoming 'citizens' of a modern nation-state, and on the other hand, continued to suggest how women are symbols of traditional values. Accordingly, women should uphold their traditional roles of holding the family together in times of crisis, and receive education in order to educate their own family and children, and live their ambition to achieve through their sons.

New Developments in the 1980s: The Rise of Women's Activism and New Gender Identities

Şirin Tekeli points out that 'state feminism' led to a 'schizophrenic identity' for women where the early republican women defined the boundaries of their lives within the framework of the national ideals and the zeal for duty assigned by the state, at the expense of their own personal wishes (Tekeli, in Göle, 1999. p. 81). While the earlier generation of Kemalist women were comfortable in being part of a populist project and 'serving the new nation-state', the younger generation of feminists in the 1970s and 1980s began to discover and voice the contradictions between their public roles and private lives. When private lives and interpersonal relationships were questioned, hierarchies and controls hitherto ignored now surfaced.

The 'progressive' Turkish Civil Code was revealed to be permeated with patriarchal concepts of gender roles. The underlying norms defined women as the inferior partner in marriage, who was to be guided and protected by the husband. The Civil Code legitimized the dominance of the men in the private sphere by defining the male as the 'head' of the family. The husband decided where the couple would live, and his permission was needed if a wife sought employment, or wanted to travel abroad. In case of divorce, he had priority for the custody of the children. Even though, polygamy was outlawed , the Turkish policy-makers have ignored its continued practice by clan leaders and landowners; we should also note that some of the clan leaders and landowners *are* the policy-makers in the National Parliament. The continuity of high number of marriages by religious ceremony only are likewise ignored, despite the law requiring a civil ceremony for a marriage to be legitimate. One could argue that when the secular, bureaucratic elites had difficulty penetrating society to achieve compliance with, participation in, and legitimation of new gender rules, they struck a bargain with local strongmen, what Migdal calls a 'hands-off policy which allowed the strongmen to build enclaves of social control' (1988, p. 32). This social control continued to be structured on the basis of control of female sexuality and women's isolation. Such an order measures its integrity by the honor of its women, which requires, in turn, the untouchability, as well as invisibility of women. Polygamous marriages, even though they were banned in the 1926 Civil Code continue, as well as restrictions on women's right to freedom of movement. The Penal Code, which was ultimately revised in 2004, further demonstrated the strict norms of control over women's sexuality. Crimes committed by male members of a family in the case of sexual transgressions by female members, allowed more lenient sentences. Such crimes were called crimes against public decency, rather than crimes against an individual.

Until late 1970s, there was little questioning of the Kemalist position on women's rights and gender equality. Up to then, women's groups in Turkish society had followed the Kemalist interpretation of gender identities and expressed gratitude to the secular state for having granted them their rights. Thus, the problem was perceived as the need to spread modernization to the women in the periphery as the majority of the women in rural areas were virtually untouched by these reforms. With the spread of leftist ideologies in the 1970s, some women in the universities were politicized as members of the leftist student movement. The revolutionary leftist ideologies in the 1970s incorporated 'female comrades' but oppressed the gender identity of women, pointing at feminism as an example of 'bourgeois deviation' (Berktay, 1991). But in the 1980s, Turkey saw the emergence of a women's movement that questioned the Kemalist version of gender equality. Most observers agree that this movement was spearheaded by the leftist university students who had already become politicized and learned to organize. With the 1980 military coup, the government cracked down on leftist and rightist movements, when many partisans were jailed or escaped abroad as refugees. All political parties were closed down, civil society organizations were tightly controlled. While political organizations were still banned, an 'autonomous' feminist movement began to flourish, meeting informally in homes, and cafes.

Many observers see the Turkish women's movement as the first democratic movement to emerge after the coup (Tekeli, 1989). When political parties were closed and all groups which were perceived to be politically active were disbanded and their leaders taken into custody, space for political debate on hitherto unexplored issues opened up. It is also possible that political suppression raised the importance of informal groups, which could continue to meet and discuss issues. When Turkey returned to 'democracy' in 1983, the new government headed by Turgut Özal did not feel threatened by the emerging women's movement, partly because it allowed the government to see itself as democratic, and partly because the government did not attach much importance to a few women speaking out on women's rights. Moreover, women's groups themselves did not challenge state authority. In fact, they preferred to have minimal interaction with the state. This is when Turkish women began to explore the meanings of feminisms, as they had been discussed in the West since the 1960s. The new Constitution was very restrictive of organizing non-govenmental associations, or public meetings. The leftist student movement of the 1970s had been crushed and many female university students active in this movement, with experience in organizing and in social movements, turned their focus to their own experiences. It is fair to say that many of the leaders of the women's movement came from the leftist movement of the 1970s and came to define women's oppression in connection with both patriarchy and capitalist oppression. These women had also been involved in organizing women within the context of the leftist movements and established organizations such as Progressive Women's Association (İlerici Kadınlar Derneği), and Revolutionary Women's Organization (Devrimci Kadınlar Birliği). The Progressive Women's Association was set up in 1975. When it was closed in 1979, it had approximately 15,000 members and 33 branches across the country. Its newspaper The Voice of Women (*Kadınların Sesi)* published 30,000 copies. Thus, this was the first women's organization that spanned Turkey. It can be called a socialist feminist organization, focusing on social struggle, and giving priority to women's workers' organization within that struggle. Ultimately, the priority was socialist revolution first, women's equality was assumed to follow.

The Turkish women's movement started in the 1980s in informal settings with meetings in homes, cafes, around book and journal clubs in Istanbul and Ankara. For the first time some Turkish women were defining themselves as 'feminist', meaning that they raised questions and concerns that stemmed from their shared identity as 'women'. They were identifying the source of the discrimination they experienced as the patriarchal system in Turkey. This was a period of consciousness-raising, of women acquiring a feminist consciousness regardless of their backgrounds, in understanding gender-based discrimination and examining their identities as women. As one observer puts it, the Turkish women began to question the separation of the public and private, and the continuation of gender hierarchies in the public realm (Timisi and Gevrek, 2002). Thus, the slogan 'the personal is political', a slogan that Western feminists had used in the 1960s, became popular in Turkey in the 1980s as some women began to question what it means to be a woman.

Why did this activism take place in the 1980s? Tekeli (1989) has argued that as Turkey chose economic liberalization and integration into the global economy, and as the military coup of 1980 lost its place to a limited democracy, some space was opened up for a women's movement to flourish. It is interesting to note that researchers have pointed to the same type of process in other countries. For example, Alvarez's (1990) research on Brazil demonstrates that in transitional regimes, gender-specific demands stand a greater chance of being met if women's mobilization is seen as necessary to consolidate the regime, solidify its legitimacy and achieve larger developmental goals. Goetz (1995) also shows that in countries undergoing a period of transition, such as in Uganda and in Chile, some political space to promote women's issues is more likely to present itself. Sawer (1995) discusses how women's machinery in Australia and Canada were assisted by a political machinery, both reforming governments eager to expand the policy agenda and the economic prosperity of the 1970s.

The 1980s also led to a new type of politics where mega ideologies have been replaced by 'identity politics' into which women's movements fit. According to Ertürk (1997) during the 1980s and particularly since the breakup of the socialist bloc, mega ideologies have been replaced by particularistic values in determining the basis of 'identity politics' world wide. She defines 'identity politics' as the legitimate right to produce alternative definitions and symbols of identity in public space. She notes that with the coming on stage of new centers of power asserting their own gender discourse, the previous dichotomy of traditional versus modern no longer holds. In the political sphere, while leftists and even liberal-minded intellectuals were censured, traditional/particularistic centers of power along with new actors came on stage as competitors to assert 'identity politics' in the public sphere. At the expense of being too categorical, three such competitors can be distinguished: radical religious groups, Kurdish nationalists, 'marginal' groups among whom the feminists occupy a primary place. The radical religious groups challenged the secular principles of the state; the Kurdish nationalists challenged the unitarian character of the state; and the feminists challenged the latent patriarchal order of the state. Obviously, the Turkish bureaucratic secular elite could no longer dictate the terms of the gender discourse with a free hand. While the state continued to reject claims made by the Kurdish nationalists, they have had to share power with elites who support religious values and who have openly begun to redefine the gender discourse along the lines of their values and beliefs. 'Identity Politics' has created new dichotomies of legitimate images for women, Moslem versus secular being the most assertive. Likewise, feminists and other women's groups have actively sought alternative definitions of identity. Thus, the modernist gender discourse promoted by secular state elites was challenged by a broader discussion over women's place within society.

Agreeing with Ertürk, Sirman (1989) argues that the 1980s was a period marked by new attempts to define and regulate the social order in Turkey through efforts to redefine modes of legitimate participation within the political domain. She suggests:

> In the process, the very identity of the individual as a Turkish citizen was being called into question. This search for new conceptions of democracy and individuality was (and still is) a process that involved all sections of the political spectrum and is indeed productive of new forms of political participation. This search for 'democracy' can perhaps be best understood as producing a new balance between the drive towards modernization and individual aspirations for social mobility that will not be unduly disruptive of the social fabric. That such a search also includes a search for female identity has been noted by many observers. (pp. 16-17)

This process was distinctly Turkish, in the sense that the activist women were seeking a way to bring together, to resolve the dualisms inherent in 'the traditional and modern', 'the public and private', 'the individual and collectivist definitions of identity', and for those coming from an Islamist perspective, between 'modernity and Islam' as these applied to their own identities and life experiences. But, they also engaged with the rising feminist movements in the West, and the global agendas that prioritized women's human rights and gender equality. There is no doubt that Turkish women were influenced by the rising feminist movements in the West and by feminist authors such as Simone de Beauvoir. Many Western feminist authors' works such as J. Mitchell, A. Michel, L. Segal and A. Oakley were translated along with feminists from the Middle East, such as Nawal el Saadawi (Sirman, 1989). According to Sirman, Western feminism had a significant impact on the burgeoning women's groups: non-hierarchical and independent forms of organizations, consciousness-raising groups, issue-oriented ad hoc committees are clearly reminiscent of the Western experience. Moreover, most of the women in these groups or at least the most active organizers, had first hand experience of life in the West, and were aware of feminist activities abroad. They met to discuss feminist authors from abroad, and they became politically and ideologically aware of different feminisms during this period. Kardam and Ecevit (2002) also claim that the Turkish women's movement in the 1980s was substantially influenced by the Western feminist movement. In 1989, the conclusions of a weekend feminist event pointed to the three major concerns of Turkish women, which also incorporated liberal, socialist and radical feminisms major principles in that order: 'We have to own our identities as women, our own labor and our own bodies' (Kardam and Ecevit, 2002, p. 89-90). The first public campaign of the emerging women's movement was a petition campaign in 1987 which collected 7,000 signatures and presented them to the National Parliament demanding the implementation of CEDAW.

Women's groups during this period begun to formulate a public agenda, and raise their voice through public campaigns and media, but they did not yet engage with the state in any direct way. There was very little in the form of policy advocacy or partnership with state institutions up until the 1990s. In terms of influencing the public agenda, a major contribution of the 1980s women's movement has been to bring the discrimination and violence that women experienced in the private sphere and make it public. A public campaign against gender-based violence took place in 1987, interestingly enough, well before gender-based violence was placed on the global agenda in 1993. This choice of issue area, violence against women, seems to reflect a particular Turkish context, the continuing sexual harassment and discomfort that women alone faced in the public arena, in the streets and public places. The widespread violence against women affected all women, regardless of class, ethnicity or education. This campaign was organized on Mothers Day in 1987, and therefore, many people on the street apparently perceived it as part of Mothers Day Celebrations. The slogan they chose is noteworthy as a strategy, using women's traditional roles and collective identities, and moving from there to the individual right to be free from violence: 'Do you love your mother and beat up your wife' (Timisi and Gevrek, 2002, p. 23)?

Even though many of these activities remained within the big cities, the dynamism of the women's movement was unquestionable. As one of the leaders commented, there was a new dynamism among women in Istanbul and Ankara. The burning issues that energized women were also different than before:

> These women were not trying to organize for the welfare and support of needy women. They were not satisfied with struggling solely for future social equality or rights and freedoms. Rather they diligently questioned women's issues that had until then not been addressed...Doubtless, the feminists were the motor power of women dealing with such taboo issues such as 'honor killings', domestic violence, battering of women, harassment, assault and rape. All kinds of discrimination against women, including those in the legal sphere were made public. (F. Kardam, 2000, p. 2)

The private sphere was no longer taboo and was placed on the public agenda. While women were only visible as mothers or wives before, now women's individual rights and identities began to be discussed more freely. After a few years, women's groups begun to diversify into different ideological persuasions: radical, liberal and socialist feminists could now be distinguished based on their emphasis. Another division occurred between those that were educated, academics, and those that were not. Yet another division occurred in the choice of type of organization. Some were ready to establish formal organizations, while others preferred to remain within informal, non-hierarchical networks, claiming that forming associations would inevitably lead to hierarchical organization. Meanwhile, the groups in Istanbul and Ankara began to define themselves differently from each other and competition ensued between them.

What we also see in the 1980s is the emergence of political Islam and Islamists who promoted their own views on women and gender norms. The political party in power, the Motherland Party (Anavatan Partisi or ANAP), supported the rise of Islamist organizations, businesses, and foundations. For example, the Ministry of Education allowed the establishment of Qur'an courses[7] and ANAP leaders followed a policy that supported an Islamist perspective. Thus, for the first time, women university students began to wear what is called the 'turban' and a long coat, to signify their allegiance to an Islamist lifestyle. They also began to debate women's place in Islam publicly in journals and newspapers. They criticized the 'modern/Western gender identity' and identified secularism, consumer capitalism and modernity as the major problems for women, leading to the disintegration of the family and turning women into commodities. During these years, Islamist women were active in publications such as Kadın ve Aile (Woman and Family), Mektup (Letter), and Bizim Aile (Our Family). Female students fought for the right to wear the turban at universities, and this struggle became the major symbol of the struggle between political Islam and its supporters and the secular state establishment. In 1988, Islamist women established an organization called Hanımlar Eğitim ve Kültür Vakfı (The Ladies' Education and Cultural Foundation). Many of these women had come from small towns to study in big cities, or they were first generation immigrants from rural areas. By entering the public sphere wearing the hijab, and becoming politically active, fighting for the right to wear it on university campuses, they felt empowered (Acar, 1990; Özdalga, 1998). In a society where women's right to be in public spaces is still questioned, and where they may be subject to harassment as they walk alone on the streets, these women reclaimed the streets in their new attire, and claimed that they were no longer harassed on the streets, and in fact were treated with respect. Furthermore, they believed that they fulfilled their obligations as Moslem women.

The appearance on the streets and university campuses of women in turbans and coats caused strong concern among the women who identified with the image of 'modern, Western, secular woman' that Atatürk's revolution had created. This image had also posited the image of a covered woman as the antithesis of the modern/Western/uncovered woman. Thus, it was obvious that those who identified most with the 'state feminism' would also be the ones who would readily put anyone dressed in turbans and coats into the 'other' category and tend to fear and reject them. Thus women who identified themselves as 'Atatürkist or Kemalist feminists' and who saw their primary role as protecting the rights women received with the establishment of the new Republic and defending women's status against the onslaught of political Islam began to organize themselves. Their objective was to provide greater opportunities for Turkish women to learn and apply their rights. Their underlying assumption was that some women were drawn to Islam because they had not benefited from Atatürk's reforms.

The Establishment of the National Women's Machinery: The Site of Contested Gender Norms

The policy process that led to the establishment of the Turkish National Women's Machinery, the Directorate General for Women's Status and Problems (DGWSP) is very instructive as it shows the expanded range of actors involved in the definition and contestation of gender norms. The obligation to establish a national women's machinery was stipulated by the Nairobi Forward Looking Strategies (1985) and CEDAW to which the government became a party without any significant involvement from women's groups. The response to these global stipulations also came from the government. The Ministry of Foreign Affairs was involved in the establishment of the first 'Consultative Commission for Policies on Women' within the State Planning Organization in 1987. According to Acuner (2002), the Ministry of Foreign Affairs then proceeded to inform the United Nations that Turkey had implemented its obligations according to the Nairobi Forward Looking Strategies. Acuner finds it striking that this commission was established in order to implement Turkey's international obligations, rather than as a response to the demand from society (2002a, pp. 126-7).

The establishment of the NWM as a separate bureaucracy had to wait until 1991 when a female Cabinet Minister, İmren Aykut, took the initiative to introduce a bill in the Parliament in order to establish the Directorate General for Women's Status and Problems. Acuner (2002a) notes that although leftist women led the 1980s women's movement and helped put gender equality on the national agenda, it was, in fact, a right of center political party representative, İmren Aykut, who initiated the process to establish a national women's machinery. She adds that ANAP did not have a conscious gender policy; it was purely a personal initiative of Minister Aykut. This is not too surprising, given the importance of individual personalities in Turkish politics. Aykut was no doubt influenced by the global attention to women's issues; she had attended the 1985 Nairobi meetings as a government representative. She had also attended several conferences organized by women's organizations where academics spoke of the need for a Turkish NWM. As Abadan-Unat, a prominent Turkish scholar put it :

A meeting was organized in December 5-6 1989 by the Association to Support Civilized Life (Çağdaş Yaşamı Destekleme Derneği), and speakers emphasized that the only member of the European Council who has not set up a national women's machinery yet is Turkey. And four months later on April 20, 1990, the NWM was established under the Ministry of Labor and Social Welfare, that Aykut headed. It is obvious that Aykut, after attending this meeting, went to Ankara and established the NWM! (in Acuner, 2002a, p. 98)

Even though Aykut may have been influenced by women academics, she did not solicit any interaction with women's groups in preparing the draft of the bill. This, again, is not terribly surprising because of the top-down nature of Turkish politics, also because of the general reticence on the part of women's groups to interact with the state for fear of co-optation. Aykut's initiative did not go through the National Parliament easily. In fact, it became a lightning rod for both competing state elites and women's constituencies. First of all, the state during this period had become the site of contestation between more liberal (understood also as secular) and conservative (understood also as Islamist) elites who, strangely enough, lived under the umbrella of the same party, ANAP, a rightist centrist party then in power. This contestation was mirrored in the writing of the Bill.

The liberal wing of the government promoted women's equality within the context their greater integration into economic development, led by the Minister of Labor and Social Welfare, Imren Aykut, very much in line with the Western liberal feminist ideas. In other words, Minister Aykut faced no problem in adopting global gender equality norms as embodied in the Nairobi Forward Looking Strategies and CEDAW, especially in the context of women's contribution to economic growth. Western liberal feminists had argued that development had ignored women's productivity, calling for women's greater integration into economic development. The 'Integration of Women into Development' viewpoint is captured well in the bill specifying the responsibilities of the Economic and Social Affairs Unit of the Directorate:[8]

1. To make sure that women participate in all decision-making.
2. To establish mechanisms so that women may be integrated into social life and contribute to development.
3. To increase employment opportunities for women in order to ensure economic independence.
4. To ensure women's training and education so that they may compete for jobs in the free-market economy.
5. To consider women in all social, economic, political decisions so that they may be fully integrated into the development process.

The women in development approach promotes increased integration of women into economic development and growth, by increasing education and employment opportunities. This bill's wording is consonant with CEDAW, Nairobi Forward Looking Strategies and the general women in development approach:

> [The new NWM will aim] to increase women's level of education, to increase their economic participation in agricultural, industrial and service sectors, to increase women's security in the health, social and legal arenas, to improve women's status, and to establish their deserved status as equals to men in social, economic, cultural and political arenas. (Acuner, 2002a, p. 100)

The liberal wing of ANAP was in favor of greater economic liberalization and Turkey's integration into the global capitalist economy. This policy, which was started by Prime Minister Turgut Özal led to many fundamental changes in Turkey. It fueled the economy, renovated society by forcing it to synchronize with capitalist markets and organizations, created economic opportunities for people who lived outside big cities, but also engendered greater poverty and deep differences in incomes and life styles. Many women moved into the public sector jobs in this period, as men moved into the private sector. These developments created opposition and resentment in more conservative and traditional groups in society who opposed the effects of capitalist integration as 'immoral' and 'threatening'. These groups also had become economically and politically more powerful. As they moved into cities, Turkey became increasingly urbanized, and integrated into the global economy. They were supported by both the powerful military and ANAP, and had been perceived as a balance against leftist and rightist radicalism of the 1970s.

Meanwhile, the same government's conservative wing, led by Cemil Çiçek, simultaneously claimed that a Turkish-Islamic synthesis was needed to save the disintegration of the Turkish family as a result of capitalist development, claiming that women's economic activities outside the home contributed to that very disintegration. They argued that industrialization, urbanization and interaction with Western cultures have harmed 'the Turkish family'. In particular, women working outside the home have contributed to the disintegration of the family, according to them. Cemil Çiçek pointed to feminism as one of the major obstacles to the formation of the Turkish-Islamic family, along with the increase in premarital relations and moral degeneration caused by increased communication, industrialization and tourism in Turkey. Another conservative member of parliament spoke against the bill to establish the NWM in these words:

> ...It is obvious that if the Turkish women's rights are supposedly going to be protected by this NWM, but, in fact, this means a step backwards. The Turkish women's rights are protected by the Qur'an. They are also protected by our traditions (örf ve adet). We are in favor of women's rights because it is women that gave birth to the Prophets. We have another concern: some feminist organizations are presented in the media, in the forefront, and these oppress our women, and we are against them. The Turkish woman is capable of protecting her own chastity. (Acuner, 2002a, p. 149)

In other words, women had again become the central focus in the debate between Islam and secularism. An Islamic way of life meant that women's collective identity as a wife and mother had to be reemphasized, her virtue and honor came first. A woman had to be protected, and her sexuality controlled by limiting her access to public spaces. An uncovered woman, working outside the home, on the other hand, is associated with the disintegrations of the family, immorality and eventual chaos. The political polarization had now become clear in speeches by politicians, but it was more rhetorical than real. The inconsistencies and tensions between these opposing viewpoints soon became evident. The economic liberalization policies of Özal had encouraged male bureaucrats to leave the public sector for the profits of the private sector, while more women had been hired to fill those positions. Furthermore, as Özal's policies created a new Islamic capitalist class in Anatolian cities; their daughters, some in turbans and coats, found themselves in public spaces, at university campuses, receiving higher education and becoming professionals.

The wording of the bill was an amalgam of the conservative and liberal views in the government and satisfied no one. In line with the strong state tradition, it proposed strong government control of women's organizations and women's affairs through this new Directorate, *and* claimed that this would be done in accordance with a 'National Viewpoint'. National viewpoint sounds like a neutral word, in fact, it connotes a conservative perspective. It was a slogan used by a rightist religious party and is widely known to represent a religious conservative stance. This bill introduced in April 1990 was almost immediately withdrawn after much criticism from women's groups and from the deputies of leftist opposition parties. Women's groups, even liberal feminist groups who might have gone along with 'Integrating women into development' as introduced by the bill, refused to have anything to do with it due to the wording of the NWM's future activities. It was worded as the following:[9]

1. [The NWM is established in order] To promote cooperation and coordination among institutions which work in the area of women's affairs, to regulate and support the activities of independent women's associations, to observe all activities of local administrations related to women.
2. To engage in appropriate activities to protect women's status and to prepare principles, policies and programs to solve women's problems.
3. To acquire knowledge on the activities and research of women's studies units of universities.
4. To direct the activities of voluntary women's associations in accordance with the *national viewpoint* to be formulated.

So the bill came to be contested on two grounds: the state was clearly claiming extensive control over women's issues and in accordance with the 'national viewpoint' to be formulated. Both of these were equally explosive: the former claimed extensive state control over women's affairs, disregarding women's groups and the emerging women's movement in society, while the latter implied religious conservatism by the words used previously in that context by the elites.

What was Minister Aykut's response to all this furor? Aykut's response was not sensitive to these fears. In fact, she believed that the state had the right to direct (yönlendirme) civil society organizations and make sure that they all behaved according to a national policy on gender. She explained in an interview:

> For example we have a national viewpoint in foreign policy of 'peace in Turkey and peace in the World.' In the case of women, our national viewpoint is that there should be no gender discrimination and women and men should have equal rights. This is the viewpoint that our society has formulated in harmony and consensus. Thus, we see it as very useful that women's organizations should be directed in line with this viewpoint. (Acuner, 2002a, p.139)

This is a striking quote because Aykut assumes that there is actually a gender policy over which there is consensus. The most favorable interpretation one can have of this quote, is that she wanted to 'protect' women's organizations from religious conservatives by directing them in line with Atatürk's reforms. Yet, as soon as 'in accordance with national viewpoint' is included, this interpretation becomes moot. It seems that Aykut may have been basically trying to overcome the opposition in her own government. Besides she may found it politically expedient not to come outright and clearly define what she meant by this 'national viewpoint' on women in the bill, hoping that once it was passed she could clarify it.

At any rate, the language of the bill frustrated many civil society leaders, members of the media, as well as opposition parties who claimed that the bill was antidemocratic. As a woman member of parliament from a center of left political party, SHP, put it:

> As has been decided at the Nairobi Conference, there is in fact a need to establish a public sector organization that has the responsibility to implement its stipulations. But what is being done here under the guise of responding to international stipulations, is to control and regulate all activities and research related to women's issues. (Acuner, 2002a, p. 142)

Women's groups protested the bill's intent to regulate the activities of women's organizations. As the English language newspaper *Dateline* observed:

> Several women's associations, among them the Turkish Women Lawyers' Association, the Association to Support Civilized Life, the Istanbul University Center for Research into Women's Problems, the Turkish Women's Union among others, issued a press release in which they objected to the decree in its present form and proposed amendments. The Women's associations objected to what Gültekin Baktır, Chairwoman of the Istanbul Turkish Women's Union Branch, called the government's intention to control the activities of the independent women's associations unacceptable. (*Dateline*, 15 October 1990)

Professors protested the bill's intent to acquire information about all activities and research on women, claiming this to be a violation of their academic freedom. Meanwhile Aykut, the Minister who had introduced the Bill and fought hard over it at the Parliament, complained how most women's groups really are ungrateful, uninformed and concerned only about their self-interests. They were unable to appreciate the lengths she had gone to promote a new bureaucratic unit for women. Even though women's groups had begun to make themselves heard in society, began to organize and mount public campaigns, Aykut's initiative had little to do with the women's movement in a direct way. She did not consult with women's groups or academics who had discussed potential institutionalization alternatives on behalf of gender equality in Turkey, or show them the draft of the bill (Acuner, 2002a, p.132-135).

What we witness here is a lack of communication between a woman who represents the state's top-down approach and the voice of resentment and rejection by women's organizations. Yet, during this period many women were reluctant to engage with the state, especially those that identified themselves as radical or socialist feminists. Others were reticent in engaging with a political party they did not support. On the other hand, Aykut's reaction was one of exasperation at the 'ungratefulness' of the women on whose behalf she was working, symbolizing the general 'devlet baba' (father state) attitude. It was clear that Aykut had to compromise in working with the conservative wing of her party by, for example, the inclusion of Mehmet Keçeciler, one of the conservative state ministers in the cabinet, in the drafting of the bill. This raised doubts about the liberal goals of the bill. Meanwhile, state minister Cemil Çiçek contributed to the furor by publicly declaring that Western values and influences were corrupting the traditional Turkish family values:

> Flirting is nothing different from prostitution. Flirting and premarital relationships are human beings rapprochement' with animal instincts. According to Law 41 of the Constitution, the Turkish family structure is to be preserved. This was not just a natural obligation after 1982, but it became a social obligation...Industrialization, urbanization and interaction with other cultures brought along social changes. It was the family which was harmed by those changes. We are an old nation, a nation of families. At first, the family was confronted with mass communication; satellites enabled us to watch the world's television programs. A lot of tourists visit Turkey, and they have a certain influence on the Turkish people which is hardly positive. Family values change...instead of taking the developments of science and technology, we are imitating the degenerated values of the West. (*Dateline*, 17 November 1990)

Women's groups, especially more secular, Atatürkist feminists, vehemently objected to these claims. One of the leaders of the movement called Cicek's views 'unacceptable' (*Dateline,* 17 November 1990). She said: 'They are trying to put women behind bars. There are human rights in Turkey, with equality of women and men.' A member of the main opposition party, the Social Democratic Populist Party, claimed: 'It is useless to try to revive the model of traditional Moslem Turkish women; it is like making rivers flow upstream'. As one professor pointed out:

> What does national viewpoint mean? As I understand it, national viewpoint has been articulated by Erbakan for twenty years (leader of the religious conservative party). Is this Erbakan's national viewpoint? If it is not, since it represents a particular political party's perspective, what is it? Does national viewpoint mean the traditional Turkish family structure where women sit at home, do not work and look after their children? Whose national viewpoint is this? (*Dateline*, 17 November 1990)

While the bill to set up the Directorate General for Women's Status and Problems articulated liberal solutions to women's problems, Islamist policies on women were being voiced by the same government. For example, a report by the Commission on the Turkish Family Structure, prepared as a reference document for the Sixth Five Year Development Plan indicates that Turkish TV should emphasize national programs. In music, literature, and folklore, the Turkish culture should be promoted and a Muslim-Turkish personality should be created. (Aile Araştırma Kurumu [Family Research Organization], 1989, p. 36). According to this report, the Turkish family structure has been disintegrating as a result of rapid cultural changes, and the roles of men and women have begun to alter. However, the report continues, in the Muslim-Turkish family structure, the father has a sacred role and women are revered as mothers. This report implies that the disintegration of the Turkish family is partly due to women working outside the home, and proposes solutions such as cottage industries in the home.

There were two main consequences of this process. One was to the establishment of two parallel bureaucracies, one dealing with the Family (Family Research Organization), the other with Women (Directorate for the Status and Problems of Women). Thus, both wings of the ruling party 'won'. The other consequence was the 'victory' of the women's groups who objected to the extensive state control implied in the wording of the bill to establish the Directorate. The bill was revised and the wording became much more conciliatory, and a clear 'secular' orientation. The following items compare the two versions as they were published in the Official Gazette dated 20 April 1990, and 28 October 1990 after it became a law on 15 October 1990:

1. Instead of to engage in appropriate activities to protect women's status and to prepare principles, policies and programs to solve women's problems as the purpose of the new Directorate , the revised version reads: to engage in appropriate activities to protect and improve women's status and to prepare principles, policies and programs in accordance with Atatürk's reforms.
2. Instead of to acquire knowledge on the activities of women's centers at universities, the revised version reads: 'to use the research and publications produced by women's centers at universities'.
3. Instead of to direct the activities of voluntary women's associations in accordance with the national viewpoint to be formulated, the revised version reads: 'to provide information to voluntary women's associations who are members of international organizations on national values as reflected in Atatürk's principles and reforms'.
4. Instead of to promote cooperation and coordination among institutions who work on women's issues, to regulate and support the activities of independent women's organizations, to observe all activities of local administrations related to women, the new version reads: 'to promote cooperation and coordination among institutions who work on women's issues, to request information from them, to support the activities of independent women's organizations and to observe all activities of local administrations related to women'.

Conclusions

Up until the 1970s, most Turkish women accepted the gender norms constructed by the state in the name of Westernization and secularization. The rights given to women were to emphasize Turkey's shift to Western/modern values, to secularism and distancing from Islam, and not necessarily for the promotion of individual human rights or democracy. In the 1970s, in the Turkish political context of rising leftist and rightist ideologies, the first feminist groups that emerged were women in socialist organizations who organized other women for the socialist cause and were definitely engaged with Western feminisms. But they began to see that socialist promises ignored the prevalent patriarchal norms and that their efforts to promote women's rights within socialism were seen as marginal or 'bourgeois' occupations by their comrades. After the military coup in 1980 when most political expression was suppressed, these women transferred their organizational skills and passion to leading the budding women's movement. As women in the big cities became acquainted with varieties of Western feminisms, they too divided into different camps: socialist feminists, radical feminists, liberal feminists. For the Turkish context, one has to also add 'Kemalist/secular feminists' whose main goal was to protect the rights that secularism had bestowed on women and fight against the rise of political Islam. As the 1980s saw the rise of political Islam and Islamist organizations, the contestation over gender norms acquired much greater importance.

The initial state response to global norms, the signing and ratifying of CEDAW, and the establishment of the first Consultative Commission on Women in the State Planning Organization, reflects a need to fulfill international obligations. The bill to set up the new NWM, represented an effort to compromise between Westernist and conservative positions and satisfied no one. Prime Minister Özal's reorientation of Turkey towards capitalist economic growth and integration into the world capitalist economy fitted well with the 'women in development approach' that dominated the global agenda. This approach called for increased integration of women into development and increased economic opportunities for women, which, in turn, would lead to increased economic growth for the nation. This view provided the framework for Aykut's proposal – that women should be given economic opportunities for the benefit of Turkey's overall economic development. Yet conservatives in the same political party simultaneously were criticizing unchecked capitalist economic growth and increased participation of women in the workforce as the basis of corruption and the disintegration of the family. The result was two parallel bureaucracies, one which acknowledged women's individual rights and pledged to overcome gender-based discrimination based on a modernist/Western perspective, while the other refused to see women as citizens with individual rights but only in their collective identities, as members of the family, focusing on the protection of the 'family' rather than improving the status of women. Women's groups by opposing the Bill inadvertently engaged with the state and prepared the ground for active policy advocacy and further engagement with the state in the 1990s, the topic of the next chapter.

Notes

[1] The following section on constructivism draws from Kardam, 2004. Please see (http://www.tandf.co.uk).

[2] CEDAW has chosen to maintain a constructive dialogue with members rather than adopt a confrontational stance.

[3] Sufi organizations that were outlawed by Atatürk but remained a part of Turkish society.

[4] The Civil Code of the time still maintained the man as the head of the household and included a number of discriminatory clauses against women.

[5] This topic will be explored in Chapter 3.

[6] The turban or headscarf should not be confused with the colorful headscarves traditionally by village women. What is being referred to here are the headscarves or turbans, usually accompanied by long coats, worn by university students and urban women. Such attire became a political symbol, usually identifying the wearer's affiliation with specific religious groups and 'tarikats'.

[7] Qur'an courses taught young people Arabic, and how to read the Qur'an, as well as social and behavioral norms.

[8] Published in the Turkish Official Gazette, 20 April 1990, p. 2.

[9] Published in the Turkish Official Gazette, 28 October 1990, p. 2.

Chapter 3

Institutionalization of Women's Human Rights

Introduction

Government obligations in a number of different issue areas such as education, health, economy, media, access to decision-making power, and violence against women are spelled out in CEDAW and in the Beijing Platform for Action to which Turkey is a signatory. How has the Turkish state fulfilled its obligations? According to the Platform for Action and the Beijing Declaration that came out of the Fourth World Conference on Women in 1995, the actions to be taken by governments include:

1. Create or strengthen national machineries and other governmental bodies.
2. Integrate gender perspectives in legislation, public policies, programs and projects (gender mainstreaming).
3. Generate and disseminate gender-disaggregated data and information for planning and evaluation.
4. Present progress reports to the Committee on CEDAW.
5. Ensure equality and non-discrimination under the law and in practice.
6. Collaborate with civil society organizations and increased responsiveness to civil society. (United Nations, 1996, pp. 115-120)

How did Turkey do in the above categories? After signing and ratifying CEDAW, the establishment of a Consultative Commission on Women's Issues within the State Planning Organization in 1987 marks the first state response to fulfill international obligations. The Ministry of Foreign Affairs supported the establishment of this Commission, and afterwards notified the UN that Turkey had fulfilled its obligations, as indicated in the 1985 Nairobi Forward Looking Strategies and CEDAW. The first World Conference on Women, in 1975 had called for the establishment of national machineries for the advancement of women. By the end of the World Decade for Women (1976-1985), 127 member states of the United Nations had established some form of national machinery.[1] The process to set up the national women's machinery (NWM) in Turkey, called the Directorate General of Women's Status and Problems (DGWSP), had to wait till 1990, and it was a top-down initiative of the female Minister of Labor, İmren

Aykut, at the time. Her initiative was more a response to international mandates than the demands of women (Acuner, 2002a).

The process of the establishment of an NWM in Turkey reflected the divisions within the government between more Western/liberal oriented elites versus those that favored a 'Turkish-Islamic synthesis'. This political negotiation process led to the establishment of two parallel commissions at the State Planning Organization, one focusing on women, and the other on the family, and again later to two separate bureaucratic units, one called 'the Directorate for Women's Status and Problems', acquiring the official status of the National Women's Machinery and the other called 'The Family Research Organization'. The former represented Turkey's modernist and Westernist vision and focused on women as 'individuals' and the other focused on the 'family'. Thus, for example, while Cemil Çiçek, the Minister of State, gave public speeches on how women's place is within the family, Aykut (the initiator of the bill for the new NWM) was stressing women's individual identity, and trying to secure them a place within the public sphere (Acuner, 2002a, p. 130). In the end, the bargaining between the proponents of these opposing views resulted in a compromise: the conservatives allowed the bill for the NWM to pass in return for a new organization to research the Family, and for the law that proclaimed freedom of attire at university campuses, allowing women students to wear the hijab in classrooms.[2] The two new bureaucratic units were set up within the Ministry for Women's Affairs, and are housed in the same building, competing for the same resources and personnel while different ministers in charge of the Ministry for Women's Affairs show favoritism towards one or the other. The discussion below will focus on the Directorate for Women's Status and Problems since it was named the official National Women's Machinery in charge of implementing Turkey's international obligations and since this chapter focuses on the extent of state accountability to those obligations.

Creating National Machineries and Other Governmental Bodies

The New NWM: A Weak but Innovative Bureaucracy

The Directorate General on the Status and Problems of Women was established in 1990 in conformity with the liabilities of the Republic of Turkey to international resolutions and the targets of the 6th Five-Year Development Plan. It became an affiliated body of the Ministry of State responsible for Women's Affairs, Family and Social Services in 1991. The new NWM began with no organizational law and limited human and financial resources, and this is still the case. Initially, the NWM was only allocated 20 staff members and was given no permanent budget allocation. It was first set up under the Ministry of Labor and Social Welfare; as Aykut, who initiated the bill had this portfolio in 1990. In 1991, it was transferred to the Prime Ministry, and later its portfolio was given to one of the State Ministries. In 1993 and 1994, there were attempts to strengthen the NWM and give it a permanent status, but the proposed bill was nullified twice by the

Constitutional Court. Since 1994, the NWM has been running with an extremely limited budget (its share of the national budget is 0.00012%); it has 41 staff members, and no permanent bureaucratic structure.[3] The bill to provide a permanent organizational status to the NWM is still waiting to be discussed by one of the commissions of the National Parliament. Yet, its establishment and operations served some important purposes.

The debates around its establishment, as discussed in Chapter 2, were instrumental in placing women's rights on the national agenda and contributed to public awareness. The contestation of norms on gender identities and women's place in society galvanized many women's groups of different ideological persuasions into action. They demonstrated that a draft bill could be revised as a result of public demand. Furthermore, the NWM, as a weak bureaucracy, sought to find allies and in the process became an example of innovation in the Turkish bureaucratic context. Donor funding also encouraged such collaboration. In short, even though the Turkish NWM is weak by all accounts, and has been dependent on donor funding, and some would say *because of it,* it was able to bridge the state-society divide more than most bureaucracies in Turkey. This experience is shared by other NWMs around the world. Goetz (1995), in a study of six developing country states' response to gender issues, has found that states that depend on donor funding and whose bureaucracies may be weak tend to be more responsive to international women's norms. Goetz (1995) has also pointed out that the weaker NWMs have built partnerships with civil society, including women's organizations and other stakeholders.

Even though it is seemingly a weak bureaucratic structure, the Directorate General of Women's Status and Problems fashioned itself into an innovative and unusual bureaucracy. The bureaucratic tradition in Turkey is generally top-down, rather than participatory, but the NWM was able to break from this tradition and spearhead collaboration between the state and civil society. It contributed to the growth and strengthening of the academic and activist capacity on gender issues in the country , since it inevitably had to rely on the voluntary contributions of this expertise which existed outside the state bureaucracy (Ertürk, 2004). The new NWM gave women's groups an institutional framework within which to penetrate and influence the state apparatus. They were able to familiarize themselves with the international agenda on gender equality, women's rights instruments and mechanisms and make inputs into Turkey's official reports in response to international and regional mandates. The NWM also provided diverse women's groups with a common platform for dialogue (Ertürk, 2004). According to Kümbetoğlu, the new NWM, with support from international donors, has provided opportunities for women to expand their views and brought the traditional and the modern together, two very different worlds, experiences, perspectives, behavior patterns (2002, p. 166). Women's organizations got progressively engaged in national and transnational networking, campaigning, policy advocacy for legal reforms and various types of empowerment training programs across the country. In short, as Ertürk (2004) suggests, the NWM gave women ownership of the state's agenda on women's issues.

The NWM's active collaboration with women's organizations, activists, and academics has been a new experiment that is unusual for the top-down bureaucratic structure in Turkey. This experiment also demonstrated that perhaps the traditional state-society gap is more fluid than imagined. Many women assumed multiple roles, switching between bureaucratic, academic and activist identities. For example, one of the NWM's directors was a previous leader of a women's NGO. Another director was a government bureaucrat but also an academic expert on gender issues. The NWM published a regular bulletin with NGO participation. Consultants were hired to direct projects funded by international donors. The involvement of NGOs and academics in the preparation of Turkey's country reports also increased over time. Acar's (2000) research shows that while the first country report to CEDAW sought limited participation, later reports were prepared in a participatory manner in cooperation with academics, and NGO leaders. The national machinery invited women from diverse segments of society to attend workshops where strategies and inputs for all major national reports were prepared. Most significant in this regard is the preparation of Turkey's Report to the Fourth World Conference on Women in 1994, which is the product of contribution made by over 70 women from different fields and backgrounds' (Ertürk, 2004). Thus, the report reflected view of women 'themselves' rather than an official view. The second and third combined periodic reports (1997) to CEDAW, as well as the third and fourth combined periodic report (scheduled for review by the Committee in January 2005), were prepared in a collaborative manner. In fact, the second and third combined periodic report to CEDAW (1997) was presented to the CEDAW committee by a professor from the Middle East Technical University.

Among the many activities initiated by the NWM, several stand out. The Directorate helped to establish and coordinated four commissions, with the participation of women's organizations, in law, education, employment and health. The objective of these commissions was to prepare and present policy proposals in these areas. Furthermore, a protocol agreement was signed between the Directorate and the Ministries of Education and Health to work on the following objectives: women's basic health, access to family planning, increased literacy and improved economic opportunities for women in the poorer Southeast region. With support from international donors, the Directorate supported the development of gender expertise including the establishment of gender and women's studies centers at universities, research by individuals and organizations, and projects of women's NGOs. This process led to the accumulation of knowledge, offering of new courses and graduate degrees on gender issues. The NWM in cooperation with women's NGOs and the new academic centers began to adopt gender training manuals, developed in the West, to the Turkish context and accumulated knowledge on gender training and women's empowerment. The new academic centers developed gender sensitivity training courses for various groups, such as the police, labor syndicates and others. All of these activities could not have been undertaken without donor support, among whom the United Nations Development Programme stands out as the instigator of many new programs. UNDP supported the NWM by a project titled 'Strengthening Women's Integration into Development', starting in 1993.[4] The priorities of this project were: integration of gender into sectoral planning and into development, creation of gender-based statistics, strengthening of the NWM, training and education programs for gender sensitivity, support for research and pilot projects related to women. It also emphasized strengthening of the coordination and collaboration between the government and women's NGOs. UNDP also contributed to the establishment of a number of centers for women and gender studies. Master of Arts programs in gender and women's studies and research centers were established at universities of Istanbul, Marmara, Ankara, Çukurova, Gazi, Ege, Gaziantep, Mersin, Çankaya, Atılım, and Anadolu (DPT report, 112-113). Another UNDP project focused on changing discriminatory and negative images of women in the media. Another was on women's human rights. A booklet titled 'We Have Rights' was published and widely distributed. This booklet focuses on early marriage, bride price and violence in the home. Besides UNDP, the World Bank also supported the NWM with a project titled 'Women's Employment in Turkey'. This project aimed to integrate women into non-traditional professions and to support research with the ultimate objective of providing opportunities for women for employment in all sectors. It allowed the establishment of a documentation center at the NWM offices and supported the development of gender training materials that were implemented by facilitators in different locations. It also supported the writing of a report on 'Women's Economic Status in Turkey' (Koker and Ataüuz, 1996).

Undoubtedly, donor funding has encouraged dialogue between the NWM and civil society organizations and created many such opportunities. But the dependence on donor funding has its drawbacks. The very existence of international donor support may reduce local commitment or interest or lead to the perception that gender-related activities are 'foreign imports'. Donor agencies bring their own agenda and may create dependency rather than self-sustainability over the long term. Furthermore, not all donors are equal: some donors are more influential than others. As a major supporter of gender issues, the UN system's financial resources and influence are relatively limited compared to the Bretton Woods institutions. The latter promote a neo-liberal paradigm that does not necessarily give priority to claims of equality (including gender equality) and social justice over the goals of market-based economic growth and streamlined government. When donor agencies seem to shape the development agenda and prioritize areas for funding, it is not easy to formulate a coherent national strategy stemming from local needs. As one Turkish researcher wistfully puts it, first Western donors claim that women are in a position of need and discrimination, and then provide large amount funds in order to shape what should be done for them (Kümbetoğlu, 2002). Another researcher and former NWM director points out that donor dependence may put limitations on the Turkish NWM's ability to develop self-driven, coherent gender equality policies and strategies (Acuner, 2002a).

International donor support became vital for the Directorate, partly because of lack of domestic political support. Lack of political commitment to the directorate simply means that bureaucrats will not see any incentive in putting their energies and resources into it. Bureaucrats will be attracted to gender programs only if they believe that there are opportunities to be tapped, but once funds and other incentives dry up, they are likely to fall back on traditional gender-discriminatory practices (Bangura, 1996, p.31). As mentioned earlier, the women's machinery emerged with no permanent status, and extremely limited funds. At the outset, many women's groups were ambivalent or outright against a women's machinery for a variety of reasons, including their ideological stance towards the ruling party, ANAP, reticence to collaborate with state institutions, or lack of interest or capacity to engage with a state bureaucracy. Once the NWM was established, the existence of donor funding created more stakeholders, such as university research centers and new degree programs, individual researchers and academics, and women's NGOs who benefited. The NWM has had a more difficult time creating allies and stakeholders among other government institutions, or attracting ambitious and career-oriented bureaucrats. As Goetz (1995) puts it, NWMs, in general, are still not equipped to alter the incentive structures governing individual bureaucrats or departments. According to her, they usually cannot offer material or status rewards, nor can they provide useful technical support and they lack the powers of ultimate sanction over policy and program proposals that fail to incorporate gender-sensitive perspectives (1995, p.52). Furthermore, as donor funding became more limited over time, those people working on a contract basis with the NWM departed.

Part of the problem is inherent in the nature of the NWM as a bureaucracy engaged in changing social norms when the general character of bureaucracies, including in Turkey, are more oriented towards keeping the status quo rather than innovation. For individual bureaucrats, it is very hard to be a change agent if one's priority is to keep one's position. Career aspirations often compete with the commitment to gender equality. The paradox that the NWMs face is the following: they are state institutions in the business of altering those very institutions (Kardam and Acuner, 2003). Their success requires working inside the state but sometimes against the state. This means that the NWM staff have to acquire a dual identity: they cannot be just bureaucrats; they have to bring the goals of the women's movement that are outside the state and make it palatable within the state. In the Turkish case, the director of the NWM has changed frequently, as governments changed. Sometimes the director had strong gender expertise and acted successfully as a policy advocate and other times she was a bureaucrat from another agency who did not have the relevant expertise or interest. Furthermore, there usually is ambiguity regarding the role of the NWMs: are they coordinating, resource-allocating or policy-making bodies? Should they be building human resources on gender issues? Should they promote internal policy advocacy and build alliances with other state bureaucracies? How can one bureaucracy undertake all these tasks? Should the role of the NWM be a resource for policy dialogue on gender equality, a place for establishing common ground for joint efforts among all sectoral counterparts and pertinent actors such as advocacy groups, women's movement, women's NGOs, public officials, political parties and media?

In Turkey, gender equality has generally not been perceived as a priority area by politicians and is easily manipulated for their own interests. Furthermore, the few resources accorded for gender equality are in proportion with the small political clout of women's groups. In many countries the main problem is the lack of ideological leadership. There is no stable political perspective that incorporates and owns gender equality policies. For example, in Turkey support for gender equality depends very much on the socio-political context of the times, and such support moves from center right to center left parties depending on political expediency. Under such circumstances, the NWMs find themselves in a politically precarious position. Political instability and frequent changes of government have made NWMs dependent on political fortunes as in many countries. What does political instability imply for NWMs? Instability leads to job insecurity and an atmosphere of uncertainty. Inevitably, lack of motivation and ineffective performance follows when it is not clear how long one's job is going to continue.

Overall, the picture that emerges is one of a bureaucracy that is born weak and continues with extremely limited resources. But with donor assistance, it has created and collaborated with a set of allies in society, including women's organizations, research centers and universities. It has succeeded in creating gender expertise and data, in expanding gender-related knowledge, in helping to disseminate that knowledge, in working with women's organizations at global conferences and in the preparation of proposals for legal reforms.

Further Institutionalization Efforts

With the establishment of a Gender Commission in 1987, women's issues began to be included in National Development Plans. Interestingly, as the development discourse changed from 'women' to 'gender', this was also reflected in the Five-Year Development Plans. The 1990-1995 and 1996-2000 National Development Plans adopt an approach in line with 'Integrating Women into Development' and focus on themes such as enhancing women's education, expanding women's participation in non-agricultural labor through increased access to vocational and higher education, as well as measures for eliminating workplace discrimination. The Seventh Five Year Development Plan, covering national development strategies for 1996-2000, on the other hand, specified measures for ensuring gender equality as follows:

> It is elemental that women participate as individuals of equal status in all areas of social life. Measures will be taken to improve the status of women in the fields of education, health, labor, social security and employment. Measures will be taken to eliminate existing inequalities. Efforts will continue to eliminate the factors that negatively impact women's status in society. In order to advance social welfare and to ensure that women derive maximum benefits from social welfare, emphasis on women's education and participation will be increased.

In the Eighth 2000-2005 National Development Plan, there is a new approach to gender issues. This Plan does not just focus on women's health, employment and education, but also on violence against women, law, politics and gender mainstreaming in the public sector, in line with the global emphasis on these issues. As part of this process, the State Planning Organization convened Gender Commissions on health, education, violence against women, law, politics, and institutionalization in the public sector with the participation of gender experts, academics and civil society representatives. These are significant developments that demonstrate a shift in the discourse on gender issues and in the extent of institutionalization of gender equality. They also sow a new level of collaboration between state and civil society in the work of the consultative commissions.[5]

Institutionalization of gender issues in national and local governance remains limited but some significant changes have occurred. In 1993, a Department for Gender-Disaggregated Statistics was established at the State Statistics Institute with donor funding. Several ministries have set up units focusing on gender issues. These include the Department for Women in Rural Development in the Ministry of Agriculture, the Women's Education Branch Directorate within the Ministry of National Education and the General Directorate of Mother-Child Health within the Ministry of Health. So far little gender mainstreaming training for the public sector has taken place. The NWM has developed a 'Gender Training Program' which has been used to train small groups of staff members at the State Planning Organization, the Medical Association, State Employment Agency and within the NWM itself. Within the provinces, 12 Women's Status Units have been created, housed in mayor's offices and mainly staffed by Social Services personnel.[6] Within the Department of Social Services and the Protection of Children (SHCEK), there is now a Directorate for Services to Women. This directorate runs women's shelters called 'guesthouses'. There are now 7 such guesthouses located in Ankara, Antalya, Bursa, Eskişehir, Istanbul and Samsun. The SHCEK community centers around the country offer courses to women including ones on women's human rights, courses for parents on child education and literacy. Some of these courses are offered in partnership with women's NGOs, such as Women for Women's Human Rights-New Ways (WWHR) and Mother Child Education Foundation (AÇEV) with support from international donors. The GAP Administration (Güneydoğu Anadolu Projesi) has set up 21 ÇATOMs (Multipurpose Community Centers) that mainly offer services to women in the East and Southeast regions (Fazlıoğlu, 2003), as part of a vast socioeconomic development project. These centers offer courses for women in literacy, human rights, family planning and small business development with NGO participation. The ÇATOMs maintain a participatory approach and aim at sustainable development (Fazlıoğlu, 2003).

Women's participation in local governance has increased since the early 1990s where women's organizations approached municipalities for support to open women's shelters and counseling centers. For example, for the first time in Turkey, the Women's Solidarity Foundation based in Ankara formed a partnership with a local government and opened a Women's Counseling Center in 1991 and the first women's shelter in 1993. The increased collaboration between local governments and civil society organizations has been given an impetus by global developments. Participation in local governance was brought on the global agenda with the 1992 Rio Conference and its 'Local Agenda 21' recommended that each locality form its own Local Agenda 21 with the contribution of women and youth, to participate in decision-making processes. UNDP in Turkey has supported the establishment of Local Agenda 21 groups within municipalities.[7]

Integrating Gender Perspectives in Legislation

Lifting Reservations to CEDAW

Turkey ratified CEDAW with reservations to Article 15 (2) and (4); 16 (c), (d), (f) and (g). These reservations included equal rights in freedom to choose residence, legal capacity in civil matters, equal rights during marriage, matters of children, the right to choose a family name, a profession, and an occupation. Even though the Turkish state consistently declared its intention to lift the reservations to this article, this situation lasted for 15 years. The reservations, according to Acar, reflected 'a deep underlying ideological conflict between progressive and traditional views with respect to gender equality, women's roles and particularly private sphere relations that have existed in Turkish society throughout the Republican era' (2000, p. 207). According to Acar, the adoption of the General Statement on Reservations by the CEDAW monitoring committee at its 19th session, calling for withdrawal of all reservations to the Convention by the year 2000, was an important motivation for the State Ministry for Women's Affairs to take an initiative (2000, p. 207). A Parliamentary Commission was convened to inquire into the issue of women's status and offer solutions towards the full implementation of CEDAW in Turkey. The report of the Commission, published in July 1997, reiterated CEDAW's central function and underlined its salience as a yardstick for all measures to be taken de jure and and de facto, in order to ensure recognition, promotion and protection of women's human rights (Acar, 2000, p. 212). Finally, in September 1999, the Turkish government withdrew its reservation to the above articles. The removal of reservations no doubt opened the way to more effective harmonization of CEDAW with domestic legislation. According to Acar, this action was taken by political decision-makers, cooperating closely with sympathetic bureaucrats, and academicians, without significant effort on behalf of women's NGOs (Acar, 2000, p. 207). It is important to point, however, that many discriminatory items had already been repealed or changed in the Turkish legal system with significant contribution from women activists. The intensive public campaigns organized in the late 1980s by women's groups created public consciousness and sensitivity around violence against women and discriminatory clauses in the Turkish Civil and Criminal Laws.

The first change towards removing gender discriminatory legislation occurred in 1990. Paragraph 438 of the Turkish Penal Code that reduced a rapist's punishment if the person raped was a prostitute was repealed. In 1992, the Constitutional Court annulled the law that required a husband's permission for the wife to be gainfully employed. The latter law was rendered unconstitutional as a result of a landmark case brought to court by the advocacy efforts of women's groups (Gülçür, 2000, p. 14). The Constitutional Court made extensive reference to CEDAW as those of a ratified international treaty to which national legislation should adapt. The reasoning behind the Constitutional Court's decision emphasized CEDAW's notion of nondiscrimination of women in marriage (Acar, 2000, p. 213). Married women now have the right to keep their maiden name and the right to travel abroad without their husbands' permission.

Family Protection Law

A special law entitled 'Family Protection Law' on violence against women was enacted in 1998. As one analyst comments: 'the feminist movement dared to voice and bring into the public agenda issues no one had voiced publicly before – violence against women, rape, incest, sexual harassment and wife battering'. In a society as deeply patriarchal as Turkey, publicizing these presumably 'private' matters is no minor achievement. Now we see the repercussions of this agenda, not only in the three major cities, but also impacting Diyarbakır and Urfa (in the Southeast), once unthinkable areas for the feminist agenda. Starting in the 1980s, the campaign on domestic violence built up, characterized by panel discussions, media reports, lobbying, and demonstrations, and leading to legal reform. Thus, the issue of violence against women was placed on the national agenda, but this does not automatically lead to a place on the government agenda. As Acar explained, the politicians were also influenced by the CEDAW Committee's response to the report submitted by Turkey:

> The domestic violence act, (Law No. 4320 Family Protection Law) was influenced by CEDAW in terms of not only the inspiration and ideology that promoted and legitimated women's human rights and obliged the State to take action to protect women from violations of their human rights, but also with regard to the timing of governmental efforts...The face to face dialogue between the Committee (for CEDAW) and state's representative during reporting, as well as the Concluding Comments of the Committee to the Combined Second and Third Reports of Turkey have been critical in the initiation and sustenance of efforts by the State Minister responsible for Women in drafting this legislation and ensuring its passage by the Grand National Assembly (GNA) often in what proved to be an uphill battle in the face of strong opposition from conservative members of the Parliament (CEDAW, 2002, p. 212).

A New Civil Code and Penal Code

In 1984, coinciding with the rise of the women's movement, the reform of the civil code became an issue of public debate as the Ministry of Justice published a draft law. Several women's groups submitted petitions to the Parliament urging its acceptance, but the draft law could not make its way to the Parliament, even though CEDAW was ratified in 1985 with a promise to remove the reservations in a short time (WWHR/New Ways, 2002). It was not until 2002 when the reservations were removed. In 1994, a commission was formed to prepare a new draft of the Civil Code. During that year, Women for Women's Human Rights/New Ways, a prominent women's NGO based in Istanbul, initiated an international campaign demanding full equality for women in the Civil Code. This campaign was joined by many NGOs who supported Turkish women, and Turkey's commitments to CEDAW were repeated by the government delegation in Beijing in 1995 and in the second and third combined reports to CEDAW in 1997. A new draft law was prepared by the commission and presented to the National Assembly in September 1998. The discussion of the draft law in the Justice Commission started in April 2000 and continued until June 2001. The campaign was successful in creating a general atmosphere where objections to equality simply did not have credibility. The NWM was also instrumental in achieving these changes by working on a draft Civil Code, consulting with women's NGOs and providing input to the Civil Code Commission at the National Parliament. Women's NGOs initiate international letter and fax campaigns which were joined by hundreds of NGOs which supported these demands from all over the world (WWHR/New Ways, 2002).

A new Civil Code came into effect on 1 January 2002. In addition, in October 2001, Article 41 of the Constitution was amended, redefining the family as an entity that is 'based on equality between spouses'. The new article states that: 'The family is the foundation of Turkish society and is based on equality between spouses'. The new Code establishes an equal division of property acquired during marriage as a default property regime, assigning economic value to women's labor in the family. It also sets 18 as the legal minimum age for both women and men (previously 17 for men, and 15 for women), and gives the same inheritance rights to children born outside of marriage as those born in marriage, and allows single parents to adopt children.

The new Civil Code, especially the division of property clause, met with strong resistance from conservatives; the party that voiced the most objection was MHP, the Nationalist Action Party who claimed that the legal system should not intervene in family affairs and that the family should be kept within the realm of culture, tradition and religion (*Radikal,* 11 November 1999). They objected to removing the clause that stipulates that men are the heads of households. The strongest objections were raised against the notion of 'equal division of property acquired during marriage'. It was claimed that this would lead to immoral, extramarital affairs just like in the West, and to the corruption of the family institution. Women would now have an incentive to marry many times in order to accumulate wealth! Obviously, traditions and culture were being invoked for another purpose, the purpose of maintaining existing power relations that privileged men over women (women own about 7% of property in Turkey). Tripp's comment below is applicable to Turkey:

I argue that those who defend practices that are harmful to women in the name of preserving their religious, ethnic or other cultural identity are also often protecting certain political and/or economic interests. They have a vested interest in maintaining the status quo and a set of power relations that are tied to certain practices. This is not to say that cultural preservation and identity concerns are not real, but rather they are often tied to a broader political and economic context that affects their sustainability. (2002, p. 414)

The process that led to the new Civil Code is a good example of collaboration between the NWM and women's organizations, which took five years of hard work. Starting in 1997, activists, academics and bureaucrats put together drafts of the Civil Code and brought it to the attention of the relevant Parliamentary Commission in charge of drafting the new Civil Code. Obviously, Parliamentary attention to reforming the Civil Code substantially increased as Turkey became an official candidate to the EU in 1999, but the preparations and advocacy for reform had already been under way.

In 2004, the Penal Code was revised in accordance with Copenhagen Criteria, in anticipation of opening negotiations for membership in the EU. The new code no longer gives lighter sentences for 'honor crimes' under provocation. Rape in marriage and sexual harassment are also treated as crimes. A rapist will no longer receive lighter sentences or allowed to go free for marrying his victim or for raping a 'woman', rather than a 'girl', meaning a virgin. The new code calls for severe consequences for men convicted of such crimes, almost completely eliminating the extenuating circumstances a killer can claim. It also punishes men who send their adolescent brothers to slay the offending female relative. (Minors usually escape prison time or get much lighter sentences.)

The efforts to provide a constitutional basis for gender equality, however, have not met with great success. To establish this, women's organizations initiated a campaign calling for an amendment of Article 10 of the Constitution, to include a clause on gender equality making the state responsible for taking all legal and institutional measures to realize gender equality. In Turkey paragraph no. 4a of CEDAW, which provides the grounds for legitimizing special measures or priority of equal opportunity policies in signatory countries, was taken as the basis in efforts to bring an 'Equal Status Act' to the political agenda. This initiative came from 11 women's NGOs.[8] In spite of women's groups advocacy efforts, and the support of the opposition party in the Parliament, 'positive discrimination' for women was rejected. Also, to the consternation of women's groups, virginity tests were not banned but instead the right to carry them out was limited. The most striking controversy occurred when the Justice and Development Party attempted to reinstitute adultery as a crime in the new Penal Code even though an anti-adultery law was overruled by the constitutional court in 1996, on the grounds that it penalized women unjustly. Prime Minister Erdoğan claimed that the plans to criminalize adultery were aimed at buttressing the family and that 'Turkey must not always blindly imitate Europe'. He also insisted that such a law, since it would treat men and women equally, would boost equality between the sexes. Turkish media interpreted the plans as a nod by Erdoğan's Justice and Development Party toward its conservative and often religious electorate. The EU protested, claiming that this broke its human rights policy. Some EU officials said that outlawing adultery could breach article eight of the European Convention on Human Rights, creating a new legal obstacle to begin membership negotiations. EU enlargement spokesman Jean-Christophe Filori in Brussels said that the plan could harm Turkey's image and cast a shadow over its EU bid (*Reuters*, Ankara, 7 September 2004). Women's groups protested vehemently (*The Humanist*, 7 September 2004). Ultimately the Justice and Development Party retreated.

Growth in Civil Society Networks and State Responsiveness

In the 1980s, some women's organizations either worked very closely with the state, almost as arms of the state, while others stayed away completely. The 1980s was the decade when women's groups emerged, meeting at homes and forming informal networks. The reasons for such behavior must be sought in the history of Turkey. Historically, the state has controlled and shaped civil society. During the Ottoman Empire period, the state was highly centralized. Although civil society organizations started to develop in the 19th century, they could not flourish under heavy state control. They remained small in number and were mostly social aid and cultural associations; those with political aims remained underground. The declaration of the Constitutional Monarchy (1908) opened the way to new organizations but they remained basically under the control of İttihat ve Terakki Party (Unity and Progress Party), which was the political party in power. Greater participation by civil society organizations was manifest only at times of gaps in political power, such as in the years of the independence war. After the declaration of the new Republic of Turkey in 1923, it consolidated itself by closing some of the organizations, especially the tarikats (sufi organizations) and restricting the activities of the others. With the establishment of the Republican People's Party as the state party in 1926, there began a long period where only those organizations that served and strengthened the state ideology were allowed to exist. Many of the existing organizations were closed or put an end to their activities by themselves in 1930's based on the reasoning that their goals were already achieved by the state party. The Turkish Women's Union was among these organizations. This situation lasted until the establishment of the Democratic Party in 1945, which came to power in 1950. Although the way to pluralism was opened, the traditions of holding civil society organizations under control were already strongly established in the political culture. This was reflected also in the legal framework regarding the rules and procedures to organize. The instability of the governments leading to military interventions also narrowed the public space left for civil society and curtailed democratic rights and freedoms. Although the right to organize was stated in every Constitution of the Republic from the beginning, it was never absolute. The organizations were left relatively free at certain periods, but were heavily restricted at other times (Yücekök, Turan and Alkan, 1998).

The women's organizations of the 1980s that worked either under the state umbrella or preferred to stay away completely started to look for new forms of organization and new relationships with the state. A common strategy to set up a formal organization is to form a 'dernek' (an association), but the government has the right to monitor its activities. Foundations are relatively more independent but they are expensive to establish. Some women's organizations have preferred to set themselves up as a business (a limited company) in order to avoid some of these issues. The first initiatives of formal organizing centered around the issue of violence against women. In Ankara, the Women's Solidarity Foundation established a women's counseling center and women's shelter focusing on gender based violence. In Istanbul, Mor Çati (Purple Roof) Women's Foundation and shelter were set up. Women's Rights Commission within the Ankara Bar Association, the Istanbul Women's Rights Commission and Turkish Women Lawyers' Association began to provide legal and psychological counseling to women. A Women's Library and Information and Documentation Center was established. These were all institutional responses to the 1980s public campaigns against gender-based violence.

According to the Turkey Country Report presented to the Commission on CEDAW (1997), women's NGOs have expanded their spheres of influence and formulated strategies that work towards women's empowerment, building gender-sensitive public opinion, and towards gender-sensitive policy-making. An empirical study of 40 women's NGOs confirm the above view, and show that their focus has begun to change from service, charity, volunteer-based elite organizations, to service and advocacy orientation, global networking, external fundraising, and increased professionalism (Ataüz, 1993). The same study also shows that the recently founded women's NGOs tend to be relatively more democratic internally, function in many fields rather than in one field, and have a global orientation.

The nature of women's organizations began to change from charity to service delivery and policy advocacy in the 1990s. Some deliver services such as literacy classes to women in low income areas, others organize participatory workshops for rural women to enable them to identify their own problems, and still others focus on increasing women's political participation, lobbying and political advocacy efforts to change legislation and policy, or to raise awareness on important issues such as honor crimes. By 2000, according to the European Commission in Ankara, there were 211 women's organizations in Turkey. These organizations have begun to play a significant role in developing an agenda for gender equality, creating space for public debate, promoting gender sensitivity in the media and on public agendas (Avrupa Birliği ve Eşitlik [EU and Gender Equality], 2000). By 2003, a project supported by the British Embassy created a database on 320 women's organizations, established as associations, foundations, groups, initiatives, platforms, companies, and cooperatives.[9] The NGO Forum of the June 1996 Habitat Conference held in Istanbul reflected this development; it included more stands by women's NGOs than in any other category. They were very noticeable in their numbers, diversity, interest and involvement in the conference.[10] The women's NGOs that were represented included professional women's organizations, organizations focused on culture, religious values, women's rights, health, family planning and employment. Some were umbrella organizations called 'women's platforms' that include many local branches. A major outcome of the growth of women's organizations and attention to women's rights has been increased communication among women themselves from different regions and different social classes. As Belkis Kümbetoğlu pointed out in an interview at the CEDAW Civil Society Forum of April 2003:

> Last night I had a chance to talk with several women from Hakkari and Diyarbakır (Southeast Turkey). For example, some friends from Hakkari say that women could not easily walk around at the street markets up to two years ago, and that women who belong to ağa families (aşirets) are subject to heavy pressure and control. These experiences are now being discussed openly due to women's efforts, their centers, their research, and the groups and platforms established. This meeting gives us the possibility to enter the worlds of women coming from different groups. Women form relations with different women and they learn to listen to other women. I noticed how participants use concepts like 'gender' and 'inequality' now. I saw that our efforts to emphasize such concepts have achieved the main purpose here (*Flying News*, 2003, p. 13).

Women's Organizations: Invoking CEDAW and Using Global Forums and Networks to Demand State Accountability

In countries around the world, women's groups drew strength from the global women's human rights regime and began to pressure their own governments for change. In Western industrialized countries like Canada, Australia, and New Zealand, Sawer (1995) argues that international pressure has been used by female bureaucrats (she calls them 'femocrats') to press home policy change at the domestic level. Jehan (1995) discusses how women's groups supported by international networks of donors and NGOs have begun to shape the national policy agenda in Bangladesh and Tanzania. Many feminists believe that the documents from conferences such as the Vienna and Beijing documents, the UN declarations and conventions give them leverage with their governments. They have begun to engage in accountability politics, demanding that their governments come through with their promises. CEDAW, despite its shortcomings, does at least encourage compliance. Latin American rights advocates now more regularly invoke international human rights law to press for local compliance with new global gender equality norms, and they appeal to the UN and OAS conventions in their quest to promote women's rights locally (Alvarez, 2000, p. 7).

Acar's study reveals that those NGOs in Turkey with international connections are very much aware of CEDAW and refer to it. These include Women for Women's Human Rights, Ka-Der (Association for the Support and Training of Women Candidates), and Uçan Süpürge (Flying Broom), and others. But other NGOs that are strictly locally oriented may have limited awareness or direct involvement with CEDAW. Acar also indicates that even though the priority of many women's organizations was the amendments to the Civil Code, demands for change were never framed in terms of Turkey's obligations to CEDAW (Acar, 2000, p. 208). This has changed substantially as the network of NGOs around the country has expanded and regional meetings on CEDAW have taken place. Women's NGOs prepared alternative reports or 'shadow reports' to the CEDAW Committee. This process started in 1997 when a few Istanbul-based women's NGOs prepared a shadow report and a representative of WWHR/New Ways attended the CEDAW Committee session when the Government Report was presented. By 2000, a women's NGO, Uçan Süpürge (Flying Broom) based in Ankara organized a National Women's Meeting of women's NGOs to prepare a shadow report, and this process was repeated in 2003. The meeting in 2003 was named the CEDAW Civil Society Forum and attended by more than 400 women from different organizations.[11] Also, training programs on women's human rights have introduced CEDAW across the country to more than 1,500 women who have participated in these programs (Kardam, 2003). Thus, awareness of Turkey's international obligations and the invocation of CEDAW gradually increased

At the global level, the official delegation of Turkey, represented at the Beijing Plus Five Conference in New York in 2000 as well as the regional preparatory meetings in Geneva, included women's NGO representatives elected by the NGO community. It included feminist bureaucrats who played a bridge between government and the NGO leaders. This was first of its kind: a government delegation that included representatives of civil society. Up until the Beijing Plus Five conference, NGOs were not permitted to participate in Turkish government delegations for UN Conferences. According to İlkkaracan:

> Through intensive lobbying of the Equality Watch Platform, a network of feminist NGOs that were democratically elected by the NGOs themselves, were invited to join the government delegation for Beijing Plus Five in June 2000. This development has led to an increased recognition of activist NGOs by the Ministry for Women's Affairs and since then they have started to consult us regularly in development and implementation of their programs and policies (2001, p.3).

At the Beijing Plus Five conference, the Turkish NGO representatives succeeded in including references to honor crimes and forced marriages for the first time in the final document of the conference. Clearly, some Turkish NGOs became quite effective in utilizing transnational networks and global conferences in order to include relevant women's human rights issues in intergovernmental processes and documents. They then lobbied at home towards the implementation of governmental commitments at the national and local levels. One good example is the Women for Women's Human Rights/New Ways Foundation. This organization was founded by activists who already had experience working at the international level and had participated in the 1993 Vienna conference. As one of the founders says, they were inspired and encouraged by the success of the international women's movement and were determined to translate this success into real gains for women in Turkey and in the Middle East (İlkkaracan, 2001).

According to İlkkaracan, WWHR participated in the Beijing Plus Five preparatory meetings held in Geneva in January 2000, and then in the conference itself in June 2000 in New York:

> WWHR with other NGOs lobbied the official Turkish delegation intensively. We established contacts with sympathetic members of the delegation, facilitated networking among Turkish women's NGOs and participated in the international lobbying efforts. As a result, the Turkish delegation played a key role in the formulation and support of language on our issues, which were finally included in the outcome document. (2001, p. 2)

After they returned home, the WWHR prepared a booklet to disseminate information, engaged the media and integrated this information to their already existing programs. Interestingly, women's human rights activists ran into opposition at home from other human rights organizations. As Acar notes, human rights in Turkey has mostly been conceived exclusively in the context of protection from torture, maltreatment and promotion of ethnic (Kurdish) political and cultural rights. She points out that their work has not reflected a 'women's rights are human rights' mentality:

> In general, human rights and women's rights are highly compartmentalized, and the conventional approach treats women's rights as a separate issue...The idea of 'women's human rights' is still largely an alien concept and is only being introduced to Turkish society, in the last few years, through mainly the activities of a few internationally oriented women's NGOs, and universities' women' studies programs/centers and feminist scholars. (2000, p. 210)

More recently, women's organizations are beginning to be represented in the human rights policy-making process and the planning of human rights education. A National Committee on Human Rights Education has been established by the High Coordination Board for Human Rights Education to prepare a draft program for the implementation of the United Nations Action Plan for Turkey. This committee has adopted women's human rights as one of the four fundamental human rights education areas.

As the political savvy and effectiveness of women's groups to hold the government accountable have increased, partly due to international donor support, the nature of this assistance is also threatening to turn them into 'gender experts' or 'project feminists'. Some observers lament that the women's movement has lost its momentum of the 1980s and instead, turned into 'project feminism' (Kardam and Ecevit, 2002; Kümbetoğlu, 2002). The same lament has come from feminists around the world; competition over funds has lead to changes within the women's movement and its NGOization, as it was called in Latin America (Alvarez, 2000). Concerns have also been raised about the 'NGOization of the Turkish women's movement' and the potential for being drawn towards donor priorities rather than indigenous ones in search of external funds. Many Turkish NGOs receive funding from the European Commission, bilateral donors of Northern Europe and Canada.

These donors have the ability to shape project objectives and activities. NGOs may seek projects that do not fit their goals and objectives just because funding is available. Thus, instead of the enthusiasm and fervor to change the political system through public campaigns and protests, donor assistance tends to create 'gender experts' who instead write project proposals to get funding for projects whose goals are set by donor agencies. Some become so popular with donors that they have no time to consider their own priorities. For example, one NGO leader admitted that she had become very popular with donors due to the geographical location of her NGO and the ethnic groups she worked with, and she had more offers from donors than she could handle.

In Turkey, women's NGOs may approach donor agencies to ask them to put pressure on the government on their behalf. But who are the donors and what are their agendas? One observer commented that while she was involved in gender mainstreaming conferences organized by the World Bank, UNIFEM and other regional donors, she increasingly became aware that the women's NGOs were asking donors like the World Bank to help broker negotiations with their own governments.[12] This is really a major shift in terms of the social contract where the major actors do not just include the state and civil society anymore.

Islamist Women's Organizations and State Responsiveness: A Different Discourse and Different Concerns?

Since the mid-1980s, Islamist women's groups have also formed their own organizations. The first one was created in 1987 and was called Parents Mutual Help and Support Organization (Öğrenci Velileri Yardımlaşma ve Dayanışma Derneği). It focused on women's roles as mothers. According to one Islamist writer, there are now more than 300 Islamist women's associations, clubs, foundations and informal groupings. These are organized under several women's platforms, including the Gökkuşağı women's platform in Istanbul, and Çınar women's platform in Bursa, Başkent Women's Platfom in Ankara and Southeast Region's Women and Culture Platform (Eraslan, 2002).

According to Eraslan, Islamist women's organizations manifest their members desire to redefine their identity as 'individuals and human beings' rather than in relation to just the family or the state. She laments how women's issues are politically manipulated, by modernist and Islamist ideologies alike. She further argues that Islamist women are looking to define themselves as 'citizens' and are in the process of renegotiating their identities with the state, as they organize their own civil society organizations (Eraslan, 2002, p. 242). Women who wear the hijab find themselves in a bind as they claim that secular elites find them traditional and backwards, while traditionalists (and mostly their families too) find them too modern because they are not like them.[13] In a way, they incorporate the modern/Western and the traditional. They can be covered, yet employed outside the home; they can be Muslim and feminist. Thus, the dualisms that we see in political statements seem to erode when we talk to Islamist women themselves, or observe Turkish families who observe a variety of dress codes, from jeans to turbans, and sometimes the same woman may wear jeans and cover her head with a headscarf or turban!

Despite this eclecticism, the hijab issue has became a hotly contested issue, propelling women who want to wear it in public places to become politically involved in defense of their rights. A number of organizations have been formed to protest the rules against the hijab and to help the women who cannot study or practice their profession. These include Association of Women's Rights against Discrimination (AKDER: Ayrımcılığa Karşı Kadın Hakları Derneği) and ÖNDER (alumni of İmam Hatip schools).[14] Both of these provide education to women who are barred from regular schools and place them in universities in Europe and the US. Many women who were barred from universities and employment filed complaints with the European Court of Human Rights.

This is an example of how political space has opened up for individual women to become visible participants in international relations and subjects of international law (Sassen, 1998, p.15). As Sassen comments, once the sovereign state is no longer viewed as the exclusive representative of its population in the international arena, women and other nonstate actors can gain more representation in international law and contribute to its making (Sassen, 1998, p. 94). Another example is the Optional Protocol to CEDAW which allows complaints to be filed with the United Nations against states that do not protect the human rights of women. This mechanism may only be used against states that have separately ratified the optional protocol treaty. The Protocol allows individual women or groups to submit claims of violations to the Committee on CEDAW and a procedure that allows the Committee to initiate inquiries. After Turkey ratified the Optional Protocol treaty in 2001, it became possible for the first time for individual women to take advantage of world forums to appeal for justice. But this Protocol was resisted by some members of the Turkish delegation for fear of individual complaints on the right to wear the hijab. For some secularist women, women's rights do not include the right to wear an Islamic-style dress, such a possibility has been perceived as a threat to the secularist reforms of Atatürk. But even in seeking rights to wear the hijab, one sees a common ground between Islamist, feminist and leftist activism. Eraslan talks about how leftist university students, male and female, supported the covered students' cause. She recounts how an uncovered woman student came up to her to support her protest and give her advice:

> A young woman who looked about nineteen came near me...she was wearing a t-shirt that had the female symbol. She held my hand and shaped it into a fist and said: we are not playing a game here, raise your hand and shout – enough is enough. Also put your scarf under your coat so that the police cannot grab and drag you by the end of your scarf, you must also wear pants underneath in case you are thrown on the ground and wear boots rather than shoes so that when the police chase you, you can run better!! We are not picking pears here!! I had never seen a woman picking pears but I still did what she said. Meanwhile, she was muttering to herself: these people are going to be activists some day and we will see !! (2002, p. 249)

Eraslan herself wonders how different she is, as a committed activist of the Refah Party, from the socialist feminists engaged in grassroots activism in the 1970s! Here is an excerpt from her insights:

> She was an old Maoist and feminist who signed her book she gave to me. It said: with feelings of mutual support. I was very surprised. What kinds of mutual support could I have (an Islamist woman) with an old Maoist and feminist? She answered: the passing of years and life. After a while, I observed that in fact, we are becoming similar. She was the 'comrade' (bacı) of the Workers Party in boots – but didn't I live the same process, the same commitment in my party, my own community (Eraslan, 2002, p. 250).

Islamist women's concerns may be summarized as a need to assert their individualism, and the right to the political activism in the public sphere, but within an Islamic worldview. For instance, one of the Islamist women's publications, *Mektup (Letter)*, advises women to get education and acquire self-confidence, claiming that the history of Islam is also the history of women and calling them to become active nationally and internationally (Eraslan, 2002, p. 252). Similarly, the Başkent women's platform has criticized the anti-woman views within Islam. The Southeast Women and Culture Platform has provided employment in handicrafts for young girls and works in the area of women's and children's health. Women in these groups have also attended global conferences such as the 1999 World Religions conference, and the United Nations Millennium Forum in 2000.

Grassroots Organization: Refah Party Women

The grassroots activism of women in low and middle income neighborhoods who worked for the Welfare (Refah) Party's election campaign in 1996 constitutes a significant form of political mobilization. According to Sevindi, this was the most politicized women's movement in the history of Turkish politics. She notes that 'Women from the Welfare Party succeeded in grassroots mobilization, where neither the feminists nor the other political parties succeeded' (Sevindi, 1998: p. 150). She and other observers have noted that women members of the Welfare party broke all stereotypes of Islamic women as passive, apolitical and confined to the home. Instead, these women created a new model for the Turkish woman, a Turkish-Islamic woman who was politically aware, against male authority, and for women's rights. Sevindi observes that the Welfare Party women first changed themselves and then their family members. They did this within the legitimate framework of working for their religion – the Welfare Party gave them a legitimate identity, turned the women's feelings of uselessness and discrimination into rebellion and political action.

In a sense, their fight for the right to wear a turban had politicized them. As they have been turned away from universities, they have defined the right to wear Islamic garb as their 'human right'. They felt committed to a utopian vision of Islam. For instance, Havva was trained as a public speaker who traveled to 56 different cities as a Refah Party spokeswoman, and visited many homes. Instead of the 'solcu bacı', (leftist sister/comrade) the female leftist militants, the Refah Party women were the 'mücahide' (fighter for Islam).

Some claim that Welfare Party women campaigned not as individuals, but as servants (kul) of God. But studies found that as they became more politically involved, the women also began to examine their gender identities. They began demanding their rights, and furthermore, they based their demands for women's rights on Islamic philosophy. They wanted to be feminine, to look beautiful and to be attractive and yet still be politically active outside the home. They see Islamic-style dress as a way for saving themselves and their beauty for their husbands. In this way, sexuality is excluded from the public sphere, so that they can still be virtuous and work outside the home. According to Sevindi's study, the Welfare women that she interviewed claimed that there is no male superiority in Islam and that they cover out of their own free will.

Unfortunately, when the Welfare Party came to power in 1996, it did not appoint any women to important political posts. This political mobilization of women turned to be not different from other examples of political mobilization of women for a cause, whether it be a leftist or religious cause. There are many examples around the world of how women are asked to go back to their families and to their kitchens after political goals are attained.[15]

The Response of Secularist Women

Since 1994, a number of new Atatürkist social organizations have been established by groups of secularists who worried about threats to their lifestyle as a result of the Welfare Party's electoral victories. One example is the Association to Support Modern Life (Çağdaş Yaşamı Destekleme Derneği). This organization began primarily working with women, construing the Islamist politics of identity as one primarily based on changing or 'reconstructing' women's identity. They began to implement training and education programs for women in low income areas. Thus, a significant outcome of the successful grassroots organization of the Welfare Party was the galvanization and response into greater activism by the secularist women and their creation of education programs for women in shanty towns around the big cities and other low income areas. As Navaro-Yashin writes:

> As an effort to reach out and ground themselves in society, activists of The Society to Support Civilized Life started 'houses of learning' in various shantytowns around Istanbul. In these centers, 'women from the people' would be taught all sorts of skills, from sewing to embroidery, childcare to hygiene. They would also be educated in the principles of Ataturkism. The Ataturkist women who paved the way for these local centers often admitted that they modeled their practice on that of Welfare Party activists who walked from door to door in shantytowns in order to recruit people to their electorate and worldview. Central to the Welfare Party's campaigning strategy was the distribution of food and other resources (coals, burning wood, clothes, etc.) to the people they reached out to. Activists of 'Civilized Life' started to follow a similar strategy. Whenever they introduced themselves to women in shantytowns, the activist

women would first offer their gift or donation packaged in cloth bags with the emblem of their organization (2002, p. 145).

Another example of such efforts is the Marmara University's Center for Income Generation and Employment for Women and their projects with the Kadiköy Municipality in Istanbul on women's training and education. According to Pur who led the Center:

> After the 1994 elections (that brought Welfare Party to power), we thought that the central values of the Republic of Turkey and secularism were under threat. Therefore, we organized a group of women under the name of Kadıköy Women's Platform and started work on educating women in the surrounding shantytowns. In partnership with the Kadıköy Municipality's Family Counseling Centers project, we have reached about 15,000 women since 1994. Our programs focused on the adaptation to urban life (this was an area where migrants from rural areas lived), on topics such as hygiene, citizenship education, the values of the Republic of Turkey, communication in the family, and consumer education. (Ankara Universitesi, 2000, pp. 7-8)

Istanbul University Women's Center for Research and Application also implemented training programs to women in low income areas where topics included: Women's Place in the Turkish Republic, Women's Human Rights, Hygiene, Legal Literacy, Women and Employment. They showed films such as 'Love of Atatürk' and 'Atatürk and Independence'. In many cases, they collaborated with the Association to Support Modern Life. They implemented a project on income generation for women in low income neighborhoods. (Ankara Üniversitesi, 2000, pp. 29-32).

Conclusions

In the 1930s, the implementation of gender policy by a secular bureaucratic elite which granted Turkish women certain rights served not only to demonstrate to the international community that Turkey was becoming a 'Western' nation, but also to establish control of gender norms within Turkish society. The elites mainly wanted to disown the symbols of Islam in gender rules and norms. They did this by outlawing polygamy, giving women the right to divorce, and changing the dress code to Western dress for both women and men. The wish of the state elites to appear 'modern' to the international community coincided with their wish to define gender roles in their own terms as one way to establish dominance over society.

In 1985, Turkey became a party to CEDAW and other international platforms for action on gender equality since the Western-looking elites wanted to continue looking 'modern' to the rest of the world. But by the 1990s, the political and economic context in Turkey and abroad had changed dramatically. The new political actors in Turkey professing competing ideologies, liberal capitalism on the one side, and Islamist conservatism on the other, interpreted gender equality and women's rights in competing terms. Add to that the fear on the part of secularists for the advent of Islam, and the potential threat to the existing order, the draft bill to set up a mere bureaucratic unit or 'an institutional mechanism for the advancement of women' turned into a bombshell! In this political context, the potential implementation of global women's human rights norms sparked an enormous debate, and in a way, provided the space where women's human rights could be placed on the national agenda. This debate did not result in eventual consensus. Neither did it result in powerful bureaucracies on each side with their own supporters! Instead, it led to the establishment of two parallel and weak bureaucracies: The Family Research Organization and the Directorate for Women's Status and Problems. But neither had much resources and power, and were left to compete with each other for very limited government resources. The coming to power of an Islamist party, the Welfare Party, further accelerated these debates and fears.

The interesting outcome was that both Islamist and secularist women organized themselves to defend their values and beliefs. The Welfare Party mobilized women's grassroots organization and activism while secular women mobilized in response to Welfare Party women's successful grassroots organization and to the threat they perceived to their secular lifestyle. But they ended up learning form each other and mimicking each other's tactics! While the Islamist women became more aware of their human rights as individuals and began to seek their rights, the secularist women adopted the grassroots organization strategies of the Welfare party women. The Welfare Party did not include women in its higher ranks after it was elected, even though it benefited greatly from women's grassroots campaigning on its behalf. In 1997, the Welfare Party was forced to give up power by the military establishment.

The National Women's Machinery (The Directorate for the Status of Women's Problems), ostensibly established to respond to Turkey's international obligations, emerged as a weak bureaucracy and still awaiting an organizational law that would give it a permanent status. But despite this weakness, (and perhaps also because of it), it came to represent a new style of bureaucracy for Turkey, one that is more open, flexible and willing to collaborate with civil society representatives. The NWM was able to help build gender expertise with donor support, which led to the emergence of new stakeholders for gender equality at universities, research centers and stronger women's NGOs. As Acuner notes, although it has a limited budget and human resources, it could mobilize international resources and through its ties with women's groups and academic circles, it could achieve considerable gains in terms of gender expertise and data collection (Acuner, 2000a).

There is no doubt that state accountability to gender equality has increased as a result of the maturation and policy advocacy efforts of the women's movement, who succeeded in putting women's rights not only on the public agenda, but also on the government's agenda. The emergence of a global women's human rights regime and international donors certainly helped women's groups and organizations in Turkey, by providing support, networking opportunities and the sharing of information and advocacy skills. Thus, women's groups, organizations and their academic and bureaucratic allies have been pivotal in the advocacy for legal reforms. It would have been unthinkable, even a few years ago, that there would be a new Civil Code, or a law to deal with violence against women. In their advocacy efforts, women's activists invoked CEDAW, the Beijing Platform for Action, and filed lawsuits with the European Court of Human Rights. It would also have been unthinkable a few years ago, for women's NGO leaders to join state delegations at United Nations conferences, as it occurred in the Bejing Plus Five Conference. As Acar has noted, there is now a greater public consciousness of women's human rights as a concern of the international community, and Turkey's obligations under international treaties, of which CEDAW is fast becoming a popular reference in Turkey (2000, p. 213). The implementation of new laws and gender mainstreaming within different levels of the government, however, still remain weak. The legal reforms are very recent and there are serious gaps in implementation. Women's organizations have organized gender-sensitivity training programs to public sector employees, but they remain limited, sporadic efforts without greater political commitment.

Turkey's response to global women's human rights would probably have been more limited, without the added incentive of potential EU membership. As Turkey became a formal candidate to the European Union in 1999 and the war against Kurdish guerillas ended, attention to human rights issues inside the country increased. In order to be accepted to the EU, Turkey began to enact a series of reforms that reduced the power of the military, gave rights to Kurdish minorities, and lifted the death penalty. The Copenhagen political criteria state that a candidate state has to achieve stability of institutions guaranteeing democracy, the rule of law, human rights and respect for and protection of minorities. European Union laws also emphasize providing equal opportunity for men and women, including equal pay, equal opportunities for employment, promotion and social security. The European Parliament and the European Commission have clearly indicated that greater efforts towards these goals needed to be implemented during the accession process and that there would be no accession without equal opportunities between men and women (Acuner, 2002b). The reports prepared by the European Commission in Turkey have also stipulated that there is a need to mainstream gender equality changes in the legal system, as well as in the institutions responsible for making policy and implementing them, supported by adequate human resources, budgets and other mechanisms.

The European Commission in Turkey has furthermore been a major supporter of programs for women's empowerment. Beside greater equality in work conditions, especially in the area of social security, the EU accession requires more efforts in bringing family life and work conditions in greater harmony, by establishing more kindergarten in work places, and providing paid leave to both mothers and fathers at the birth of a child. European Union countries themselves subscribe to the global women's human rights regime and many are its major supporters. The 2000-2005 EU Structural Funds stipulate their use for greater incorporation of gender equality into all major policies (Acuner, 2002b). The Amsterdam Agreement (141/4), in parallel to CEDAW's 4/1, urges the implementation of equal opportunity for gender equality through 'positive discrimination', and special policies that empower women.

Turkey's interest in joining the European Union and the readiness to make the needed legal and policy changes have no doubt influenced and accelerated state accountability towards greater gender equality. The globalization of the Turkish society and economy, the crossfertilization that takes place between the Turkish diaspora in Europe and other parts of the world, the greater openness and permeability of Turkish society to influences from abroad, the greater networking abilities through travel and the internet have all promoted greater discussion and openness to new ideas, including in terms of gender norms, and human rights. But it is also important to note that political reforms do not happen without real life actors; it is the policy advocates who work to make it happen. Turkey's accession to the EU accelerated the process, but it cannot be considered its primary driving force. The Turkish women's movement had already started policy advocacy efforts that led to legal reforms before the EU accession process. For instance, Turkey was officially named as a candidate for EU accession, in December 1999, after the preparation of the draft Civil Code and after the repeal of several gender discriminatory articles, and the passage of the Family Protection Law.

An exploration of Turkey's engagement with global women's human rights cannot be complete without tracing some of the more specific norms, from their introduction to the Turkish context, to its interpretation and implementation. Therefore, the next three chapters will investigate this engagement with three norms in greater depth: women's empowerment, overcoming violence against women, and their participation in local governance.

Notes

[1] As listed in the Directory of National Focal Points for the Advancement of Women, quoted in Women 2000, No. 3. 1987, p. 7.

[2] In 1997, this was no longer the case and women students wearing the hijab were banned from university campuses.

[3] State Planning Organization Report, p. 103.

[4] UNDP, Turkey, National Program for the Enhancement of Women in Integration in Development. This program has supported the following outputs since the early 1990s: establishment of a gender data base; more than 24 income generation pilot projects for rural and urban women; starting Gender Studies Programs at three major universities; more than 30 gender sensitization training provided to legal officers; police, social workers, etc., establishment of an Advisory Council for Gender Policy Development; and support of gender research and policy formulation activities in areas such as women's human rights, women's entrepreneurship and violence against women.

[5] Please see "Kurumsallaşma ve Kadın Alt Komisyonu Raporu" (Institutionalization and Women Subcommission Report), State Planning Organization, 2000 for detailed information on institutionalization of gender within the public sector.

[6] The effectiveness of these units has not yet been studied.

[7] For further discussion on women's participation in local governance, please see Chapter 6.

[8] Eşitlik icin Anayasa Değişikliği Paketi, (Constitution Reform for Gender Equality Package) 8 March 2002.

[9] See Flying Broom's website: www.ucansupurge.org

[10] Personal observation from attending the conference.

[11] Flying Broom (Uçan Süpürge) is an NGO set up in 1996 as networking organization.

[12] Personal communication with Simel Esim.

[13] Many young women who took up the hijab did so against their families' wishes.

[14] The Imam-Hatip schools have become the focus of a big political controversy, as the secular establishment sees their graduates as potential political Islamists. The AK Party proposed to allow all graduates of Imam-Hatip schools to compete in university exams, but amidst protests by secular elites, the proposal was dropped.

[15] See, for example, Bystydizienski, 1992, especially section 3 on national liberation and development movements.

Chapter 4

Empowerment Through Training

Filiz Kardam[1] and Nüket Kardam

Introduction

'I think now I have the power to fight with injustice. And my family cannot oppress me as before. They are aware that I'm not alone, I have friends and an organization behind me...'

These are the words of Zeliha[2] from Ka-Mer, the Women's Center in Diyarbakır, which was established mainly to support women confronted with domestic violence. She is a 37-year-old Kurdish woman who has gone through hard days of abuse and mistreatment in her husband's family by him and his relatives. She was left alone with her children when her husband deserted her and she also had to face various kinds of oppression in her own parents' house where she sought refuge. Wedded to her husband through a religious ceremony without an official marriage contract, she could not demand anything when he wanted to take a new wife. She was not even allowed to see her own children by her husband's family. The laws did not apply to her, and she could not seek her rights in divorce since she was not considered legally married. She was feeling totally downtrodden and lost when a friend brought her over to Ka-Mer. After a while, this organization became the most important turning point in her life. Sitting at the porch of Ka-Mer's restaurant, where Zeliha works currently, Filiz Kardam had a long interview with her, trying to understand how she was feeling now and what gave her back the strength and desire to live and to build up trust in herself. Is not this what we would call empowerment in the personal sense and how was it made possible?

This chapter examines several training programs offered by NGOs in different regions of the country, some in partnership with the government, and should provide an insight into the nature of how 'women's empowerment' was understood and applied in Turkey.[3]

The Concept of Empowerment: One Word, Many Interpretations

As aptly put in the title of Jo Rowlands' article, 'A Word of the Times, but What Does it Mean?...' (J. Rowlands in Afshar ed. 1998, p. 20) empowerment has been one of the most frequently used, but least well-understood words in women's international conferences and in the development discourse since the 1980s. It has been used by feminists, non-feminists and by people with different ideologies from countries at different levels of development. Empowerment emphasizes bottom-up processes instead of top-down, women's self-reliance and the mobilization of women's organizations (Moser, 1993, pp.56-57). Women's organizations have worked to attain justice for women not only through legal changes, but also through political mobilization, popular education, consciousness-raising in order to challenge women's subordination (Moser, 1993, p.76). It has become obvious from the experience of many developing countries, including Turkey, that legal changes are necessary but not sufficient. Women were given rights that remained unimplemented or minimally implemented. It is the grassroots women's organizations that contributed to the development of this concept, especially those in South Asia and Philippines. Yet, 'empowerment' is now referred to in many of the policy documents of the international development agencies although usually it does not carry the political connotation that it had in grassroots women's collectives (Kabeer, 1994, p 224).

The concept of 'empowerment' started to become more popular after the Beijing Fourth World Conference on Women in 1995 since the Conference documents had declared the empowerment of women and gender equality as a prerequisite to achieving political, social, economic, cultural and environmental security of all people. 'Empowering women' especially in the critical areas designated in the action platform of this conference was accepted at least in discourse by all participants. But it was not necessarily used with an awareness of the theoretical debates and the historical realities which have contributed to its development. Rather, it was usually employed with a broad understanding which simply meant supporting women economically or socially through different measures so that they become more visible in social, political and economic life, so that they acquire 'voice', apply their 'rights' and gain resources to become active in the public sphere. In this sense, empowerment is the necessary first step to the achievement of gender equality.

Different Forms of Power

The critical issues for feminists have been the form or meaning of 'power' in the word 'empowerment' or the kind of power training programs should focus on. To put it differently, there are different ways of understanding power. This understanding reflects itself in the way we approach society and societal change. For example, the women in development (WID) perspective, which has predominated women and development literature since 1970s has mainly adopted an instrumentalist, 'power over' view. It states that through certain programs or support systems, women can be empowered to gain access to economic and political institutions. Later, a feminist model of power has emerged which is inspired more from the thinking of Michel Foucault who considers power as something that is complex, relational and everywhere. It exists only in exercise, that is in a network of relations (Foucault, 1988, pp.101-107). Feminists have expanded Foucault's definition with a gender analysis of power relations that includes 'an understanding of how internalized oppression places internal barriers to women's exercise of power' (Rowlands, 1998, p.12).

'Power within' is the strength which resides within all women, but it is hidden or rather inhibited through socially structured and culturally patterned behavior. Since it remains hidden, the conflicts in relations with men are prevented and the pervasiveness of male dominance continues. According to Kabeer, 'the multidimensional nature of power suggests that the empowerment strategies for women must build on the power within as a necessary adjunct to improving their ability to control over resources, to determine agendas and make decisions' (Kabeer, 1994, p.229). Since it is important to go beyond formal equality with men in order to bring a radical change in women's lives, one should take into account women's oppression in different situations and levels such as class, ethnic groups, religion and international economic order. Forms of subordination may differ depending on women's position in social life so that each woman may have different needs to fight oppression. Therefore, the empowerment approach recognizes the need for women to gain power for themselves and increase their capacity and self-reliance through programs that pay attention to their needs, considering their differences and caring for their individual experiences.

Empowerment strategies also stress the recognition of the shared aspects of subordination and encourage women's self-recognition that their experiences are not just personal. Many women also live through similar experiences. Since the problem concerns a collectivity, it can be changed through collective action. Therefore, understanding other people, getting together with them in solidarity, forming alliances become important. This is what is understood as 'power with'. The ultimate goal at this point is what is called 'power to', that is, women acting together for a change in their practical and strategic interests (Kabeer, 1994, pp. 253-256). Practical gender needs are usually formulated from the concrete conditions of women. These are immediate necessities and inadequacies in living conditions such as insufficient health services, child care facilities or lack of employment. These are easily seen and expressed as needs by women themselves. However, strategic gender needs are those needs formulated by the analysis of women's subordination to men. They are issues such as legal rights, domestic violence and equal wages. Women achieve greater equality when the strategic gender needs are met (Moser, 1993, pp. 39-40).

Most definitions of empowerment emphasize two main issues:

1. A change at the personal level which involves movement to more self-confidence and independence to make choices and decisions.
2. Collective change through cooperation with others and organizing for social and political action.

However, the theoretical discussions and the real life experiences have shown that it is not so simple to produce change in women. It is even harder to transfer this personal power to collective action.

Strategies of Empowerment

As the goals of empowerment are defined differently, so are the strategies. Bottom-up approaches, needs assessment, interactive adult education techniques, experiments, peer visits, and learning from one another are emphasized. The experiences of Grameen Bank or Self-Employed Women's Association (SEWA) demonstrate that through participatory approaches, it is possible to change the initial set of needs for more hidden needs during the process of training and organizing. These experiences also reveal how organizations approach women. Do they see them only as 'passive clients in need of enlightenment and uplifting or as real actors who can make their own decisions' (Kabeer, 1994, p.235)? Being considered 'real actors' helps women feel more responsible, as well as increase their self-esteem.

Both feminist epistemology and Paulo Freire's method of learning and problem solving have contributed to the design of empowerment training programs as a setting for mutual learning (Mies 1995, p.55; Stanley and Wise 1995, pp.67-98; Collins, 1995, p.104; Freire, 1991). In feminist epistemology and in Freire's method of learning, the training process is participatory. The trainer and the participants inform one another and share their experiences. The participants may be a subordinated, disadvantaged or oppressed group, which is usually the case, but this does not mean they are looked down on or make them 'passive clients' who must be taught and directed. The trainer builds the program on the valuable experiences they have. The more she understands the world of these women in which they have accumulated their knowledge and the more she is in solidarity with them, the more the training programs will have a chance to be successful. Thus, towards the end of 1990s, in a few projects, especially those planned by feminist women, training for empowerment started to be discussed not only with respect to what was aimed, (outcome) but also how it was going to be achieved (process). Programs on gender sensitivity training or training on women's human rights started to be conceptualized by considering the role of the trainer and the trainees, and an attempt was made to learn and use active participatory techniques. The aim was to make women more aware of their potential and to support them 'to help themselves'.

Strategies for empowerment can also be conceived in terms of taking care of practical and strategic gender needs. The experiences of the grassroots organizations especially in the Third World countries have shown that women need resources and they need to fulfill some of their practical needs before they can change their situation. So the practical and strategic needs can be regarded as different aspects of the same problem. (Kabeer, 2000, p.32). However, after the practical needs are taken care of, it cannot be taken for granted that women have now have reached a position to question and change the status quo, and that they have the power to transform it. Power to transform requires women's awareness of their inner strength and a redefinition of their identity. In the empowerment process women become more aware of their self-worth and of the causes of their problems and the problems of women like them. Through capacity building, this awareness can lead to more participation in decision-making processes and may be transformed into collective action. Capacity-building programs usually include training to increase the capacity of women to negotiate, articulate and communicate, cooperate, to collect information and analyze, to make plans, to manage vocational/economic activities; to undertake various aspects of sustainable development and participate in decision-making as was experienced in the Self-Education Process (SSP Project) in India (Purushothaman 1998: 116).

Empowerment Discourse and Practices in Turkey

In Turkey, the concept of empowerment was initially introduced by international donors, and it was first used in income generation projects for women. In the 1990s, international donors started to include gender criteria in the evaluation of rural development projects implemented by NGOs working in this area.[4] In these projects, involving women in the production processes was not considered sufficient. It became important to bring them to a position where they could contribute actively as individuals in the decision-making mechanisms and could benefit from the results of the development processes. In order to accomplish this, various training programs for empowering women were integrated into the projects.

Although training for empowerment is new, training has always been an important element in women's as well as other civil society organizations in Turkey. Starting with the early Republican period, training and educating people to become better citizens or supporting them by providing their practical needs has been the aim of civil society organizations. However, such programs have traditionally been controlled by the state whose primary objective was to create citizens in accordance with Atatürk's modernization project. Training women was also part of this grand objective and served the purpose of raising women's status, educating them to be good wives, mothers and citizens (Sirman, 1989). Especially for the young women of the Republic or those who are born into and grew up with the ideology of Atatürk's reforms, educating other women to be literate, it was an important endeavor to be enlightened mothers as well as good citizens aware of their legal rights in the new, modernizing Republic. The populist discourse of the time was, on the one hand, to support a smaller group of women from middle or upper middle classes to get educated and enter public life as professionals, but on the other hand, to make sure that the majority of women accepted their roles as good housewives and mothers (Kandiyoti, 1997 and 1998; Arat, 1998). Whether in public or in private life, women were going to play the roles defined by the state ideology not for themselves, but to serve the modernization efforts of the new Turkish Republic within the principles defined by Kemalism. In this context the training programs to educate 'other' women can be denoted as a rather instrumentalist, top-down process, combined with a service orientation.

There has been some break away from the state-directed organizations during the 1960s and 1970s with the establishment of mass democratic organizations of students, workers and women espousing various leftist ideologies. Their activities were mainly against the existing political and economic system. Although they had a definite stance against the establishment and worked with larger masses, these organizations could not succeed in creating more autonomous and flexible structures or more participatory forms of management. During the 1960s and 1970s, some Turkish women, especially those who were high school and university students in those years, found themselves in different Marxist circles. They organized women's associations from a socialist or Marxist perspective. These associations were primarily anti-state and especially mobilized middle or lower-middle class women in activities against class domination and subordination by the existing social and economic system. In order to mobilize the masses of women, these organizations also carried out training activities, albeit without a socialist feminist perspective. Women's question from a feminist perspective and gender-based subordination by men were missing subjects in these training programs. These were amateur experiments in using interactive techniques of education. The training usually took place in the areas where women lived, sometimes in their homes to increase the participation. Informal networks were used to mobilize women successfully for political activism and public campaigns. In each of the above cases, training for women served purposes other than empowering them per se, either serving the state ideology to achieve the goals of modernization and Westernization, or the achievement of a socialist state through the mobilization of the masses.

After the mid-1980s, there has been some change in this picture with the increase in the type and number of different civil society organizations, as well as women's. The economic, political and social changes in Turkey within the context of globalization have opened up space for a variety of civil society organizations. Feminist organizations that were established in this period tended to ·focus on women's issues in the private sphere which remained unsolved in spite of legal gender equality. In their efforts to build an independent women's movement 'with women and for women', the feminist women of 1980s did not carry over the experiences of women in the 1970s into their movement especially in terms of mobilization of women from lower-middle and lower classes. They also largely preferred to stay away from the state in an effort to keep their autonomy. As such, most of the new NGOs were not interested in mass membership or mobilization or 'educating' and 'directing' other women.

By the 1990s, women's organizations entered a new stage. They not only increased in number, but were also organized in new forms for new functions. While a few preferred to stay informal and loosely structured, others were set up as, or turned into, 'professional NGOs', learning how to raise funds for specific projects. This professionalization of women's NGOs and their project orientation in search of donor funding is one that is raised by observers around the world

(Alvarez, 2000, INSTRAW, 2001). Women's organizations were no longer just charity-based or volunteer-based organizations but were providing specific training programs , such as on women's legal rights, reproductive rights, or mother-child education (Kardam N. and Ertürk, 1999). Such programs can be divided into three categories: a) programs that focus on skills training such as literacy, income generation, adaptation to city life b) programs that focus on self-empowerment, investigation of the social construction of gender roles, and long term collective action c) gender sensitivity training for public organizations, such as labor unions, political parties, or municipalities (Eğitim Yoluyla Güçlenme, 2000). Another study on women's organizations classified them according to the values they espouse (Esim and Cindoğlu, 1999). According to this investigation, they were classified as Kemalist (those supporting the reforms of Atatürk which had introduced important legal and political rights for women), Islamist (those supporting women's role in Islam) and Feminist (those attempting to dismantle patriarchal attitudes).

In terms of training programs, the Kemalist organizations followed a strict commitment to Kemalist reforms and secularism in their training programs, while they became more service oriented in the 1990s. They focused on gender equality and implemented various vocational training programs, so that their development strategy may be identified as emancipatory. Islamic women's organizations also have focused on training programs in which they taught women the importance of their role in the family and other institutions within the framework of Islamist ideology, while at the same time carrying out aid programs of various kinds for poor women. Their development strategy could be classified as welfare, although they also began to question their individual rights within Islam (Eraslan, 2002). The activities of feminists mainly dealt with the strategic gender needs of women focusing on issues such as domestic violence, economic empowerment of women, consciousness-raising on women's issues and rights. They challenged the social and political structures to change the existing gender inequalities.[5] Kemalist women's organizations have been interested in maintaining and defending Atatürk's reforms and principles of secularism. They were galvanized into greater service orientation in response to Islamist women's activism and perceived threats of the advent of political Islam. The feminist organizations are directly interested in overcoming gender hierarchies, challenging these hierarchies in all institutions, and addressing women's strategic needs by encouraging self and collective empowerment.

The interest in training other women started among some feminist organizations only in the late 1990s with training programs for empowerment. While gaining from the experiences of the women in other developing countries in empowerment training, they also drew from their experiences of women's democratic mass organizations of 1970s especially in terms of establishing links with grassroots women's groups and using informal networks.

Experience with Training for Empowerment Programs in the 1990s

Turkish feminists encountered the concept of empowerment and learned about the empowerment programs through their international contacts and networks with international women's organizations. By the end of 1990s, besides trying to adopt the programs used by different international organizations, some groups of women started to develop their own materials that incorporated gender training to other types of empowerment training, making use of adult education techniques. At the beginning of 2000, a few of the graduate programs or women's studies centers in universities,[6] various women's organizations and projects and the National Women's Machinery (Directorate General on the Status and Problems of Women) had already accumulated some knowledge and experience on gender and women's rights training. This experience was shared with other women's organizations which design and implement training activities at a workshop organized by KASAUM (Women's Center at Ankara University). A resource book reflecting the discussions in the meeting was published in 2000. This workshop revealed that the training programs differed in content and implementation according to the general perspective, goals and expectations of the recipient organization. The training programs were mainly directed to women from lower or lower-middle socio-economic classes. Although still very small in number, there were also some pilot programs of gender training for NGOs or for bureaucrats in central or local governments, as well as training programs for women members of political parties and trade unions, and for rural women. The topics covered included training on gender roles, domestic violence, reproductive rights, legal rights, women's health problems, participation in political life, communication, organization, planning, lobbying, on issues of feminism, women's movement and solidarity, on children's rights, on developing personal identity and assertiveness, on establishing and managing small businesses (KASAUM, 2000). In most of the training programs, there was an attempt to make use of some form of participatory adult training techniques such as learning by experience, visiting, sightseeing, learning from peers, and role-playing.[7]

In short, global forums and particularly the Beijing International Conference on Women have given the impetus especially to feminist women to design and implement training programs. These may in the long run affect more traditionally organized women's associations and make them perhaps reconsider their own training programs. However, for the time being, these experiences remain relatively limited. In order to gain more insight into the processes of empowerment through training, we will now examine several specific training programs for women's empowerment.

Contemporary Women and Youth Foundation (Çağdaş Kadın ve Gençlik Vakfı): Training Programs[8]

This organization was established in 1994 to provide services for women and youth in the socio-economically poor regions of Ankara. The word 'contemporary' implies furtherance of Atatürk's reforms towards a modern and secular Turkey. Its objectives are to provide information and services to women and youth so that they could participate in the social life of the city more effectively and could learn and apply their rights. The activities include literacy courses, courses that support secondary education, vocational and women's legal rights courses. The goals and structure of the Contemporary Women and Youth Foundation bear many similarities to the Kemalist, service-oriented organizations that serve women's practical needs. On the other hand, it is quite different because it is unusually open to participatory learning, mainly as a result of the background and training of one of its principal founders who has had both extensive experience as a government social worker and close relations with women's organizations. The establishment of this NGO constitutes a first in the Turkish context. Its activities were designed and implemented with the participation of the people living in the neighborhood and benefiting from its programs. Before it was formally established, Zuhal Arnaz, the founder and coordinator, individually visited the women who might use its services to make sure that the new NGO would be responsive to their needs.

We will focus on two short-term projects of this organization as examples of Empowerment through Training. The first one is 'The Training of Women for Participation in Decision-Making Processes', supported financially by the NWM. This was a four-month project that offered training on women's rights, as well as field visits to various government agencies and women's NGOs. The participants were trained by experts on women's rights; they also made field visits to various agencies, including the courts and women' advocacy centers, allowing them to learn directly where to seek legal help. They visited women's organizations in different cities such as Diyarbakır, Gaziantep and Kocaeli to share experiences. It was also an adventure for these women to be away from Ankara and travel to other cities without their family members for the first time for some of them. After the training session, the women collected their experiences in the cities they visited in a journal, as well as the stories of their lives with their original handwriting in a book called 'My Knees Were Shaking'. This book offers some very poignant stories that demonstrate their newly found self-empowerment. Some of these women had also learned how to read and write in the courses offered by the same organization.

The second project was the 'Human Rights Training Project', which was again a short-term project, supported by the British Embassy. This project incorporated information sharing sessions, films, visits to human rights organizations in Ankara, Istanbul and İzmir, as well as sightseeing tours and cultural events. The story of this training program was also collected in a book with the participants' original handwriting. They included incidences from their own lives under the titles such as 'The Father's House', 'The Husband's House' and tried to evaluate the situation regarding their individual rights before and after they were married. Also the visits in Istanbul and İzmir were recorded with a video camera because the women wanted to share their experiences with their friends who could not be there. Most of the women in this project are also from economically lower or lower-middle class families in that neighborhood. Their ages varied between 18 and 54 and most of them are elementary school graduates.[9] They have been participating in the activities of the organization for several years now.

The most important characteristic of the above projects was their participatory nature. The coordinator discussed the project design in detail with potential participants, and the daily activities were planned together. Some of the participants were themselves involved in organizing the sessions and other activities. Thus, the women felt that it was their project from the beginning. Learning by peer group experience and field visits to agencies and other women's organizations were also a strong part of the program. Discussing the visit to the Women's Advisory Center of the Ankara Bar, the coordinator recounted how surprised the women were to meet a group of sympathetic woman lawyers in a small cozy room in the huge, gloomy and serious-looking courthouse where they felt lost. But now, they would not be afraid to go there for advocacy. Also they paid visits to the governor and the municipal leaders. They expressed their concerns in front of authorities and learned to make demands and defend their interests. Various guest speakers, including experts on different issues, women from the women's movement and community leaders were invited to come in and share their viewpoints. These speakers were not necessarily trained in adult education techniques or in empowerment training. But interestingly enough, it was the participants themselves who planned to make the situation as informal as possible so that they could ask questions and discuss issues with the guest speakers. They even had tea and homemade cookies available to add to the informal setting. This was an arrangement they were used in other information sessions as well, which they called 'yemece-içmece-konuşmaca' (eating-drinking-talking).

The coordinator played a vital role in these projects. The trainers or guest speakers for different sessions were there only once, but the coordinator Arnaz was there throughout the duration of the project. She participated in every activity and therefore the constructive dialogue between her and the participant women proved crucial. The participants respected her and were aware that she was experienced and knew what she was doing. They trusted her because she treated them as equal partners, listening to their needs and wishes and motivating them along the way. A woman participating in the activities of the Foundation expressed this by saying: 'If they had looked down on us as, disadvantaged, inferior people who need help, I would never have come here. Even the inclusion of the word "contemporary" in the name of the foundation reflects how they look at us here'. Other participants referred to her high level of tolerance and lack of any kind of imposition on them. The coordinator was also very careful not to discriminate among the participants. In the case of selection of women to participate in certain activities such as visits to other cities (when the funds were limited and only a certain number could go), they discussed it openly and decided together on the candidates. The coordinator was careful not to create any resentment.

The Impact of the Training Programs

The impact of the programs on the participants can be analyzed at several levels. First, the participants made a switch from their collective identity as a member of family to an individual identity (I am now a person in my own right). Second, they made a switch from the private sphere (to which they felt mostly confined) to the public (by traveling, visiting other cities and government agencies). Third, they realized that the roles accorded to them as natural and immutable, are, in fact socially constructed. They saw that the problems they experienced were not just personal but were shared by other women. Thus, they gained greater confidence from this sharing. Thus, empowerment for them constituted a change at the personal level towards greater self-confidence and exercise of choice in making their own decisions.

For the coordinator, the most significant result of these training programs is that most of the women were able to value themselves more. She explained that participants receive greater recognition and respect in their families and communities, and therefore value themselves more:

> Their children see them differently; they think their mother is more informed now. Also their worth is higher in front of their neighbors. Their husbands, even those who were somewhat resistant at the beginning, accept that their wives' participation in the Center's activities. They themselves now say to others that Friday is the 'community center day' for their wives. And the women are proud to see such acceptance from their families. (Interview with Zuhal Arnaz, Ankara, March 2001)

The participants emphasized how much more self-confident they had become: 'I feel it even when I walk on the street', one woman has expressed, 'that I'm stronger now'. The women have interpreted this feeling of power as a result of 'learning more about themselves and their bodies', 'learning to share, friendship and solidarity', 'learning that there are many other women like themselves, with the same problems that could be overcome', 'learning that they have rights and the ways to use these'. As they stepped into the public sphere, they were empowered by new activities, a first for most of them, such as travel outside their own city, meeting new people, visiting a theater, staying at a hotel and eating at restaurants and doing these without the husband and family. A woman who had also contributed to the project books with her poetry has stated with excitement: 'I have felt the pleasure of writing, I wrote poetry; I sang and acted in a theater group. I have done things which I had no opportunity to do before.'

This new self-perception and newly gained 'voice' influenced the women's relationships with family members and others in their lives. They could see the change in their relations with family members and others in their daily lives. 'I have the courage to say no to certain things that my husband and children want now and spare some time only for myself. I can convince them now that this is important for me' was a statement made by one of the participant women while another expressed that she had more tolerance now for her family. She was not as stressed as before and that her family was also aware that she was behaving differently toward them. Personal empowerment not just contributed to self-confidence and overall better family relations, but also to the women's greater self-expression in the public sphere. They felt that through understanding themselves better, they could understand other people better. They found the courage to express themselves better in front of strangers, even those in front of those in positions of authority, and not be embarrassed speak up in public.

This newly found self-confidence was carried even further by some of the women, as in the case of Emine from Mamak. She is in her late thirties and has taken many courses at the Center, and is now its director of activities. She has expressed with confidence: 'I wanted to become a leader, because I was aware that in this organization they were listening to what we were saying. I manage this center now, but this is not sufficient for me. I know that I can carry the responsibility of higher positions. I can work more now with a higher tempo and can plan better.'

As mentioned earlier, the first step in empowerment is change in self-perception, to gain 'power within'. The second step is to move towards 'power with' or collective action. After the training program, the most important collective action achieved by the women themselves was a petition to get one of the main roads in their district repaired by the municipality. The women, putting their efforts together succeeded in collecting about 300 signatures, and forwarded it to the municipality with an appeal. The women have expressed that they were aware of social problems before, but this training has helped them to feel responsible for seeking solutions and engaging in action.

Mother Child Education Foundation (Anne Çocuk Eğitim Vakfı): Training for Leadership Program[10]

Women's Training for Leadership is a small project implemented in 2000 by one of the coordinators of the Mother Child Education Foundation (AÇEV). ACEV, established in 1993, focuses on both women and children, and works with women from lower socio-economic groups. ACEV also has functional literacy programs and educational programs supporting fathers. Obtaining its financial resources from different institutions, it currently implements mother-child education programs and other activities in 58 provinces of Turkey in collaboration with the Department of Adult Education of the Ministry of Education and with the Social Services Administration (SHCEK). It trains volunteers from other NGOs and Teachers Unions to become trainers in its programs.

The Training for Leadership project was a six-month project. During this time, 15 women underwent a two-week training program to become leaders in their community. These women had already participated in the mother-child education programs of AÇEV, and were all from the same district in Ankara. The training included topics on group dynamics, leadership, communication, legal rights of women and health problems. It was not a systematic and formerly tested empowerment program for women, but one that was put together by the coordinator, using her experiences working with women in low income neighborhoods. The training was mostly delivered by the coordinator herself, with the help of a few guest speakers. The participants shared some important characteristics besides similar socio-economic status. They had all completed 8 years of formal basic education or high school education. After two weeks of training, each of these women visited women in their neighborhood to do a needs assessment. Each 'leader' had to make at least one home visit or training program. In total, each woman who received the training implemented a similar program of training to about 15 women, but in their homes and in smaller groups. The trainers had reached 205 women at the end of the project period. Although the project has ended formally, the trainers still communicate with each other and with women they have trained, trying to respond to some of their practical needs such as medical or legal help. Also they are still in contact with the coordinator; they continue to discuss the needs of the women in the neighborhood, sometimes asking for help, sometimes suggesting ideas for new projects, and expecting the continuation of the work they have started with new projects.

The role of the coordinator, Seda Yılmaz, was again very important for this project because she was not only experienced in her area of work, but she was also someone whom they knew and trusted. She was a person who had accumulated experience in working and training people from lower economic groups and a person with lots of enthusiasm and deep engagement in her work. These qualities helped her to create an informal, genuine atmosphere where learning could take place by sharing experiences. As one of the participants said:

> I think that the most important thing during training is the feeling I had that she (the coordinator) understood us. She knew what we knew; she was aware of our potential that was even unknown to us. She started with what was familiar to us, what we knew and built on that... The information she gave came after. Also she knew how to listen to us and taught us how to listen to others. She never looked down on us or scolded us like a teacher. But somehow we learned to listen and learn from one another without any directives.

Another woman from the same program stated that the atmosphere created in the training sessions was important because it turned them from passive listeners to active participants.

The Impact of the Training Program

The participants first learned to trust themselves more and built self-reliance through this project. They were afraid to train other women at the beginning, but they overcame their fear once they started their own training programs. The fact that they were paid some money, however little, to undertake this training, also contributed to their sense of self-worth. It helped to increase their self-esteem. This gave them also a higher status in their family since most of them were housewives and had no personal income. Change in terms of more self-confidence was expressed in the following words: 'discovering our identities and importance of our role in the family as women', 'learning to be more decisive in our behavior' and 'having more confidence in our relations with other people'. They think that this personal change has helped them first of all in their relations in the family. Since they have more confidence in themselves, their husbands and children also trust them more. In addition, this change has become the motivating power increasing their interest in what is going around them and widening their horizons. As one participant pointed out:

> I was not so interested in what's happening in the world or in the society. Now I feel that I have become more sensitive to political and social issues and I can see things which I have disregarded before.... Now I'm not only more sensitive, but I also feel that I have to learn more. I read the newspapers more carefully, because women around me ask questions and want to get information. I have to develop myself.

Still another woman commented that people come and ask her views or ask for advice. She and her friends in the group have initiated some action or established relations with the public authorities in several cases. For example, they solved a problem with the community sewage system and a problem related to the distribution of electrical power by contacting authorities. This has led to the feeling of greater responsibility about community concerns and especially problems related to the practical needs of women. To have trust in themselves has come to mean not only the ability to solve personal problems but also seek collective solutions in the community. In their efforts to act as genuine leaders, the women have related success stories in terms of solving some problems with the municipal services, and initiating action towards the implementation of consumer rights. However, in all these activities, there are also constraints which slow down their work. They think that 'to help other women help themselves' is no easy process. They have mentioned specifically two factors which constitute barriers: the need to educate men and the extent of their poverty.

Trainers mentioned that some women resisted any kind of training or support (although they knew that they needed it) because they believed it would not be of any help unless their husbands were ready to change. 'First of all our husbands should learn these and change' was a frequently encountered comment. Changing an individual woman's self-perception puts all the weight on her to change her husband and her family. The other factor was the economic situation of the families. Most of the women they visited stated that their husbands or other adults in the family needed jobs or better paid jobs, rather than themselves. They seemed to close their ears to anything which did not seem to solve this issue. So, unemployment and poverty, being such a big problem which could not obviously be solved by our 'leader' women, made them feel powerless.

Ka-Mer Women's Center: Human Rights Training[11]

This center was established in Diyarbakır, in Southeastern Turkey, in 1997 to support women who are confronted with domestic violence, as well as to raise consciousness around women's issues and to inform women about their rights. The founders were a group of local women who believed in the autonomy of women's movement and approached women's problems from a feminist perspective. Because of political tension and armed conflict in the region due to the Kurdish problem, these women had to work under extraordinary restrictions and very unfavorable conditions. Ka-Mer, as an autonomous women's organization, met with resistance and pressure. In fact, it was the first organization that focused on discrimination against women in the region, a taboo subject in the traditional culture. It was furthermore criticized by other human rights NGOs which perceived any form of issue-based organization as a luxury when all kinds of human rights and freedoms were in danger in the region.

In spite of the drawbacks of the political climate, Ka-Mer succeeded in organizing small consciousness-raising groups and established an emergency relief line for women suffering from domestic violence in 1997. Besides providing counseling and various forms of support to women, they tried to bring together women in different social and cultural activities. In 1998, Ka-Mer also managed to establish a child-care center and a restaurant serving local food at its new premises. With these two enterprises, Ka-Mer aimed to offer services to women in its immediate circle, provide employment for women, especially for those who had to leave their homes due to various kinds of mistreatment and violence. The founders thought that a well managed restaurant could be an important basis for the sustainability of the other services and activities of the organization, such as the emergency line and counseling until other means of support could be found.

Consciousness-raising for women's human rights in small groups and group discussions were consistently used by the founders of Ka-Mer even before it was formally organized. Since 1996, about 600 women have participated in these group discussions. Twelve women from the organization taught themselves to become facilitators in these training sessions, preparing and using materials developed by others, and inviting experts to join the sessions. The facilitators in the sessions are women from the region, who had a feminist perspective and who were aware of discrimination against women, besides other forms of subordination in the area. Some of them have also worked in other NGOs and have attended training sessions on different topics such as communication or management, offered by other organizations. The fact that they can speak Kurdish was an advantage especially when they are working with women who express themselves in Kurdish. All the women working in Ka-Mer participated in this group training as well. In these sessions women learned from one another and developed more empathy for each other's problems, instead of being formally taught by experts. The groups usually consisted of 10-12 people depending on the topic of discussion. The training program was designed after an initial stage where a needs assessment was conducted. The content of the training sessions included women's human rights, domestic and other forms of violence, sexuality, communication, economic rights, gender roles, education of girls, feminism and women's organizations. There are now training documents on 14 topics (Ka-Mer'in Hikayesi , Ka-Mer's Story).

Each training group underwent 10-14 different sessions which were usually once a week and each individual session lasted about 3-4 hours. The topics are selected according to the participants' wishes and then the trainers prepare the materials. At the end of the training period, the participants were asked to evaluate the training and its contribution to their learning. Although a general evaluation report on the training programs is still to be completed, the participants' views on the training program guide the facilitators in the subsequent sessions. Also, some sessions on critical issues may lead to unexpected discussions, conflicts in the groups and may disturb women psychologically. In such cases the trainers seek professional help.

The coordinators of the training programs at Ka-Mer consider that empowerment for women begins when they become aware and start to act as individuals, as individual citizens informed about their rights and ready to use them. Therefore, they do not only inform women about their rights, but also make it a point of supporting them in various ways in their efforts to change their lives. At times this may mean providing opportunities in terms of their practical needs such as literacy or employment. The trainers themselves may need to be empowered at times. So they find it important to build their capacity not only in terms of getting information on certain issues and keeping track of developments in the women's movement but also in terms of human relations and communication within the organization. Emphasizing the need for an harmonious and efficient work environment, as well as of individual motivation, they have periodic group discussions where they talk about their problems, about group dynamics, interpersonal relations, and conflicts. under the supervision of a professional psychologist.

Impact of Training on the Participants

A group discussion session with the participants of Ka-Mer could not be arranged; therefore, the evaluation of the programs is based on individual interviews, documents and observations. According to the evaluations based on the forms filled after the training sessions, the participants have not only learned to define the violence of different types on women, but they have also gained the courage to fight against it. They no longer accept their situation as their 'fate'. They are slowly starting to question the traditions and norms which have defined their roles and their subordination. They start to feel that they can communicate better now with other people and can also be more insistent on their rights. To have a job and to have an independent income becomes a real yearning and they start to be more aware of the importance of economic independence.

Zeliha, who was introduced at the beginning of this chapter and who has regular employment in the restaurant of Ka-Mer, has expressed the changes in herself since she has come to Ka-Mer: in the way she dresses, in her speech and in her increased participation in social life. She said in interviews that: 'I am a different person now. I can go outside the home; I don't have to stay at home. I also have the power to struggle with injustice. Wherever I go, whatever I do, I will never be the former Zeliha…' Zeliha's thoughts and plans on the possibility of a prospective marriage also reflected her resolve to control her own future: 'Of course I'm not against a new marriage, but I want to state my rules from the beginning. First of all I want to work; secondly, I am against any form of abuse and torture at home. Whatever we do at home, we must share the work, and I don't ever want to be oppressed again. If he accepts these rules, then we can get together, if not he should go on his way...'

The training, support and solidarity given to women like Zeliha at Ka-Mer opened a window to a different world for them. For this reason they had trust in the organization and were grateful. However, it seemed that the women needed to get their wings repaired very strongly before they were left to fly away from this window. They needed to have a good base where their practical needs are fulfilled. Some of them like Zeliha were illiterate, with no skills which could be of use in the labor market, no individual resources to rely upon. They suffered under various kinds of social pressure from family and relatives. Therefore, the person in Ka-Mer with whom they had the closest contact was seen as their saver; they depended on her and had high expectations. The danger lies in the fact that in time they may depend on this person more than on themselves, especially when their trust in themselves is not strengthened through fulfillment of basic needs. In the cases of women who still face discrimination from the larger society and are still deprived from the basic means to support themselves, such dependence on Ka-Mer for everything may become a barrier for further emancipation. Personal power may be too fragile and wavering without a supportive social and political context.

Women for Women's Human Rights/New Ways: Legal Literacy and Women's Human Rights Education Program[12]

The Women's Human Rights Education Program is being implemented in partnership with the Department of Social Services and Children's Protection (SHCEK) in 24 Community Centers across Turkey since 1998. These community centers are mostly located in low income areas of big cities, and serve populations that were displaced from their villages in the Eastern and Southeastern region and had to migrate as a result of the armed conflict in the 1990s. This program was designed by the staff of the Women for Women's Human Rights - New Ways (WWHR), a women's NGO based in Istanbul. Its staff includes women educated and with work experience abroad including the US and Germany. WWHR is active in training, advocacy and networking; it organized numerous workshops and conferences in Turkey and the Middle East especially related to women's sexuality and honor crimes. It has participated actively in political advocacy both in Turkey and at global conferences on behalf of women's human rights. So far this program is the most comprehensive women's empowerment program in Turkey and has reached more than 1500 women around the country. WWHR trains social workers who work for SHCEK, who then facilitate training on Women's Human Rights in the community centers.

The objectives of this program are: a) to learn about spoken and written laws, including CEDAW and other international conventions that Turkey has ratified and to gain critical consciousness; b) to share experiences and search for common solutions to problems and c) to take action to promote women's rights and grassroots organizing. The topics for training include: women's human rights, strategies against gender-based violence, constitutional and civil rights, reproductive rights and women's sexuality, gender-sensitive parenting and children's rights, communication, women's economic rights, women and political participation, women's movements and feminism, and strategies for grassroots organizing. These training sessions used participatory methodology and were offered over three months on a weekly basis at the community centers.

Impact of the Women's Human Rights Training

An evaluation of the training program was undertaken in the spring of 2002. A sample of 300 former participants from around the country filled out questionnaires and participated in focus group discussions. The evaluation assessed the extent to which women had learned their rights, the extent of personal changes they experienced. It also assessed how their self-perceptions had changed, and whether they began to apply their rights on an individual basis and finally, the extent to which they had become active in grassroots organization and political advocacy.

The questionnaire results showed that about seventy percent of the sample of former participants had learned a great deal about their rights through this program. The level of learning and previous lack of knowledge about one's rights was higher in the Eastern and Southeastern regions, where literacy rates are lower. The participants felt personally empowered as a result of learning about their rights. The learning environment in which they freely exchanged personal stories and learned from each other was also deemed essential for self-empowerment. Ninety-three per cent of respondents said that they now have greater self-confidence as a result of the training, and seventy-four per cent said that their self-perception had changed in a positive way. This self-empowerment usually led to greater respect towards them by their families and communities. Similar to the results of the training programs discussed earlier, many women mentioned how they were able to express themselves better now, how they believed in themselves more, and how they were now approached for help and advice by their family and community. This did not mean, of course, that their families accepted these changes without resistance. Seventy per cent of respondents said that their husbands and other family members' attitudes towards them had changed for the positive. The rest had either stayed the same or worsened. The respondents in focus groups discussions frequently mentioned the resistance they faced from husbands, mothers-in-law and even neighbors who remarked: 'Why do you need to learn about women's rights? Are you going to divorce your husband? Are you going to become a feminist? Why do you have to go out?' At the same time, many women said that over time, and with some patience, they were able to turn around negative attitudes of family members, especially with the help of communication strategies they had learned in this training program. However, women also pointed out that too much burden was placed on them; they had to learn their rights and teach their families and neighbors as well. They insisted that the men in their families also should undergo this training. A few had become so disheartened that they had to seek professional help claiming: 'what is the point of learning about one's rights, if one encounters strong resistance in the family and community and is not able to implement them?' They said that they wished they had not learned them at all.

It is also worth noting that 'women's human rights' was not a concept the women and their families were familiar with. Many of the women who participated in the program did not know what 'women's human rights' meant. They and their husbands assumed that it only had to do with their rights as a wife, the right to divorce, the right to child custody etc. rather than rights as a citizen. Some husbands were afraid that their wives were going to the training sessions, so that they would learn how to exercise their right to divorce them. One woman, even after having gone through the training, remarked in the focus group discussions that she was getting along fine with her husband and therefore did not think she needed this training, but she came anyway in order to be able to help her friends and neighbors.

Moving Towards Collective Action

The main objective of this training program is collective action. In other words, did the participants practice and/or seek their rights, first on an individual basis and then collectively? The evaluation results showed that individually, the right to education and the right to work were practiced to a greater extent after the training sessions. About one third of the participants exercised their right to work after this training by finding employment or setting up their own businesses. About half of the participants exercised their right to education by either continuing their interrupted education, taking other courses at the community centers, or going on to higher education. Did the participants approach state institutions (courts, police and others) to exercise their rights? Only twenty-five per cent of the respondents answered yes. There were, however, individual cases reported such as where a woman sought legal advice for divorce, or filed a complaint against a husband who battered her, or who went to the police because her father would not let her sister take the university entrance exams.

While achieving personal empowerment was relatively easier, taking collective action was more difficult. Challenges occurred because of patriarchal norms, together with the collective identities and perceptions of women themselves as wives or mothers, rather than individuals in their own right. The establishment of formal organizations was the result of a long term learning process. The women first learned to organize events under the auspices of the Community Center (such as theaters, performances, March 8th celebrations), to set up committees to determine their needs, and over time approach government organizations and donors in order to set up a formal organization (an association, a foundation or a business). These stages constitute a learning process and gaining experience over time that may lead to establishing an actual organization. Such efforts also required the strong and sustained support of the Community Centers, and especially the social workers who facilitated the training.

The experiences of seven NGOs that were established in different parts of the country (Istanbul, Çanakkale, Antalya, Ankara, Van, and Diyarbakır) after the training program provide us with the following lessons. Good rapport with the facilitator and social worker made a big difference. The motivation of the social worker herself to assist participants and yet her willingness to stand back and not to overpower them was very important. Once leaders emerged among the participants themselves, they were able to organize the others. But many participants also wanted the social workers/facilitators to tell them what to do.

What emerged as one of the most important factors for success was the undertaking of needs assessment and the identification of concrete objectives. For example, women from the Gazi Community Center (in Istanbul) conducted a needs assessment in the neighborhood and found out that a kindergarten was most needed. They then went to the municipality and got public land on which to build the kindergarten. They sought the Community Center's help to become their legal sponsor, and they wrote a project proposal to the European Commission. They were about to receive funds to set up their center as this evaluation was being completed. In the same vein, the women from Fatihpaşa District in Diyarbakır also did a community needs assessment and set up a kindergarten with the mayor's support; they furthermore set up a candlemaking atelier to generate income in partnership with a women's NGO, and now make and sell candles.

The evaluation of the Women's Human Rights Education Program revealed several conditions that together have contributed to grassroots organizing. These conditions are (Kardam, 2003, p. 52):

1. Emergence of leaders among the participants.
2. Identification of concrete and achievable objectives.
3. Support of trainer/facilitator.
4. Family and spousal support.
5. Collaboration with and support of existing women's NGOs.
6. Learning and applying policy advocacy and negotiation strategies in dealing with government institutions.

Conclusions

As in the case of many international concepts or norms, empowerment as a popular concept of 1990s found its way into the Turkish women's organizations by way of international organizations and donors, and women's own interaction with global networks. CEDAW calls for women's empowerment through positive discrimination and for governments to take active policy measures to redress specific forms of gender discrimination and exclusion. Without policies and programs that promote equality in education and access to information including legal literacy and women's human rights, how can women in Turkey empower themselves? Are the empowerment training programs undertaken by women's organizations destined to remain sporadic and limited experiences, without political commitment?

The underlying goal of many empowerment programs is precisely to prepare women to take political action to demand accountability and bring about greater political commitment. But this assumes that there is an enabling environment for civil society activism. The female adult literacy rate is eighty-eight per cent in Turkey and it goes down to sixty-seven percent in rural areas (UNICEF, 2003). In other words, a massive overhaul of education policy and educational institutions would be needed while community programs that involve families would investigate why families stop sending girls to school at puberty, and force them into early marriages. It would involve redefining incentives together with families so that their own value system and cost-benefit analysis would change in favor of girls' and women's rights. A UNICEF-funded Advocacy Campaign for Girls' Education Project (in partnership with the Ministry of National Education) is being implemented since 2003. The project team investigated these issues, prepared reports, and organized a campaign that started in Van in Eastern Turkey.[13] In Van, girls who had learned to read and write through community programs, had written a play that examined and questioned gender roles, and performed it in front of the guests. When the Minister of Education spoke at the opening of the campaign, he said that they (the government) was not in the business of creating a revolt of women against men, and that they were going to respect traditional norms of the people.

There is no overall government policy for women's empowerment that establishes incentives to discourage discrimination by gender and active measures to empower them through education and access to information. Women's organizations (women's centers at universities, women's NGOs) with support from international donors) have undertaken themselves to redress this imbalance and in the long term create a political constituency that would demand accountability and political commitment to gender equality. These programs also include information on CEDAW and other global conventions to which Turkey is a signatory, information on laws, on policy advocacy and on how to approach government institutions individually or collectively. Thus, so far a small number of empowerment training programs have been implemented but, by all accounts, have made a significant impact by creating a shift in women's self-perception. These programs have created an environment where women began to gain power for themselves and increased their capacity and self-reliance because programs paid attention to their needs, and to their individual experiences. These are all new developments for Turkey.

Empowerment training programs are obviously limited efforts that have helped pockets of women in different parts of the country, and the whole number of women who underwent any kind of empowerment training would probably not exceed several thousand. Although their scope is still quite narrow, they make an impact in the participant's families and communities. Turkish women's organizations have started to record their preliminary experiences with such training programs. It is clear that these programs have created some important spaces where at least some women have started an investigation of existing gender norms, and experienced significant changes at the personal level, first step at empowerment. They have been able to investigate their situation with other women and share stories. Organizing for social and political action has begun to appear and just the fact that it has, and the conditions that have made it possible, deserve careful investigation.

The central findings of this chapter are that women's empowerment training, even though they are not widespread, are beginning to rupture the dualisms that traditionally relegate women to the 'collective rather than individual identities', to 'private rather than the public sphere'. Yet, the experience of these empowerment programs show that participants begin to shift towards individual identities, becoming aware of their human rights as individuals. They are also moving to the 'public sphere', stepping out of the private sphere of the home, to travel, to organize collectively and begin to participate as citizens, demanding accountability from a traditionally top-down state.

The participants no longer see themselves just as someone's wife or mother, but as individuals in their own right. They overcome an internalized sense of inferiority and begin to perceive themselves as worthy individuals. This happens in a participatory process, where the trainer is a 'facilitator' rather than teacher. This personal empowerment is then reflected in the readiness to defend one's individual rights and make personal choices. Participants now spare time for personal interests without feeling guilty, whereas before their entire days had been dominated, without any questioning, by the needs of others. They find a new balance between individual and collective identities as they redefine themselves. Empowerment training programs created spaces for women to speak with each other, share their stories, and find out that they are not alone. This helped them to realize that it is not 'their fault' but there are socially constructed gender norms that they have hitherto come to accept as 'given' and 'natural' that relegate them to an inferior status, and that can be changed. Empowerment strategies also stress the recognition of the shared aspects of subordination and aim that women see by themselves what they have gone through is not just personal. Many women have indeed found out that their problems are not just 'personal' but are shared with other women. Since the problem concerns a collectivity, it can also be changed through a collective action. Therefore, understanding other people, getting together with them in solidarity and forming alliances becomes important. And as Kabeer noted, the ultimate goal at this point is what is called 'the power to', that is women acting together for a change in their practical and strategic interests (Kabeer 1994, pp. 253-256). And this also began to take place as a result of empowerment training programs in Turkey.

When women leave the private sphere, and claim their individual rights, they encounter opposition in the family, and other institutions, including the bureaucracy and judicial systems, as these institutions continue to operate under norms that see women belonging in the private sphere, and in their familial roles. With an invisible inertia, they push the women back into their former positions of compliance, obedience and unquestioning passivity. For many, these norms are very hard to resist when we know that so many women still strongly identify with them and have internalized inferior roles defined for them by the society. Yet, the results also show that even though participants encountered initial resistance from husbands, mothers-in-law, and neighbors, they were able to overcome it over time. Family members began to see that they benefited from these changes as well. There were a number of cases where the husbands thanked the facilitators, telling them how their relationship with their wives had improved, including their sexual relationship.

As told by the women themselves, their personal empowerment was often recognized by family members and in the neighborhood. The participants became more skillful in negotiating with people around them, and as a result of their newly acquired information about many new topics, they were regarded as resource people and accorded more respect by family and community. They began to follow current affairs and become more interested in political and economic affairs in Turkey and abroad. However, it should also be noted that this change sometimes distanced them from their former friends in the neighborhood. Their relationships are negatively affected when the women do not want to pass the time embroidering and chatting with friends all day long.

In short, such training programs, however small and limited, have provided some opportunity spaces for the participants redefine their individual identities and step into the public sphere. The experiences of training programs show that personal power that is gained needs to be pampered and nurtured continually with other programs of support including programs aiming practical and strategic needs. Therefore, empowerment training programs demand consistent and continuous work and readjustment. This also means that the sustainability of the projects is of utmost importance. For many women, stepping into the public sphere for the first time takes a great deal of courage. Furthermore, for women to become political actors and to work on their 'strategic needs', they must have their practical needs (housing, food, clothing) taken care of at least at a minimum level. When they do not have access to education, health, work or housing, learning and training about their rights may be perceived as a luxury. Many new women's organizations have solicited help from established ones. It is also important for participants to see other women's NGOs as potential partners to work together. However, as was stated openly by one of the women who participated in LACAP (Project for Leader Women), some of them were reluctant to work with existing women's organizations because 'their issues are different and they are talking a different language.' This reflects the limitations of feminist organizations in making themselves better understood by grassroots women and engaging in issues which are of primary concern to these groups such as poverty or unemployment. It also reflects the weaknesses of some of the empowerment training programs in introducing and discussing the women's movement in its variety, with its successes as well as failures in these training sessions. Furthermore, the NGOs themselves compete among each other. There are frequent battles over funds, territories, constituencies and documents as the legal and informal rules and processes are still in flux and are in the process of being established.

Such training programs also begin to redefine the perception of the 'top-down, authoritarian state'. The findings show that participants expected a great deal from the state. As Filiz Kardam pointed out, she seldom heard queries such as: 'how can we get together and achieve this particular objective?' but the expectations are for the state and 'rich people' to provide for them. She notes that there seems to be an internalized sense of helplessness. The state is perceived in the role of a caretaker and a stern, authoritarian 'father'. It is, therefore, not surprising that for women, as well as for men, the notion of collective organization for services (when the expectation that state provide them) for advocacy (when the perception is state is an authoritative, top-down institution), may not be immediately clear or natural. The case of the Women's Human Rights training delivered in Community Centers established by the state is an excellent example of how new ways of combining individual initiative and participation are possible within the context of state-supported community centers. The social workers who facilitated these programs played a central role in supporting women to organize themselves. For the women, the social workers bridged the gap between them and the state. However, the role of social workers as change agents has to be carefully balanced. Many social workers also indicated how dependent the participant women could easily become, expecting them to come up with new ideas and projects and help them realize them. Thus, they have to walk a fine line by giving participants the motivation and direction they need, and yet the space to go the next step on their own.

The women who receive the empowerment training need to be nurtured and supported by family members and their community in order for the changes to become permanent and sustainable. In many cases family members have responded positively and begun to change as well, but in other cases, the change in women's identity is perceived as a threat, especially to husbands since the relationship has to be redefined. This puts the burden on the women that receive the training to be very patient in creating long-term change in their spouses and children's self-perceptions, as well as perceptions of them. Empowerment of women requires changes in men. Women express and emphasize the role of their husbands or other male authority figures in their family during and after these training sessions. A negative reaction at home or a lack of understanding and respect for what the women have gained in these programs may act as a disempowering factor. This reflects the need of gender training programs for women and men together.

As Temelkuran notes:

> Both the government and NGOs know that in the last few years, many of the social development projects in Anatolia have been directed at women. Women are being empowered but what good is this? Those in power are still the same men, and they own the legal and illegal weapons to sustain the existing order, and those women that have become aware that their suppression is not the 'natural order of things' are in more pain now. So you tell these women: go ahead and claim your rights from men!!

One wishes, however, that someone was brave enough to educate the men! (Milliyet, 1 March 2004)

Notes

[1] Filiz Kardam received her Ph.D in sociology from the London School of Economics, and is currently on the faculty of Cankaya University, Ankara, Turkey. Her research areas include women's organizations and movements, poverty and gender and honor crimes.

[2] The names of the participants of empowerment training programs who are quoted in this chapter have been changed for privacy purposes.

[3] Filiz Kardam conducted a small exploratory study during February-May 2001 and she examined training projects in three different organizations, the Mother and Child Education Foundation, the Contemporary Women and Youth Foundation in Ankara, and Ka-Mer in Diyarbakır by using qualitative research techniques. Personal observations in the organizations, focus group discussions with women who participated in various training programs, in-depth interviews with the coordinators of the projects, as well as several participant women were accomplished during this period. The discussion on these three organizations draws from F. Kardam's article. 'Training for Empowerment in Turkish Women's NGOs: Processes and Impact', Kadın Araştırmaları Dergisi, Sayı 8, Kadın Sorunları Araştırma ve Uygulama Merkezi, Istanbul Üniversitesi, Istanbul, 2003, pp. 43-68. The fourth organization discussed in this chapter is Women for Women's Human Rights - New Ways. N. Kardam conducted an evaluation of WWHR's Women's Human Rights Training Programs in 1999-2001.

[4] Interview with S. Demir, Turkish Development Foundation.

[5] Esim and Cindoğlu's study is valuable in terms of giving a general categorization of women's organizations and the way they can be related with the concepts of the development literature on women. However the picture is more complicated than this. These general categories not only include organizations with different structures and different histories of development, but also they are influenced from one another's activities in various ways. The positions of these organizations in terms of their relations with the state (and in turn with one another) also changes as affected by the political situation in Turkey and the state policies. There are some Islamist women who have defined themselves as feminists, and there are Atatürkist women who have engaged in both skills training and empowerment training for women. In other words, the boundaries are blurred

[6] The institutionalization of women's studies started in early 1990s in Turkey. In the year 2000, the number of women' programs and research centers in universities had reached 13. (Zeliha Ünaldi in *Flying News Women's Communication Bulletin*, Special Issue in English, March 2000).

[7] Interview with Aksu Bora from KASAUM.

[8] The interviews were conducted by Filiz Kardam with Zuhal Arnaz, coordinator, and participants during March-April 2001.

[9] Elementary school in Turkey goes from Grade 1 to Grade 8.

[10] The interviews with Seda Yilmaz, coordinator, and participants of the program were conducted by Filiz Kardam in Ankara during March-April 2001.

[11] Filiz Kardam interviewed Nebahat Akkoc, coordinator of Ka-Mer, and participants of training programs in Diyarbakir in April 2001.

[12] Nüket Kardam directed an evaluation of the Women's Human Rights Education Program during Spring 2002. The evaluation results may be found at www.wwhr.org N. Kardam would like to thank WWWR-New Ways for permission to use excerpts from this evaluation.

[13] Nur Otaran, Ayşe Sayın, Feride Güven, Ipek Gürkaynak, Satı Atakul; Eğitimin Toplumsal Cinsiyet Açısından İncelenmesi, Türkiye 2000, (Evaluation of Education in terms of Gender, Turkey 2003), *UNICEF Report* 2003. It can be found at the address www.unicef.org/turkey. See also 'Education of Girls and Development, *UNICEF Turkey Bulletin*, Say Yes, Winter 2003.

Chapter 5

Violence Against Women

Global Norms on Violence against Women

The focus on human rights and democratization around the world after the collapse of the Soviet Union, and the ability of global women's networks to coalesce around the issue of 'violence against women' provided a window of opportunity to incorporate it into the global human rights framework. As the East-West conflict subsided, new central concepts emerged: democratization, civil society participation, and respect for human rights. Human rights are no longer divided starkly as civil and political rights on the one hand, and economic, social and cultural rights on the other. Now that 'human development' has become a core concept and human dignity is at its center, it is impossible to overlook human rights, including women's human rights. Just as the Cold War hampered the agenda-setting efforts of women's organizations, its thaw provided opportunities for the same groups. It freed up agenda space:

> In the absence of East-West conflict issues, what UN policymakers had once considered important began to appear meaningless. Looking for new issues to fill the vacuum, UN policymakers decided to hold a series of conferences in the early 1990s, starting with the UN Conference on Environment and Development in Rio de Janeiro in 1992, followed by the World Human Rights Conference in Vienna in 1993, and the International Conference on Population and Development in Cairo in 1994. (Joachim, 1999, p. 151)

The United Nations also became more accessible to NGOs with the end of the Cold War, when it relaxed standards of accreditation and granted consultative status to regional and grassroots NGOs. Previously relegated to the visitor balconies and corridors, NGOs were now allowed on negotiation floors. The global women's networks took advantage of these 'windows of opportunity' to incorporate gender issues into conference agendas. As a result, violence against women has been hailed as a global concern and a new focus on violence forced a redefinition of the boundaries between public and private. Violence against women, once a private matter was redefined as a public human rights issue and a matter of state accountability.

Violence against women and girls had become a priority issue within the feminist movements of developed countries by the end of the 1970s and women's organizations around the world embraced this issue during the United Nations Decade for Women (1975-1985). But CEDAW did not specifically address violence against women and the majority of states and international organizations were slow in acknowledging its importance until the early 1990s. It was addressed at the UN Conference in Nairobi in 1985 as a major concern, and governments were urged to take action to prevent violence. But during this period, the main focus was on domestic violence. Thanks to the women's movement, before the end of the 1990s, all forms of violence against women became challenged. In 1991, the CSW recommended the convening of an expert meeting on what international instruments are needed to confront the problem. In 1992, the CEDAW Committee adopted General Recommendation 19 that strongly linked violence with the general framework of discrimination against women, thus making states responsible for reporting on and taking measures to eradicate violence.

The turning point was the activism of women's networks in preparation for and during the UN World Conference on Human Rights in Vienna in 1993. They petitioned the UN World Conference on Human Rights to 'comprehensively address women's rights as human rights at every level of its proceedings' and to 'recognize gender violence, a universal phenomenon which takes many forms across culture, race and class...as a violation of human rights requiring immediate action' (Bunch and Reilly, 1994, p. 5). The impact of the Vienna conference within and outside the UN was monumental; within six months of the Conference, the General Assembly adopted the Declaration on the Elimination of Violence against Women. This Declaration identified gender violence and all forms of sexual harassment and exploitation, including those resulting from cultural prejudice and international trafficking, as incompatible with the dignity and worth of the human person and called for their elimination. Thus, violence against women, including domestic, societal, and war-related violence, was brought into the public arena and made a human rights issue as a direct result of lobbying by the women's rights networks. The main demands of the network petition campaign were that the UN comprehensively address women's human rights at every level of its proceedings and that it recognize gender violence as a human rights violation. The final document explicitly recognized gender-based violence, including rape and sexual slavery, as human rights issues. One of the more specific accomplishments of the women's rights networks is the appointment of a special UN rapporteur on violence against women, an idea endorsed by the conference. According to Keck and Sikkink (1998), violence against women acquired special prominence when two separate transnational networks focused on human rights and women's rights converged. They also point out that the issue of violence against women resonated across significant cultural and experiential barriers, and therefore represented a common experience around which women's networks could come together.

The term 'violence against women' as defined in the Declaration was integrated into the Beijing Platform for Action (1996) as 'any act of gender-based violence that results in, or is likely to result in physical, sexual or psychological harm or suffering to women, including threats of such acts, coercion or arbitrary deprivation of liberty, whether occurring in public or private life. Accordingly, violence against women encompasses but is not limited to:

1.   Physical, sexual and psychological violence occurring in the family, including battering, sexual abuse of female children, dowry-related violence, marital rape, female genital mutilation, and other traditional practices harmful to women, as well as non-spousal violence, and violence related to exploitation.
2.   Physical, sexual, and psychological violence occurring in the women's community at large, including rape, sexual abuse, sexual harassment and intimidation at work, in educational institutions and elsewhere, trafficking of women and forced prostitution.
3.   Physical, sexual and psychological violence perpetrated and condoned by the state, wherever it occurs. (Platform for Action and the Beijing Declaration, 1996, p. 74)

The Beijing Platform for Action identified violence against women, along with women and armed conflict, and human rights of women, among its 12 critical areas of concern. The wartime rapes in the former Yugoslavia and other conflicts around the world where women were systematically subjected to various forms of sexual assault galvanized action on international forums. At the Beijing conference, forms of sexual assault on women that were not specifically mentioned in the Declaration became specified. These are: systematic rape and forced pregnancy during armed conflict, sexual slavery, forced sterilization and forced abortion, female infanticide and prenatal sex selection. As the 2000 review of the implementation of the Platform for Action showed, violence against women had become a priority issue on the agenda of many states and significant steps had been taken to address the problem, in some cases including in Turkey's case, pre-dating the adoption of the Platform.[1] Also in the year 2000, the Security Council addressed the issue of women, peace and security and adopted SC resolution 1325. In 2002, the GA adopted resolution 57/179 on 'Working towards the elimination of crimes against women committed in the name of honor'. The Rome Statute of the International Criminal Court (ICC) includes rape, sexual slavery, enforced prostitution, forced pregnancy in the definition of crimes against humanity and war crimes.

The Beijing Plus Five Conference in 2000 reaffirmed the strategic objectives of the Platform of Action with regard to violence against women, but the Outcome Document went a step further in calling for the criminalization of violence against women punishable by law (69c; 103b). Paragraph 69c states: 'Treat all forms of violence against women and girls of all ages as criminal offense punishable by law including violence based on all forms of discrimination'. This document also identified honor crimes as a specific form of harmful traditional practice (paragraphs 692 and 95a) in need of being eliminated by implementing law and other measures. Ertürk (2003a) points out that honor crimes were listed among harmful traditional practices earlier and were addressed by the CEDAW Committee in its concluding comments on Turkey in 1997 and on other countries, but it was not until the special session that the subject became a highly debated and contested issue in intergovernmental forums. This was especially the case as the issue gained a presumed linkage with Islam, owing to the showing of the film 'Crimes of Honor' prior to the circulation of a resolution on honor crimes in 2000. As a result, the resolution tabled by Netherlands was received with much opposition and could only be adopted by 120 in favor and 24 abstentions. In 2002, the General Assembly adopted Resolution 57/179 'Working towards the elimination of crimes against women committed in the name of honor' by consensus. This resolution asks 'to investigate thoroughly, prosecute effectively and document cases of crimes against women committed in the name of honor and punish the perpetrators (para 3c); to intensify efforts to raise awareness of the need to prevent and eliminate crimes against women committed in the name of honor, with the aim of changing the attitudes and behavior that allow such crimes to be committed by involving community leaders'. (para 3e). The resolution also invited the Commission on the Status of Women (CSW) to address this subject at its forty-seventh session, but the Commission, for the first time in its history, failed to reach a consensus on the agreed conclusion with regard to this theme. According to Ertürk, this was an indication of increasing difficulty among member states to reach consensus on critical issues concerning human rights (2003a, p. 5) Another indication is the lack of reference to the Declaration on the Elimination of Violence against Women in the Outcome Document of the GA special session on Beijing Plus Five conference. Also, there was a noticeable reluctance to strongly link CEDAW as the legally binding instrument on women's human rights to the Outcome Document. Ertürk further comments that there is a lack of specific time-bound measurable targets to end violence in the Outcome Document and that there is a weakness in the language concerning state accountability and attention to non-state actors who violate women's human rights (2003b, pp. 8 and 9).

The first UN Rapporteur on violence against women, Radhika Coomaraswamy, indicated that the greatest achievements in the struggle against violence against women in the 1990s have been awareness-raising and standard-setting and persuading states to accept international standards to pass appropriate legislation (Ertürk, 2003b, p. 9). She continues to argue that it is now time to focus on innovative strategies for effective implementation. Indeed, this is the most critical challenge, and the key factor for implementation lies in demonstrating the compatibility of culture and religion with the global human rights of women. Turkey presents a fascinating case study for a detailed examination of this challenge.

Violence against Women on the Public Agenda

Violence against women was the first issue with which women in Turkey took to the streets several years before the UN Declaration on the Elimination of Violence against Women was adopted.[2] The first public campaign took place in 1987 when a judicial decree rejected the application of a woman for divorce on grounds of domestic violence in Çankırı, citing a Turkish proverb 'a woman must always have a baby growing in her womb, and a stick on her back'. It was striking that this proverb was used by a judge to justify an 'objective' decision, a judge who is trained to uphold and defend the legal system in Turkey under which women and men were deemed equal. Lawyers in Çankırı protested, and women sent protest telegrams to the judge, followed by a public campaign in Ankara which then spread to other cities. The first campaign took place on Mothers Day, May 10, 1987. The choice of the day is a creative one, as it shows that the campaigners wanted to highlight the incongruity of honoring mothers and battering wives. Women carried pickets that said: "how can you love your mother and beat your wife?' (Timisi and Gevrek, 2002, p. 23) The public was not used to seeing women activists on the streets. People first thought that this was a celebration ceremony for Mothers Day. When the purpose of the campaign was found out, the response from the press was a mixture of surprise and ridicule as the headlines show: 'There is little interest in the public campaign on violence against women' 'Seven beauties under the rain', alluding to the seven women carrying pancarts in the rain (Timisi and Gevrek, 2002, p. 23). This campaign became a turning point for the women's movement. For the first time women took to the streets with a feminist identity. The campaigners themselves were not quite sure how this would all turn out: They planned to sell flowers and carry pancarts that said 'how can you love your mothers and beat your wives?' on Mothers' Day. But as Bora points out:

> Unfortunately that day it started to rain. We couldn't organize ourselves. Some of us got together in front of the Altındağ Municipality's Culture Center, put pins on passers by, had billboards. The press talked about us, but we were unhappy about the results because we couldn't really access many women. (Bora in Bora and Günal 2002, p. 24)

The campaign against violence spread to other cities. A protest march in Istanbul attracted more than 2,500 women from all walks of life. This was the first legal street demonstration organized after the military coup of 1980. More campaigns and activities followed in different cities, including the 'Purple Needle Campaign' where women sold needles with purple ribbon, to be used by women to stick any harassers. As İlkkaracan (2002) notes, this was an excellent strategy, in that it turned a traditionally private response employed by women in Istanbul, carrying needles to stick harassers with, into a political campaign tactic in the public realm. Another campaign used the slogan: 'We demand back the streets and the nights', signaling the readiness to reclaim public spaces without harassment. In 1989 there was a strong protest by women's groups when a rape case was brought before the Supreme Court challenging Article 438 of the Criminal Code, which granted a rapist reduced sentence if the victim is a prostitute. The Court ruled that the Article was not in After the first time that women took to the streets in 1987 in Ankara, the violation of the equality clause (Article 10) of the Constitution since it aims to protect 'respectable women'. The mounting public reaction ended in the abolishment of the Article 438 in the National Assembly.

The campaign against domestic violence in the 1980s included many activities, such as panel discussions, media reports, articles in academic publications and in popular magazines, lobbying and street demonstrations. These activities played a major role in sensitizing the public, as well as pressuring governments to create shelters for battered women. The media was utilized to disseminate information and raise public consciousness around violence-related issues. Meanwhile, the National Women's Machinery also supported projects that investigated media images of women, and sponsored a panel discussion, and later the publication of a book on honor crimes. The NWM became a strong ally of women's groups, in moving the public agenda on domestic violence forward, by helping to draft a bill which later became the Law on the Protection of the Family.

Why did the first public campaign of the women's movement focus on violence against women? One reason, according to one of the activists is that the leaders of the women's movement of the 1980s had mostly come from socialist backgrounds and had been actively involved in the student protest movements in the late 1970s. They had personally witnessed or experienced violence on the streets or when they were taken into custody (Işık, 2002). As Işık (2002: 44) indicated, she and other women in the same situation who lived with violence on a daily basis in the 1980s, felt compelled to question violence in the private sphere as well. Another reason according to Işık is the combined result of the socialist feminists' engagement with the political repression and violence in Turkey, as well with the Western feminist movement. She adds that the women's movement in Turkey was distinctly local in the sense that it arose from Turkish women's own experiences and backgrounds. It may thus be called the local manifestation of a global movement (2002: 34).

The fundamental characteristic of this movement was that for the first time, Turkish women were defining their own agenda. 'Violence against women' was one that all women could agree on because it cuts across generations, classes, ethnicities and regions. In Turkey, in spite of women's equal rights granted in 1926 in matters of divorce, child custody and divorce, violence against women continues to persist. A survey conducted by Bilgi University in 2003 on violence against women revealed that out of the married women surveyed, thirty per cent in urban areas, fifty-two percent in rural areas, and fifty-eight percent in shantytown (gecekondu) areas suffered from violence by their husbands. As the level of education of the women went up, the violence they experienced decreased. Only fifteen per cent of university-educated married women experienced violence at home, while fifty-seven per cent of high school-educated women, and seventy-one per cent of women with grade school education and seventy-three per cent of women with no education experienced violence at home. Violence continues to be a pervasive problem that women experience in their families before marriage as well; fifty-two per cent of the respondents indicated that they encountered violence in their families before they got married.[3]

Social Norms Supporting Gender Based Violence

Violence against women is embedded in social norms so that it becomes an accepted part of life. Male superiority, natural leadership, and the male right to control female behavior, including and perhaps most importantly her sexual behavior, are deeply entrenched in the psyche of the society. This is reflected in many folk sayings, such as the ones below, that denigrate women to an inferior position compared to men, in which women are deemed irrational, overly emotional, incapable and in need of guidance by men, whereas men are naturally stronger, smarter, more rational, fit to rule over women:

> Those that don't beat their daughter end up beating themselves in the head' (kızını dövmeyen dizini döver); 'he is your husband; he loves you and he beats you too' (kocandır – döver de sever de); 'beating originated in heaven' (dayak cennetten 'çıkmadır); 'a woman must always be pregnant, and have a stick on her back' (kadın dediğin karnında bebek, sırtında sopa olacak).[4]

This male protection and control of female sexuality may be exercised with greater ease if women's freedom of movement is restricted and they come into contact with males (outside their own family) as little as possible. This then is the view, taken to its extreme, which leads to women being restricted to their homes or close neighborhoods, or covered up in 'burqas' or 'çarşafs', so that they do not come in contact with males. As we have seen in extreme cases such as in Afghanistan women tend to stay at home, or are hidden under burqas when they are on the streets, so that the only men they come in contact are their male family members. A male who is not part of the family may be criticized for just asking the name of a female family member.[5] Coming in contact with males outside a woman's family always creates the potential for sexual activity, threatening a husband or father's control of the female family member. When male identity, the definition of manhood or masculinity, is centrally located in the control of women's sexual behavior, and when he is threatened with ridicule, with loss of his 'manhood' or 'honor', then obviously, such control will continue unless a redefinition and renegotiation of these identities occurs by the stakeholders themselves. Some men in Afghanistan have jokingly claimed that 'women are their misery and their honor'.[6] In other words, men lose their masculine identity, their 'honor' if a female family member is judged by the community as having misbehaved. Paradoxically, this bestows power on the women, whose behavior could 'make or break' a man. Both men and women seem to be caught in this web of power relationships based on 'honor and its loss strictly tied to women's sexuality'.

If a male family member is considered to have the right and responsibility to control a female family member's sexual behavior according to social norms, it also follows that he may discipline her in whatever way he deems necessary, should she transgress her boundaries. Lack of public policy and government intervention against domestic violence has been justified in the name of not coming between the husband and wife, and that whatever happens in the home is a private matter. In fact, neighbors are usually reticent in intervening, because it is a matter between the husband and wife, really meaning that this is the husband's territory, controlled and ruled over by him. Ironically, Turkish society is very much an 'interventionist' society where neighbors are always curious about what is happening in the next apartment and are perfectly capable of prying into the most private aspects of each others' lives and giving advice. But in the family, the man tends to be considered the ruler of his household, and the female members to be under his rule, even his possessions.

If women encounter violence in the home, the perpetrators explain that it was deserved by the woman because she was disobedient. In one study, the men who beat their wives were asked to explain their actions, and the most common reason cited was the 'disobedience' of the wives (İlkkaracan et al: 1996: p. 37). The Research Association of Women's Social Life has found in a study conducted in 2004 that forty-five per cent of men in Turkey claim they have the right to beat their wives/girlfriends/daughters if they are disobeyed. The findings also reveal that during the first three years of marriage, seventy-three per cent of university-educated women and ninety percent of women who live in rural areas, or in shantytowns in the cities suffer from violence in the family. Twenty-three per cent of the men force sex on their wives (ntvmsbnc.com, March 8, 2004). Since sex is considered the right of the husband, forced sex (or rape) in marriage has been considered to be a non-issue by many.

This reveals a fundamental power dynamic between the partners in marriage, that of a master-slave dynamic in which the husband has the power to exert his will over his wife, and that disobedience can lead to punishment. One simple way to manifest power is through physical force. Other ways may include withholding what the other party needs and making sure there are no alternative ways to acquire it, be it economic resources (economic violence) or respect and recognition (psychological violence). Men who perpetuate violence against women tend to believe that women's obedience and service to them is their natural right. Thus, these hierarchical structures and male superiority then become 'inescapable' and 'unchangeable' facts of life, internalized by women as well.

These norms and the underlying assumptions of the nature of gender relations imply that if a woman does suffer from violence, it is her own fault. It is assumed that she deserved it and/or brought it to herself by defiance and disobedience of the male members of the family, either by venturing into the public spaces alone when she should not have, or by disobeying her husband in the home. If a woman disobeys a mother-in-law, this may also bring on violence against her, sometimes by the mother-in-law herself, or by the husband. Older women perpetuate this dynamic themselves, by deriving their own power from their sons, and controlling their daughter-in-laws' behavior. Such a sexist and hierarchical social order that condones violence against women is then perceived as 'natural', the way things are and going to be in the foreseeable future. As such, it leads to the internalization by women themselves that they are inferior to men and may deserve punishment. A comprehensive survey titled 'Population and Health Research in Turkey' conducted by Hacettepe University and the Ministry of Health reveals the internalization by women themselves of their husbands' right to beat them. According to this survey, thirty-nine per cent of the respondents agreed that they deserved to be beaten if they were remiss in one of the following areas: if they were profligate in spending money, if they talked back at their husbands, if they burned the meal they were cooking, if they did not take care of the children well, or if they refused sexual relations with their husbands. This survey included 8,075 women between the ages of 15-49. In rural areas, fifty-seven per cent of the respondents agreed that their husbands had the right to beat them under the above circumstances, while in urban areas this number went down to thirty-two per cent. Again the influence of education seems pivotal in these views: while sixty-two per cent of the women who have little or no education felt that husbands have right to beat them, only nine per cent of the educated (high school level or above) indicated agreement with such a right (*Radikal,* 21 October 2004).

The legal system and implementing bureaucracies, including the courts and police, on the whole, have condoned and reflected the gender norms discussed above until recently. Adopted from the Italian Criminal Code and enacted in 1926, it does contain provisions related to violence against family members. Article 478 calls for imprisonment of up to 30 months, if a family member maltreats another family member, in ways that contravenes accepted understanding of mercy and affection. However, a woman subjected to violence must file a complaint herself in order to make use of this law. Charges may be filed by the public prosecutor if she gets a medical report saying that she needs 10 days of rest as a result of the assault by her husband, and the assault has to leave a permanent visible scar in the woman's body. Research findings show that few women who suffered from domestic violence have filed complaints against their husbands. Gülcür (1996) reported that among 155 women in Ankara, none of the women who experienced violence filed a complaint, and Yıldırım (1998) reported that out of 112 women residing in women's shelters, only 9.8% filed a complaint. İlkkaracan (2002) gives us some insights why that is the case:

> They (Women) are often faced with policemen who refuse to file their complaint or tell them to go home and make up with their partners; or with doctors, who either do not, or chose not to, recognize that a woman has been subjected to domestic violence, which prevents women from obtaining the medical report needed to file a criminal charge. They are afraid that the incarceration of their partner will result in a loss of social status for the family; they do not wish to place their children in a situation where they will have to see their father in jail; they are frightened that their partner will become more violent before or after his imprisonment; they fear that the husband's family and their own community will apply pressure on them for having caused the imprisonment of the father; and they are often worried that when their partner is in jail, they will be left without a source of income, especially if their family has only a single income earner.

Crimes of sexual assault have been classified under the category of 'Felonies against Public Decency and Family Order', rather than as crimes against individual women. The suffering party is not considered to be the victim of violence, but the man whose honor has been compromised, and by implication 'public decency and family order' has been compromised. The suffering party is not 'her' but the community, and the harm done is not against her but the harm *she* has caused by compromising her husband's or family's honor, and by implication 'public decency and family order'. If an unmarried girl is found not to be a virgin, the suffering party is the family because the lack of virginity of an unmarried girl goes to the heart of Turkey's traditional moral code. The legal code reflects this code by increasing the sentence for a rapist if the victim was a virgin, and lifting it if the rapist marries the victim, thereby saving the honor of the family. The key point here is the legal system's treatment of gender-based violence which reflects gender norms where women are not perceived as 'individuals' but in their 'collective identities' and implicitly accepts men's control of women's sexual behavior.

If a woman becomes 'sexually defiant' by engaging in any perceived sexual activity before marriage or outside of marriage, or that there is even gossip that this might be the case, violence against her may be considered 'unavoidable' by male family members to protect the man's honor. In some communities where honor killings are practiced, transgressing a norm may range from a girl's losing her virginity, to calling a radio station and asking for a favorite song, to being raped and impregnated by a cousin who threatens her and her mother with death if she discloses what happened. Once her family and the community make a judgment about her moral standing, and her name, her male relatives cannot walk in the village with their heads held high. To reclaim their manhood in the eyes of other men, they cleanse their honor by stabbing, or stoning their own daughter or sister or wife. The legal system has condoned these norms by reducing a murderer's sentence if the act was done 'under severe provocation'. Women of the family, having internalized these norms and the rules about their own behavior, also tend to agree to the necessity of these crimes. They grieve more for the male member of the family who committed the crime and went to jail, than the victim who is dead. Any activity to protect a man's honor may be interpreted by judges as worthy of a reduced sentence because it was done under severe provocation, the interpretation of which widely varies.

A recent newspaper article covered the news of a 15-year-old girl in Diyarbakır, being raped by her cousin who came to her home while she was alone and repeatedly raped her afterwards (Milliyet, 23 November 2003). She got pregnant and was afraid to disclose this to her family because he threatened to kill her and her mother if she told anybody that he was raping her. When her family found out, they spoke to the rapist's family and asked that he marry her. The rapist's family refused. The result was that one day, the girl's brother invited her outside to have a talk and killed her. When the journalists visited her home to find out what had happened, they found that the mother was grieving more for her son than her daughter and the family members said that they could not have held their heads high in their community if the daughter was still alive. The journalists posed many questions to the family and the community and the answer they always got was that it was normal for the brother to kill his sister under such circumstances. Another sister also agreed that this was the normal thing to do:

> Of course I was very sorry about this but I forgave my brother. Whoever was in my brother's position would have done the same thing. I would have too. A person lives

for their honor, their virtue in this world. My sister deserved to die because she hid this situation. If she had disclosed it, she may not have died. (*Milliyet*, 23 November 2003)

The concept of 'honor' is clearly rooted in traditional social norms, and in fact, it is found across Christian cultures of the Mediterranean, such as Spain or Greece. Thus, it is not confined to Islamic cultures. Does Islam and the Qur'an justify women to be treated like this? A women's rights activist who met with local leaders, including religious leaders in Diyarbakır, challenged the concept of honor killings by arguing that the Qur'an does not permit women to be treated like this. A religious leader's response was: 'This is honor, what has that got to do with the Qur'an? Men's honor comes before the Book' (Pervizat, 2003). As Pervizat (2003) notes, challenging these power dynamics is complex since they are so imbedded in interpersonal relations, family, community, and culture, as well as in economic and political relationships. They are also part of the bargaining and accommodation between the state and the clan (aşiret) leaders. In order to investigate this further, it is useful to adopt the definition of the state found in Bratton's work (1989, pp. 408-9): 'The state is an organization within society where it coexists and interacts with other formal and informal organizations from families to economic enterprises or religious organizations. It is, however, distinguishable from the myriad of other organizations in seeking predominance over them, and in aiming to institute binding rules regarding the other organizations' activities.' Third World states, as Migdal (1988, p. 27) points out, struggle to achieve certain goals: 'The central political and social drama of recent history has been the battle pitting the state and organizations allied with it (often from a particular social class) against other social organizations dotting society's landscape.' Within this context, those who make the rules acquire social control. In the emerging Turkish Republic, the controversy over what kind of hat men should wear or whether women should cover, in fact, were about who had the right and ability (religious elites or bureaucratic elites) to make rules.

The hegemony of the state over the gender discourse was not absolute, however. The policy-makers ignored instances of polygamy practiced by clan leaders, just as much 'honor crimes', verdicts handed down by them on the women who 'misbehaved' and smeared the family or clan's reputation and honor. When the secular bureaucratic elites had difficulty penetrating society to achieve compliance with and legitimation of new gender rules, they struck a bargain with local strongmen what Migdal calls a 'hands-off policy which allowed the strong men to build enclaves of social control' (1988, p.32). State elites do not necessarily achieve predominance of the state: 'The most subtle and fascinating patterns of political change and political inertia have resulted from the accommodation between states and other powerful organizations in society. Such accommodations could not have been predicted using models and theories of macro-level social and political change' (Migdal, 1988, p.31). What this perspective shows is that political life is not simply a struggle over the allocation of resources, or the competition of interest groups, but is also a struggle over the rules of the game and underlying ideology. In fact, the rules over the gender discourse and the discourse on violence against women is precisely a reflection of this very struggle, and continues even today. As a journalist in a recent article reiterates:

> The authorities have taken a hypocritical stance against customs (töre) supported by clans (aşirets). Such a dishonest stance has oppressed this society for hundreds of years, and supported such customs on the basis of cementing society. The Turkish state has used such clan organizations to build a national identity: the Anatolian person is emotional, hospitable, holds chastity (namus) dear; one must not hurt these people's feelings, and if the finger of 'töre' (customs and traditions) points towards murder, this must be the right thing to do. Thus, this bargaining between 'töre' and governments have laid the road filled with bloody victims. (Türker, March 1, 2004)

In the last fifteen years or so and especially since 2000, what could be termed revolutionary changes on the 'rules of gender discourse' have occurred in Turkey. On 1 January 2002, Turkish women became the legal equal of men. They were granted an equal say in decisions regarding home and children, while property assets are to be divided equally in a divorce. The new Penal Code declares that 'provocation' is no longer a defense for honor crimes. Honor crimes will be defined as voluntary manslaughter and will be punished by life sentences in prison. Anyone who kills a family member will be punishable by a life sentence. It also sees that rape in marriage and sexual harassment are treated as crimes. Rapists no longer escape sentences by marrying their victim, and victims may not be forced to marry their assaulters. For the first time, incest will be treated as a crime. The rest of this chapter investigates the process that led to these monumental legal reforms and the extent of implementation so far.

Influencing the Policy Process

The Turkish women's movement used the following strategies to shape the national policy agenda, and to influence the process of legal reforms:

1. Mounting campaigns – lobbying at the national, regional and international levels, petition drives, gathering evidence, etc.
2. Building coalitions and consensus by holding strategic planning meetings such as CEDAW civil forums, meetings to prepare CEDAW shadow reports;
3. Preparing policy documents – draft bills, drafting of resolutions, platform documents.
4. Influencing public officials – publishing reports, holding briefings, forging alliances, lobbying members of Parliament; lobbying at the United Nations level.
5. Bridging norms – use of political strategies to bridge differences among political parties.

As discussed above, domestic violence was already on the public agenda in Turkey starting from the late 1980s. Several events at the global level took place in 1997 that brought together favorable factors leading to a new law on domestic violence. Turkey presented its Country Report to the CEDAW Committee in 1997. The Turkish delegation was composed of feminist academics, bureaucrats and headed by the Minister for Women's Affairs, Işilay Saygın. Furthermore, a group of NGO representatives also presented their own report and had the opportunity to bring their point of view to the CEDAW committee. Both the official report and the NGO report made references to the issue of violence against women. The CEDAW committee questioned the delegation on this specific issue, asking what the Turkish government had so far done about gender-based violence, and what its future plans were. Saygın returned home with 'domestic violence' as a priority issue on her agenda. As a longstanding politician with a strong traditional and conservative line, domestic violence may not have necessarily coincided with the Turkish minister's own priorities. Regardless of the underlying motivation, however, once she announced domestic violence as the most pressing problem her office is confronted with, this not only placed the issue in the center of mainstream politics but connected it to the women's movement. Eventually she resigned from the cabinet as well as her party (DYP – True Path Party) on the grounds that her efforts in passing a bill against domestic violence was being blocked by the Islamist wing (RP – Welfare Party) of the coalition government. The impact of this political move was twofold: a) it enabled the minister to join ANAP (Motherland Party) which is one of the partners of the current coalition government and thus regain her ministerial position; and b) the issue of violence and sexual abuse of women gained an official platform in Turkish politics.

Women's NGOs followed up on the government's promises by extensive lobbying, by keeping the issue alive on the public agenda, by presenting its demands to the Parliamentary Committee in charge, and organizing panels and conferences. One example is Women for Women's Human Rights–New Ways which played a significant role in this process. This organization had focused on an amendment of the Criminal Code that would increase the punishment to the perpetrator of violence in the family, but the Justice Commission of the National Parliament did not approve it. At the same time, İlkkaracan from WWHR/New Ways recounts how they first started a campaign for preventive measures against domestic violence, such as protection orders. They enlisted the support of the NWM, whose director, fortunately, was a member of the women's movement against violence and a co-founder of the Women's Solidarity Foundation in Ankara, which opened the first autonomous women's shelter in Turkey. According to İlkkaracan (2002), the process unfolded as follows:

> A draft law on protection orders was prepared and presented to the Parliamentary Justice Commission, which represents the first stage in the process of legislative changes. As soon as the draft law was presented to the Parliamentary Justice Commission, we contacted the 21 members. We wrote them a letter containing all the information about this law, sent them materials we had on the issue and asked for

face-to-face appointments. In the meantime, we provided the NWM with a list of countries, which had a law on protection order on their statute books together with the texts of protection orders in these countries. Throughout this period, we had the support of our friends in the media. There was extensive press coverage with invitations to television and radio programs.

This is an excellent example of how policy advocacy in the form of lobbying, networking, publicity, bringing the relevant information and facts to the table have been employed. Coupled with these, the support of the political leader, Saygın, and the international-level pressure holding Turkey accountable have clearly led to the new legislation. But WWHR and their allies were politically savvy in one more very important way: the competing definitions of individual versus collective identity of women were brought together in the same legislation, satisfying the Islamist Welfare Party, as well as the other more Western liberal-oriented parties. The Welfare Party refused to support the passage of the draft Bill, saying that this law was contrary to the unity of the family, and therefore, against Islam. İlkkaracan (2002) says that they collaborated with the NWM, and informed the members of the Party that the protection order was also used in Malaysia, another predominantly Moslem country, to protect the unity of the family. They provided the text of the protection order in Malaysia, which proved to be critical in enlisting the Welfare Party support.

There is now a new law on the Protection of the Family enacted on January 17, 1998. Under this law, any member of a family subject to domestic violence can file a court case for what is known as a protection order against the perpetrator of the violence, and if the latter does not comply, he can be put in jail. Before this law, domestic violence cases were considered under the general provisions of the Criminal Code, but in fact, the private sphere of family life remained largely outside the regulatory mechanisms of the existing legislative framework. The wife could not raise criminal charges against an abusive husband simply because no such crime was recognized or defined by the law. The issue of abuse in the relationship between husband and wife was treated as a private affair; therefore, the state did not assume a protective role. The new law is significant in that it has made a private matter 'public' for the first time under the law. The offender is now subject to various punitive measures, such as forcing to abandon the house, confiscation of arms owned by the offender, payment of temporary alimony, ban on disturbing the family through means of communication, and prohibition of the destruction of the possessions of other family members. Violation of these measures would be penalized from 3 to a maximum of 6 months of jail. The law was revised to be applicable not just upon complaint by the victim but any other person. This law is also in line with the laws and regulations of the European Union member countries.

Other important legal reforms also took place as a result of direct lobbying by women's groups. Article 159 of the Turkish Civil Code, which required a husband's permission for a wife to work, was declared unconstitutional as a result of direct lobbying by women's groups. In 1998, adultery was dropped as a crime for both sexes. Adultery, which establishes a ground for divorce according to the family law, was considered a threat to public morality and pronounced a criminal act. The unequal treatment of the husband and wife also was part of the law, as the definition of adultery was different for each. For the wife, one incident of sexual intercourse was enough to be charged for adultery, while the husband could only be prosecuted for adultery for having a continuous relationship with another woman that resembles a marriage relationship. Moreover, the husband can only be charged with adultery by his wife if the accomplice is an unmarried woman. If she is married, then the wife's complaint is not adequate for a charge; the adulterous wife's husband was required to file the complaint. All of this is no longer valid, as adultery is no longer considered a crime for either women or men. Yet, during the discussions of the new Penal Code in September 2004, the AK party brought a proposal to the Parliament to criminalize adultery again. This time it would be embody gender equality, the Prime Minister said, as both the husband and wife would be allowed to file a formal complaint and the sentences would also be equally applied to both genders. This proposal was defended on the basis of protecting the family: 'The family is a sacred institution for us. The stronger the family, the stronger the country. If the family is weakened the country is doomed to destruction' (TrkNewsE, News from Vic McDonald, 7 September 2004). Amidst EU declarations that this could cast a shadow over Turkey's EU bid, and harm Turkey's image, and strong protests from women's groups and the opposition party, this proposal was withdrawn.

One of the most controversial issues in the past decade has been the issue of forced virginity tests, which is regarded as a gross violation of women's human rights and article 17 of the constitution which states that no one's bodily integrity may be violated. But various provisions in the law have been used to justify enforced virginity testing, such as the Awards and Discipline in the High School Education Institutions of the Ministry of Education which came into effect on 31 January 1995. The statue stated that the 'proof of unchastity' is a valid reason for expulsion from the formal educational system.

In December 1997, when the issue of compulsory virginity tests became a public debate, the Minister in charge retreated to a traditional and anti-woman line. The case of five girls who attempted suicide after the director of their state foster home ordered them to undergo virginity tests when they returned late to their dormitories one night fueled a heated debate. As Washington Post noted:

Women's rights activists were infuriated when Işılay Saygın, state minister in charge of women's and family affairs, defended mandated medical examinations to verify the virginity of girls in state-run foster homes. That Saygın, a woman, is prepared to uphold the state's involvement in a practice that has caused much anguish to some young women, in the view of several women's groups. 'If girls commit suicide because of virginity tests, they would have commited suicide anyway. It is not that important', Saygın was quoted saying. Stating that she opposed a ban on virginity controls, Saygın argued that such tests were needed to help guide young people's behavior. (Couturier, 1998)

The opposing voice came from a senior aide, Selma Acuner, who declared to the press that women's bodies should be off limits to the state. Acuner, then, had to resign. But as a result of pressure from women's groups and public debate, with the recommendation of the national women's machinery, the Ministry of Education has removed the reference to 'unchastity' from the revised statute on 26 February 2002. Prior to this, on 13 January 1999, the Ministry of Justice, in response to protests and public pressure, issued a statute banning the bodily examinations of women for reasons of disciplinary punishment against their consent.

By the year 2000, the representatives of women's groups and organizations were working at the Beijing Plus Five conference as part of the Turkish official delegation (a first of its kind) and were instrumental in putting in the Beijing Plus Five outcome document wording on honor crimes and forced marriages (important issues in Turkey) for the first time (İlkkaracan, 2001) Women's activists learned to negotiate with, lobby and act as pressure groups in pressing for legal and policy changes, drawing strength from international conventions to which Turkey is party, tapping into regional and global networks and working with allies within the government. Many academics, researchers and activists engaged in transnational activities, working for international organizations, but maintaining contact with Turkish counterparts.[7]

In 2002, several proposals for changes in the Penal Code were made, including the lifting of 'severe provocation' as a mitigating factor for the offender of homicide, assault or battery cases. A working group made of several women's NGOs focused on proposals to the Penal Code from the women's perspective and continue to lobby extensively.[8] The European Commission Report on Turkey included the point that such discriminatory laws should be repealed. Article 462 of the Penal Code, allowing for reduced sentences for 'honor killings', has been repealed. However, the more general provisions of Article 51 remain, applicable to offenses traditionally viewed as being against 'virtue'. In 2003, the deep resistance to changing prevalent gender norms persists, as revealed in the remarks of the head of the Justice Commission of the National Parliament:

> We have lifted the difference between 'severe provocation' and 'ordinary provocation' but provocation is a consideration in all crimes and we chose to leave it to the judges' interpretation and evaluation. Now many MPs say that if they saw their wives with another man, they would slap their wives, or perhaps divorce them. Let me tell you, Turkish men will not behave like them, they will behave differently. In such situations, society will brand this man as 'cuckolded' and this is severe provocation. So how can we lift the factor of provocation for a man under this circumstance? (Pelek, 20 November 2003)

This remark is instructive because it shows that honor crime is not just an issue of custom (tore), understood as tribal norms of the East or Southeast regions, sometimes explained away as the practice of poor, uneducated people, but that it can be voiced by even an educated, middle class, member of the National Parliament. The 'severe provocation' stipulation in the law further makes it possible for the perpetrators of crimes against women to claim that they were provoked and get lesser sentences, thereby encouraging further crimes. Thus, there have even been cases where crimes have been redefined as honor crimes to reduce sentences or redefine agendas. For example, a man who has an erectile dysfunction and does not want his reputation to be tarnished, claimed that his wife was not a virgin and killed her, claiming it as an honor crime. In another case, the son confessed to a lawyer years later that his brother lied about their mother, claiming she was unchaste and seeing other men. The mother then was killed by the family, while the brother's sole objective was to change the family agenda and divert attention from the money he owed to the family (Uçan Haber, 2003, p. 39).

Another law under discussion stipulates that if a person rapes a virgin, and marries her, then the charge is lifted. Many women's groups have opposed this law, claiming that it encourages rape, and the forced marriage of a woman with her rapist! Furthermore, if the victim is a virgin, the rapist receives a higher sentence than if she is not. The proposals to change this provision have so far been resisted on the basis of arguments such as the one below, made by the head of the Justice Commission of the National Parliament:

> Virginity is part of Turkish traditions and customs. Therefore, our laws have to respect that. If a girl has decided to save her virginity until marriage and was raped, then the rapist must definitely get a heavier sentence. When a girl is raped, that girl is pushed outside of society, and stigmatized. No one would want to marry her. This is true everywhere, including big cities. Her family puts her outside the door, and then she gets picked up by prostitution rings and spends the rest of her life in a brothel. (Pelek, 20 November 2003)

The notion of marital rape is also fairly new on the agenda and has encountered similar resistance. As one professor maintained at a conference: (Pelek, Nov 20, 2003)

> The Penal Code must not intervene in sexual relations in marriage; such issues should be resolved within the marriage. Just because we are for freedom, if we start making forced sexual relations within marriage a crime, then there would be no end to false allegations. What if a man decides to satisfy his sexual urge while his wife is sleeping, would he be considered a rapist? What if when the wife wakes up and complains to the police that he hadn't received her consent?

Obviously this professor assumes that marriage gives a man the right to have sex with his wife whenever or wherever he wants, and even when his wife is sleeping, since her consent is a non-issue. By February 2004, forced sex in marriage had been defined as an offense upon complaint. The lobbying efforts to change gender-discriminatory laws continue, as the efforts of the Working Group on the revisions to the Turkish Criminal Code attest. This working group comprises of 10 women's organizations and groups, and 12 others have lent their support to the process. They have demanded the revision of the Criminal Code according to the principles below:

1. Sexual assault is a crime against individuals and women's bodies do not belong to society but to themselves.
2. Rape, harassment and sexual assault are crimes against a person's sexual integrity.
3. Rape is not legal even within marriage. Rape in marriage must be considered a crime.
4. Currently, the charges against a rapist are dropped if he marries the victim; a woman cannot be forced to marry her rapist.
5. In order to eliminate honor crimes, the perpetrators must receive heavier sentences like the perpetrators of blood feuds.
6. Women must be protected from sexual harassment under custody and in jail.
7. Workplace harassment should be considered a crime and should be treated accordingly.
8. Forced virginity tests should also be considered a crime and treated accordingly. (Uçan Süpürge, 2002)

The new Penal Code treats sexual assault and battery cases against a person's sexual integrity as crimes against an individual rather than as crimes against family decency. Most recently, some new steps indicate greater resolve to eradicate honor crimes. The head of the Turkish Supreme Court (Yargıtay) has publicly announced that reduced sentences for honor crimes contradict rule of law and human rights. He said that such laws cannot be defined as 'töre', based on custom, because they are rejected by the majority of Turkish society. Therefore, in the amendment of the Criminal Code, such reductions in sentencing must be eliminated (Hürriyet, March 31, 2004). The AK party government also has announced that the imams, the state-appointed prayer leaders, are now encouraged to deliver to their constituencies (15 million men who gather every Friday in mosques all over Turkey) that honor killings are against God and the Prophet's teaching on clemency. (*Economist*, 19 February 2004) As the *Economist* further noted:

> This idea came from Ali Bardakoğlu, the new head of Turkey's Religious Directorate, which 'micromanages religious life and telling preachers what to say in Turkey's paradoxical mix of official secularism and popular piety. Mr Bardakoğlu amazed women's groups by seeking their help in penning a homily in time for International Women's Day on March 8th; and the stark warning against 'honor killing' is among the results. 'It's revolutionary,' says Halime Güner, of Flying Broom....Some of Turkey's staunchest westernisers grudgingly admit that, since coming to office in 2002, the ruling Justice and Development Party has done more than its secular predecessors to advance social reform. This is at least partly because Turkey's rulers want to join the European Union, which makes social change imperative.

The Extent of Implementation

The legal reforms do not automatically bring about effective implementation. The stakeholders for policy reform are different from the ones involved in implementation. For implementation to be effective, local governments, municipalities, courts, and the police have to interpret and apply the law. In the early 1990s, when there was yet no law on domestic violence and no policy on dealing with victims, women's groups set up private shelters. This was an effort to offer services to victims of violence where the state did not. Women who campaigned against domestic violence saw forming organizations as their next step. They began to establish independent women's counseling centers and shelters. The first organization focusing on gender-based violence was established in 1990, the Purple Roof (Mor Çatı) Foundation, which then set up a counseling center/shelter in 1995 and published a book titled 'Cry out and let everyone hear' (Bağır Herkes Duysun). This book related the stories of women who were victims of violence, discussed why such violence is tolerated in Turkish society. It argued forcefully that violence in the home is not a private issue but a public concern requiring public action. A second organization also focusing on domestic violence, Women's Solidarity Foundation (Kadın Dayanışma Vakfı), was established in 1991 in Ankara.

These groups approached municipalities with requests for buildings and financial assistance to open women's shelters, but they were rejected. Municipalities claimed that they would open and administer shelters themselves ({lkkaracan, 2002). Two municipalities in Istanbul did open the first shelters in 1990, and one municipality in İzmir opened a women's counseling center. The Social Directorate for Social Services also opened its first shelters at this time. Purple Roof Foundation opened its shelter in 1995 after much search for funding. Women's Solidarity Foundation established a partnership with the Altındağ municipality in Ankara in 1993. These two independent shelters remained open in Ankara for seven years, and in Istanbul for five years. The Altındağ center was the first experiment of partnership with the government. As is common, one of the first lessons learned was the instability created by changes in political power. Once the Islamist Welfare Party won in 37 provinces in the 1994 local elections and was poised to win with a large majority in elections in 1995, the political landscape changed. Shortly after the local elections, new mayors closed almost all shelters and counseling centers administered by the local municipalities (İlkkaracan, 2002). The Altındağ shelter continued operating as a result of protest from women's groups, but it too closed down as a result of lack of funding. Even though the Altındağ shelter was closed down, the Women's Solidarity Foundation continued to raise awareness on gender-based violence and provided education and education materials to women in low income areas. Furthermore, the Foundation organized the first public panel on honor crimes and the papers from this panel were later published in a book by the NWM.

In many provinces of the country, women have established counseling centers, which increased from three in 1995 to eight in 2000, including in Mersin, Antalya, Diyarbakır, Çanakkale, İzmir, and Bursa. One important example is Ka-Mer in Diyarbakır which provides services to victims of violence. As part of their mandate to eliminate violence against women, these centers conduct research and gather data on violence and develop problem-solving strategies to respond to physical, psychological, social, financial and legal problems arising from violence. Some have been established in partnership with municipalities such as the one in Antalya. Some municipalities, especially those that are left of center, have either by themselves, or upon request from women's groups, have begun to establish women's counseling centers or shelters. Some women's groups under the umbrella of Local Agenda 21, have formed women's platforms and working groups on gender-based violence. Education and counseling services are now also provided by commissions on women's legislation which are organized within the Bars Associations in 28 provinces. In May 1999, these commissions set up the Turkish Bars Women's Commissions Network in order to work more effectively. For example, the Counseling and Legal Advice Center of the Bar Association in Dıyarbakır was able to help 96 women to start divorce proceedings. In the past, women never initiated divorce proceedings in the Diyarbakır area where traditional norms are very powerful. A recent newspaper article points out that as a result of migration from villages to the cities and counseling centers such as this one, women have become more aware of their rights. As one of the lawyers of this Center put it:

> Compared to 10 years ago, many of the women in this region have begun to seek their rights within the legal system. Just in the last year 122 women have come to us and 96 of these women claimed that they were suffering from violence from their husbands and wanted to get divorced. The rest of them came to us because they wanted to learn about their legal rights (Sabah, 12 July 2003).

The organizations established to fight against gender-based violence have also been networking and meeting at yearly Congresses on Women's Shelters since 1998. For example, the Congress held in 1999 focused on the implementation of the new law on the Family Protection, the draft of the new Civil Code, the expansion of women's counseling centers and shelters across the country. The participants have redefined violence against women to include incest, rape, honor crimes, harassment in the workplace. Governmental organizations also participated in these meetings. There are now a number of television programs on women that focus on violence and the mechanisms available to women. This is a good example of how implementation efforts may spur further efforts of problem definition, agenda-setting and renewed efforts at influencing the policy process.

The NWM and the Directorate General of Social Services and Child Protection (SHCEK) are now mandated to develop national policies and plans for governmental services and programs to eradicate violence against women and children. This constitutes an important step towards implementation. The Social Services Administration reviewed the regulations (yönetmelik) of women's guesthouses in 1997 and women's shelters were redefined as social service institutions according to this review.[9] Shelters for abused women are a relatively new initiative for Turkey, particularly for the public sector. SHCEK had opened the first women's guesthouse in 1990 and it now provides services for battered women or those at risk of encountering violence through guesthouses for women.

SHCEK operates 7 guesthouses and from 1995 to 2002, total of 3,139 women and 2,609 dependent children were housed in these shelters, and 541 women were placed in jobs. Besides guesthouses, SHCEK serves women through its 29 community centers where social workers counsel women, where different education programs are offered, and the objectives include creating a more participatory society. Those that utilize community centers' services include women who suffer from violence.

A municipality in Istanbul operates one women's guesthouse. Guidance and counseling services are offered by the Provincial Social Services Directorates of the 81 provinces, as well by the national women's machinery. The NWM has been supporting research on gender-based violence, providing training programs in other government organizations on these issues, and coordinates policy advocacy efforts such as legal reform processes. The NWM has also set up a 3B Knowledge Bank (Bilgi Başvuru Bankasi) in 1994 offering counseling. Also a direct phone line for women is currently in service in 21 provinces, providing psychological, legal and financial counseling for women. The number of shelters (13 for the whole country) and other mechanisms to deal with violence victims are not yet sufficient. A survey by Bilgi University on domestic violence showed that ninety-one per cent of the married women in the sample want to have access to a social service organization/shelter in case of need and invite the national and local governments to provide services in this area. (Bilgi University, 2003)

NWM and UNDP have sponsored a project implemented by Ankara University Women's Studies Center (KASAUM), and Women's Solidarity Foundation (Kadın Dayanışma Vakfı). This project trained 94 police on gender-based violence. Another police training project was implemented by the Women and Gender Studies Center of the Middle East Technical University where both police and students of the police academy were given training on women's human rights, gender equality, gender-based violence, and domestic violence.

A statute in the year 2000 stipulated that implementation of the Family Protection Law by the police be monitored and reported. Guidelines were published and disseminated to the police by the Directorate of Security on how to treat victims of violence at police stations. In service training was also provided to the police by the Directorate on the implementation of this Law. In addition on 15 November 2002, the Ministry of Justice has issued a by-law manual, providing guidelines for the implementation of the law. Since the Law has gone into force, an increasing number of cases have been reported. From 1 January 1999 to 31 January 2001, a total of 7,613 domestic violence cases reached the courts, of which 7,449 have been finalized. The NWM has prepared a brochure introducing the provisions of the law and disseminated it nationwide, and it is also monitoring its implementation. In a survey conducted by Bilgi University, sixty-six per cent of the respondents answered that laws and policies on domestic violence are important and will protect the family, while twenty-three per cent said that they are not important. The rest, eleven per cent, had no opinion, which may indicate that there is limited knowledge about the existence of this new law (Bilgi University, 2003)

Constraints to Implementation

Persuasiveness of Social Norms

While the efforts of the women's groups at policy advocacy were quite successful in bringing about legal reforms, implementation still remains limited as government commitment remains low. The social norms that condone violence do not disappear quickly. The most recent Amnesty International report on Turkey reiterates that the extent of violence perpetrated by men against family members is a serious concern. Estimates range from an approximate thirty to fifty-eight per cent of women who experience physical violence, to seventy to ninety-seven per cent of women experiencing a wider range of abuse. This epidemic of violence which affects all women and children who live with violent men – resulting in some cases in permanent disability and even death – appears to be condoned by the authorities and society in many situations. Family violence often occurs in public. The perpetrators are rarely tried and convicted (Amnesty International, 2004).

Chastity (namus) is an extremely important concept in Turkish society, a value that many people live by and are willing die for. As Yirmibeşoğlu, a lawyer, who has studied honor crimes across Turkey indicates, this thinking is prevalent across the country, not just in the Southeastern and Eastern regions. For instance, according to Yirmibeşoğlu, the majority of honor crime cases are filed in Adana courts, in southern Turkey (Uçan Haber, 2003). 'Namus' cannot be translated into English just as honor because it incorporates the notion of chastity of women as men's right and responsibility. The Turkish state (as evidenced by laws that allow honor crimes to receive lesser sentences and other discriminatory laws) has condoned this notion of 'namus' based on customs (töre) or traditions to thrive and continue within the legal system. This is because the cultural norms form the basis of political norms. In many cases, as Yirmibeşoğlu has observed, the men at the courts and at the National Parliament have the same values as the men on the street:

> While I was investigating honor crime cases at courts, I have come to the realization that the uneducated man who commits a murder crime on the street has the same mindset as the men who make the laws in the Parliament and implement them. Unfortunately in our society, to be educated does not mean that this mindset is changed. When I asked several lawyers about honor crimes, they said that if circumstances required it, they could commit honor crimes themselves. The Turkish state remains silent towards honor crimes, in fact silently encourages a male child (the murderers are usually underage) to kill his sister. The state that is obligated to protect the human rights of individuals, in fact, is far from protecting the rights of women and children (Uçan Haber, 2003, p.p. 38-39)

It is clear that the concept of 'honor' is a fundamental and deeply entrenched one, and not just in Eastern and Southeastern Turkey. As Yirmibeşoğlu has noted, this mindset is prevalent across Turkish society. Obviously without investigating, redefining notions of 'honor' and 'manhood', we cannot go very far. That investigation requires investigating male identities. Gürsoy (2002), who investigated how virginity controls affect women's health notes the following:

> Virginity issues affect men as well. These include inability to have a health sex life in fear of spoiling a woman's virginity, the fear of being accused of spoiling a woman's virginity, the social oppression and fears that come with marrying a woman who is not a virgin, to be forced to kill in the name 'honor' by the family.

In short, both women and men are affected by the taboos and fears and lack of knowledge surrounding sexuality. The lack of knowledge of existing laws even when there is access to information and, the reticence on the part of victims of violence remain a problem. Women who were married now or before were asked if they had heard about the Law on the Protection of the Family in 2003. Only forty-two per cent knew about it, and fifty-seven per cent had not heard about it. When women were asked whether they would report their husbands' violence or threat of violence, thirty-four per cent said yes in 2003 compared to twenty-nine per cent in 1997. This finding demonstrates that the majority of women are unsure about approaching public institutions. Twenty-eight per cent claimed that they would not report their husbands, because they believed such events should stay within the family (Bilgi University, 2003) Some of that reticence also stems may also stem from a lack of trust in security and police forces, especially in the East and Southeast where Kurdish populations have been repressed. As the Amnesty International memo rightly points out:

> In situations where the security services have lost the confidence of the population, it is difficult for women experiencing violence in the home to turn to the law enforcement agencies or to have confidence in justice. Women in these contexts may fear the consequences to their husbands or families if they report violence. Impunity of public officials who commit violence, combined with insufficient implementation of the Law for the Protection of the Family, mean that vulnerable members of the community, such as women and children, have insufficient trust that action will be taken against any perpetrators of violence. These concerns make it even more important that effective, independent mechanisms exist for women to access protection, support and shelter, and that specialist services exist within the justice system at all levels and in all branches to work with victims of family violence in every region of the country. (Amnesty International, February 2004)

Amnesty International, furthermore, calls for the comprehensive monitoring and documentation of violence against women, additional measures aimed at preventing violence, such as the provision of shelters, improved access to judicial mechanisms, appropriate health care, and measures to ensure that police, judiciary and public officials act promptly and effectively when allegations of violence are brought to them.

Conclusions

Violence against women is now on the global agenda, and honor crimes, once local and invisible, are also now a globalized problem. Women's movements in Turkey had already made violence their priority before it was placed on the global agenda. One of their first successes was the repeal of a law that gave lighter sentences to rapists of prostitutes in 1989. The next legal reform on violence, the Family Protection Law, is a good example of how favorable global norms and institutions provided a window of opportunity for women's networks in Turkey. The Minister of Women's Affairs who attended the CEDAW Committee meeting returned home with domestic violence on her agenda. With the advocacy of women's groups, the work of the NWM, and the initiative of the Minister, the law was passed. By the time honor crimes were placed on the UN agenda in 2000, women's networks had acquired a great of political savvy and international experience and served on the government delegation at the Beijing Plus Five conference. Their efforts were instrumental in the identification of honor crimes in the Outcome Document as a specific form of harmful traditional practice in need of being eliminated. International NGOs such as Amnesty International and Human Rights Watch also supported women's networks. Amnesty International published an extensive report on violence against women in Turkey, and the Prime Minister received Irene Khan, its Secretary General, personally for the first time in 2003, signifying greater responsiveness towards this issue.

The government passed the new Penal Code in 2004, which finally explicitly defines honor crimes as punishable by life sentences. This new Penal Code was passed in order to receive a positive reply to start membership negotiations with the European Union. But at the same time, women's networks in Turkey were constantly at work, lobbying both opposition and ruling parties, making sure that the new reforms did not include any gender-discriminatory wording. The AK party, for example, tried to insert a clause that would have criminalized adultery in the new Penal Code. The Party was also in favor of rapists to marry their victims in return for reduced sentences. And virginity testing is still not banned and criminalized; instead those who order virginity testing without proper authority will be penalized.

These monumental legal reforms now await implementation. But there are some signs of important changes in the making, of new actors and new alliances. Ali Bardakoğlu, who heads the Religious Affairs Directorate, has instructed the preachers in mosques (imams) to discuss honor crimes and tell the people that such acts are not just a breach of the law but also a sin against God; they contravene the Prophet's teaching on clemency. Mr. Bardakoğlu amazed women's groups by seeking their help in penning a homily in time for International Women's Day on March 8, 2004. 'It is revolutionary' said Halime Güner, of Uçan Süpürge (Flying Broom), one of the women's organizations consulted by Bardakoğlu (*Economist,* 19 February 2004). Another example is the new public campaign started in October 2004 with the cooperation of the Hürriyet newspaper, Modern Education Foundation (Çağdas Eğitim Vakfı) and the Mayor of Istanbul. This campaign will focus on several low income areas where counselors and psychologists will offer workshops held in a bus that will go from district to district (Hürriyet, 18 October, 2004). The first workshops have included sessions for both women and men and have received positive feedback. Violence in the family is an issue that receives support from both more Islamist and secularist members of society. The Prime Minister's wife, Mrs. Erdoğan, asked to visit women's shelters when she and her husband were on an official visit to the United States at the beginning of 2004. The Family Research Organization has also put violence in the family on its agenda.

While legal reforms signal unprecedented changes in the gender discourse, across-the-board implementation is another matter. Comprehensive training programs for government officials, judges and the police will be necessary. At the community level, a cultural perspective is needed to understand the causes of persisting violence and raise awareness on its detrimental impact not only on those who experience it but on the entire society by drawing on positive elements of culture. Within the concept of 'honor' lies male identity linked to female sexual control, within the concept of hierarchy, female subordination. As Pervizat (2003) insightfully comments, we must study and utilize the concepts of masculinity and its link to 'honor':

> In order to prevent honor killings, it is crucial to redefine the concept of honor within the community...When talking to families, a cultural discourse proves to be very effective. We believe that male members are also victims of the concept of masculinity – they suffer throughout the decision-making process. We try to give men what I call cultural and psychological space where their masculinity is not challenged and they do not feel forced to kill in order to cleanse their honor. To do this, and in order to create space for long-term change, we take advantage of some of the positive aspects of Turkish culture that offer individual men an excuse to avoid violence. These include special occasions and gatherings where nonviolence negotiations are encouraged or where authority figures can act as intermediaries, in which we can make use of traditions of hospitality towards guests or respect for elderly people's recommendations as tools to prevent these crimes. (Pervizat, 2003, p. 31)

Finally at the level of individual women, the types of empowerment programs to improve women's access to justice discussed in Chapter 4 need to be expanded to much wider audiences. Violence against women ultimately stems from not accepting women as individual human beings, and from the fact that the rights and responsibility to control their behavior have been transferred to men. Women have internalized these norms in many cases such that they see it as the husband's right to control their freedom of movement, or to even to beat them if they are disobedient. Thus, it seems that both gender identities are shaped by this norm: women give up some of their rights, in return for what they perceive as 'men's protection'; and men assume the role of protector and controller of female behavior and sexuality. This, of course, goes against the grain of individual rights and turns gender relations into a master-slave relationship. Male identity, masculinity and manhood too, is limited, by this very right and responsibility such that the biggest threat to their manhood is the sexual freedom of the women in their family. Any possibility of such sexual freedom must be resisted; the ramifications are that sexuality cannot be openly discussed; it is strictly confined to within the marriage for women. (Kahraman, 2004) As Ertürk has reiterated, there is a need to deconstruct hegemonic masculinity and to engage in a dialogue and alliance with alternative masculinities that do not condone oppressive uses of power.

A Turkish journalist's interpretation of gender-based violence and the norms of male superiority offers these insights:

> I think that underneath this gender-based violence lies a much more horrific truth, and that is 'misogyny' in the subconscious of the society. Misogyny is an illness, of course, but as all manifestations of societal pathologies, it reveals itself under the guise of 'naturalness' and 'normalcy'. But in reality, the manifestation of this illness abound: women are pushed aside, violently treated, pressured to remain dependent and silent. Add to this, the swearwords we use, invoking our mothers, who we supposedly revere. Let's think of how the person places himself and women in this discourse of swearing, and we will understand how we perceive women. (Türker, 2004)

Türker (2004) provides a psychological interpretation of honor crimes by claiming that underneath the murders in the name of 'töre' or customs lies a fear of women. Because in Turkish society 'chastity' (namus) as something that can be destroyed, belongs to women, and 'honor' belongs to men, men's job is to save and protect that honor. What logically follows is that when a woman's chastity is defiled, the only way to regain male honor is by eliminating the object of defilement. 'Woman' in the male psyche is someone who presents a constant threat to a man's honor because her chastity is always open to potential defilement. These underlying fears of women's freedom and the potential threat it poses to the male psyche may have led to the rejection of women from public spaces, and their harassment when they venture out on their own. That is why one of the first public campaigns of the women's movement cried out for reclaiming the streets without harassment. A woman alone means she is potentially sexually available and is not under the protection of male relatives. The relief comes when in the social hierarchy, a woman gains superiority due to her age or profession. If she is on the streets after dark, this may put her in an even more precarious situation.[10] One of the frequent explanations from women in Turkey and other Moslem countries as to why they choose to cover is that they can reclaim public spaces without harassment from men. They say that they can be on the streets safely and without fear of harassment because their appearance commands respect and signifies that they are not sexually available. But then others have argued that women take the blame for men's lewd or violent behavior by covering themselves, instead of looking for ways to change male behavior through education and the legal system. But then, one may wonder why women have to cover themselves to escape from harassment from men. In the Qur'an, it says that both women and men should dress modestly and keep their eyes down. If men keep their eyes down as advised, then the whole issue would be moot.

If there is some truth to the gender norms discussed above, it is also clear that the education of *both* genders is needed to move away from the master-slave dynamic of gender relations in the specific Turkish context. This means women's concerns cannot be relegated to the magazine/life style pages of the newspapers, by turning discourse into 'she is covered/she is not' and by showcasing a few women in politics. Türker writes that women in Turkey mostly resign themselves to be the objects of this discourse where they are limited to discussions of 'femininity' – beauty, elegance, esthetics and social harmony. He continues that those who construct this discourse and see the world in terms of power relations define women as an inferior human being who distract men but in taken in small doses, and colorful frames, they add to life to one's life. Women are mostly incapable of redefining and reconstructing their existence and they mostly inertly follow the parade of a few adjectives ascribed to them such as 'young, beautiful, mother, wife, chaste, unchaste'.

The current national debates on the revisions to the Criminal Code are extremely important because they represent several conflicting discourses that point to new opportunity spaces and their outcomes shape the new gender discourse as well as new power balances. One conflict is on the female identity: is it going be based on individual identity and respect for individual rights, or on collective identity where women's bodies and sexuality belongs to the man, family and collectivity? Another conflict is between those that would like to hang on to the fear of women, and therefore continue to want to enslave her, and those that prefer gender relations to be between free and equal individuals who come to the relationship and continue it of their own will. Yet a third conflict is between clan (aşiret) leaders and their political allies who would like to sustain their economic and political order and alliances based on women's suppression versus a growing women's movement and its supporters at the national and international level. As Pervizat (2003, p. 31) summarizes:

> Activists must use all possible advocacy tools – changing society's discourse by using some of its own terms of reference, reforming the judiciary, and incorporating a gender perspective into the human rights advocacy being conducted in Turkey, while continuing to draw on the support of global actors.

Yet, unfortunately, the mainstream human rights activists have not allied with women's human rights activists on honor crimes and do not see honor killings at the same level as other human rights violations, implicitly agreeing with male right to control of women's sexuality. According to Pervizat (2003, p. 31):

> For instance, a well known human rights activist working against capital punishment once complained to me and other activists that the recent media attention devoted to honor killings was 'exaggerating this woman thing to the level of a human rights violation and therefore diminishing the power of human rights'. For many such human rights activists, honor killings do not belong on the same level as torture, lack of freedom of expression or extrajudicial executions.

Notes

[1] See UN, 2001, From Beijing to Beijing Plus Five, Critical Area of Concern D, for an analysis of measures taken by governments to end violence against women.

[2] This chapter does not include a focus on trafficking in women. Admittedly, it is a very significant issue in Turkey that requires extensive research and policy formulation which are at the beginning stages.

[3] These findings are reported in a research report on 'Violence against Women' by Bilgi University, Center for Human Rights, 2003.

[4] Proverbs compiled by the author.

[5] One of my male students, working for an international organization in Afghanistan, recounted the story of how he asked the name of an Afghan man's sister, and the response was: 'why are you asking her name? What do you have to do with her?'

[6] Personal interview, 23 October 2004.

[7] There are now many Turkish women professionals who work in at the global level, and are also in close contact with Turkish NGOs, and research centers. Some examples of international organizations they have worked with include UNDP, ILO, ICRW, UNDAW, INSTRAW, CEDAW committee, IWHC and others.

[8] http://www.kadininsanhaklari.org/?id=882

[9] State Planning Organization, The Report of the Commission on Violence and Women, Ankara.

[10] There are, of course, big differences between urban areas, city centers, where women drive, walk around and are out by themselves any time of day or night. But overall, a woman alone may still draw stares and other unwanted attention.

Chapter 6

Women's Participation in Local Governance

Good Governance Norms at the Global Level and in Turkey

The intellectual debates of the 1980s and 1990s have focused on 'governance' as a prominent concept in the language of international public policy. It is useful to briefly discuss the concept of governance and what is meant by 'good governance' before turning to local governance and its implications for women in Turkey. Governance is used to describe phenomena that go beyond a synonym for government and the legal authority with which such polities are vested. According to Weiss (2000), governance emerged because of the disappointment with state-led models of development. Although there are diverse interpretations, governance refers to a particular relationship between state and society that stipulates the collective involvement of the government (politicians, members of parliament, public administration), civil society and the private sector. The goal of this collective involvement is to achieve 'good governance'. Good governance involves both state character (separation of powers and rule of law) and capacity (administrative effectiveness and efficiency) and the democratic concept of accountability (holding office holders to account, as well as mutual accountability of the above sectors). There is now pressure on states to reorient and restructure themselves to achieve economic growth and efficiency *with* the accompaniment of greater freedom, genuine participation and sustainable human development. Even though there are varying definitions of good governance, there is general agreement that it encompasses rule of law, political and bureaucratic accountability, transparency, decentralization and greater civil society participation in decision-making processes (Weiss, 2000).

Weiss gives four reasons why the quality of a country's political and economic governance system became an acceptable topic for debate and for intervention within international public policy (Weiss, 2000, pp. 799-800). First, there was the illegitimacy of regimes led by such international pariahs as Uganda's Idi Amin, or Kampuchea's Pol Pot. Second, both the Third World and the former Soviet bloc undertook a set of political reforms, especially when the collapse of the Berlin Wall so closely followed the collapse of the Soviet Union. New regimes saw elections as prerequisites to their legitimacy and to attract Western financial assistance. Third, the proliferation of NGOs is a striking element of contemporary international relations who have important implications for global governance.

Global networks on human rights, women's human rights or the environment have been instrumental in the shaping of legal instruments to which states are held accountable. As Weiss (2000) points out, human rights advocates, gender activists, developmentalists, and groups of indigenous peoples have invaded the territory of states, literally and figuratively. Fourth, the existence of failed states such as Somalia, the former Yugoslavia and Rwanda made it possible to scrutinize domestic policies that had led to mass displacement, rapes and killings. Even though the UN's constitution prohibits interference in the domestic policies of member states, humanitarian interventions have encouraged the insertion of responsibility as an integral aspect of sovereignty.

Not all international organizations understand governance in the same way. The World Bank defines governance as the manner in which power is exercised in the management of a country's economic and social resources. The Bank has identified three distinct aspects of governance: a) the form of political regime; b) the process by which authority is exercised in the management of a country's economic and social resources for development and c) the capacity of governments to design, formulate and implement policies and discharge functions. For the United Nations Development Programme (UNDP), governance constitutes the exercise of economic, political, and administrative authority to manage a country's affairs at all levels. It comprises mechanisms, processes and institutions through which citizens and groups articulate their interests, exercise their legal rights, meet their obligations and mediate their differences. There are some distinct differences between these two definitions. The UNDP's human development approach to government exhibits strong support for empowerment and stresses the importance of providing the tools of democracy and freedom that are integral to the political and civic dimensions of governance. As a result, UNDP has become a major donor in support of gender equality and women's human rights, including women's participation in local governance. For the World Bank, good governance is a means to improve economic performance. In other words, implementing economic reform dominates public and internal discussions of governance. But even though the formal governance agenda is narrowly defined, the World Bank has added initiatives since 1991 that have expanded the formal definition of governance to include a degree of a) the non-state (civil society) actors participation in World Bank activities; b) the discussion of corruption and its effects on good governance; as well as c) human rights understood as rights that are economic and social in nature.

The good governance debate itself has undergone some transition from the 1980s when the focus was on dismantling the state and on economic liberalization programs. The 1990s, however, have began to encompass political liberalization with greater emphasis on leadership and management as well as democracy, human rights, rule of law, access to justice and basic freedoms. What we see today is more interest in improving the functioning of democratic institutions and exploring more active and creative roles for non-state actors, including women's groups and organizations by many international development assistance organizations. Leaders are being held to higher standards of accountability and they have to contend with the forces of globalization.

Good governance cannot be attained in a society with pervasive gender inequality and that increasing gender equality provides enormous benefits in establishing a culture of human rights and participation, one of the major goals of good governance. It provides immediate material benefits through increased productivity and the human capital of the next generation. But in no country do women hold more than a very small share of the seats in parliament. A crisis of legitimacy and accountability is evident when the interests of over half the population are not reflected in the decisions that are made. Ashworth (1996) questions the legitimacy of decisions where perhaps nine-tenths represents less than half the population, and one tenth (the world average) represents 52 percent:

> Is it legitimate that the investment of their taxes and other decisions, including going to war, all of which affect all of the population, are taken without the consent of the majority? Is it legitimate even that questions of reproductive rights, population rights, medical ethics or family laws are decided without the presence and representation of child bearers?

One cannot have gender equality without good governance as well: greater gender equality requires good governance. The state has a critical role in establishing an institutional environment based on equal rights and opportunities for women and men and in ensuring equal access to resources and public services. This means some fundamental changes in the rule of law, in public sector effectiveness, in accountability and transparency mechanisms both in the public sector and in the relationships between state and civil society. Norms for gender roles and rights form part of the moral order of a community and permeate all institutions, including the state. These norms include kinship rules such as rules of inheritance and marriage. If such rules are heavily weighted in favor of men, gender equality decreases. However, if such rules are more gender balanced, women have a greater voice in the household and public spaces (World Bank, 2001). Legal systems tend to further reinforce gender inequalities unless conscious efforts are made to avoid it. They play a key part either reinforcing customary gender rights and roles – or deliberately trying to alter them. Women furthermore face discrimination in important areas such as politics, education and employment, leading to unequal allocation of resources. Thus, the public sector has to be altered so that specific efforts are made to reach women and the provision of public goods and services do not bypass them. Increased accountability, the third component of good governance, has to include women's increased participation in the public decision-making process. One might say that the signatory states to CEDAW are held responsible to make the above changes. This is what was examined in Chapter 2: the construction and contestation of gender norms that underlie the legal, judiciary and administrative institutions and in Chapter 3: the responsiveness and extent of state accountability in the legal system and the public sector to gender equality.

The formulation of good governance goals is, of course, a different matter than actual implementation. The challenges of globalization complicate the achievement of good governance goals because they produce contradictory and ambiguous outcomes. One perspective is that the market logic may lead to a restructuring in the functions and perspectives of the state, civil society and the private sector. States will then need to become more accountable to the public, more competent in their administrative capacity, and create an enabling environment for the private sector through legal and regulatory reforms. In short, good governance will follow. It is not yet clear whether there is an inevitability to this logic or whether it is mere wishful thinking. Experience has shown that economic reforms cannot be successful without an effective and accountable government and public sector, but the latter need to be in place *a priori,* not following economic reforms. It is at least clear that the relationship between economic reforms to bring about an open economy and the achievement of good governance is quite complex. Globalization has forced countries to become more integrated into the world capitalist economy. It has shrunk the world, leading to the increased diffusion of global norms of capitalism and democracy (including good governance), but we have also simultaneously seen the rise of interethnic conflict and the breakdown of societies. Economic globalization has created opportunities to create wealth both legally and illegally (including from sex and drug trafficking). It has created 'global citizens' in every country, who have benefited from this process, while relegating others to poverty and marginalization. With such unpredictable and contradictory outcomes, states are just as likely to become defensive and perceive threats from both 'above and below', or to become staunch advocates of good governance.

The challenge to states comes from above from global institutions, global social movements and communication networks, and from below, from citizens asking for greater accountability and participation in decision-making. Forces of globalization have reduced the territories over which states have traditionally had control so that many states classified as developing or in transition are faced with the necessity to give up certain areas of control to the logic of markets as well as to civil societies. As mentioned above, the success of good governance lies in the collective involvement and participation of all sectors of society. Yet, these are the very states that have traditionally built ideologies to promote unity and nationalism, that have centralized public administrations, and that have discouraged public participation in decision-making. Now a great deal of change is being demanded from them: to be flexible in allowing new actors and finding new ways of collaboration with them, but at the same time to be firm in creating a legal and administrative environment that promotes trust and greater certainty. Turkey is also in this predicament.

In Turkey, the goals of good governance, even though they are increasingly valued, have at times been overshadowed by some real or perceived threats to the unity and survival of the Republic. These threats have included the fear of political Islam, the fear of ethnic separatism, and more recently the challenges posed by the globalization process. For example, the perceived threat from political Islam and religious influence fueled a demonstration in Ankara against decentralization that would give greater decision-making power to local authorities (BBC News, March 8, 2004). Such threats, whether real or perceived, have been seen as attacks at the heart of the Turkish unitary and secular state. These threats have confirmed a strong military role in politics, as well as in other types of interventions, for example, in high-level appointments based on ideological preference rather than competence that intervene in the rule of law. Such interventions not only contradict the rule of law, but also other aspects of good governance, including administrative neutrality, effectiveness and accountability. The Turkish Constitution itself curtails individual freedoms and rights under certain conditions, including any threats to the unity of the state, to secularism, the principle on which the Turkish Republic has been built, threats to national security and to social order in general. The difficulties of upholding the rule of law also stem from the norms of Turkish political system that may allow a Member of Parliament to publicly declare, as it happened in February 2001, that 'some activities do not need to conform to law, if they are conducted in the name of state security' (Mert, *Radikal*, 15 February 2001). These norms tend to uphold a hierarchical, rather than participatory and egalitarian set of values which have made civil society building a difficult, uphill process.

How will Turkey respond to these demands in the face of potential or real threats? Can the goals of good governance be reconciled with the founding principles of the Turkish Republic, its history, its geopolitical strategies, political culture and social traditions? And if so, how? The answers will no doubt affect the potential membership of the country in the European Union since the goals of good governance are also the very ones that underlie the conditions of membership and are embodied in the Copenhagen Criteria. According to these criteria, the candidate state to the European Union has to achieve stability of institutions guaranteeing democracy, the rule of law, human rights and respect for and protection of minorities. The European Commission Report released in October 2004 has announced that Turkey has fulfilled the Copenhagen Criteria and recommended the initiation of membership negotiations. The legal reforms which encompass greater human rights and freedoms, increased civil society activity, and reduced role of the military in policy-making are all monumental steps towards the goal of good governance. An important aspect of good governance is the partnership of civil society organizations with local governments and greater participation of women in these partnerships.

Norms on Local Governance: Where does Women's Participation Come In?

Many global conferences have emphasized the need for local governments to form partnerships with civil society organizations, including the 1992 Rio Conference on Environment and Development and the 1996 Habitat conference. One of the results of the Rio Conference was Local Agenda 21. This document pointed to the importance of civil society organizations in the democratic process, and recommended that local administrations establish a 'Local Agenda 21' whereby they include the participation of women and youth in their policy-making and implementation processes. Local Agenda 21 is implemented in Turkey by the UNDP in cooperation with International Union of Local Administrations – Eastern Mediterranean and the Middle East (IULA-EMME) and the World Academy of Local Governance and Democracy (WALD). These norms were also emphasized in the 1994 Cairo Conference on Population and Development and 1995 Copenhagen Conference on Social Development. Furthermore, the Beijing Platform for Action reminded people of the importance of civil society organizations as reiterated in:

> All members of civil society, especially women's groups and networks and other NGOS should collaborate with governments so that the Platform of Action can be effectively monitored and implemented. (Platform for Action and the Beijing Declaration, 1996, p. 27)

Why women's participation in local governance? It is argued that decentralization of government functions at the local level helps redress gender inequalities because decentralization increases grassroots, thus women's, participation. For example, grassroots mobilization and political organization of women in countries such as South Africa, India and Pakistan have resulted in significant increases in representation. The quotation below illuminates the South African experience:

> In South Africa, at the early stages of preparing for the election, the advocates of systemic mechanisms to insure gender equity were laughed at, even by the President-elect, Mandela. However, the multi-racial National Coalition of Women mobilized women throughout the country to state and defend their interests – their immediate infrastructure needs, as well as their views on geopolitics – with the chiefs and community leaders. The processes of negotiation themselves in which women gained self-confidence in their difference from men, as well as their own capacities for self-expression were empowering psychologically, as well as politically. Large numbers of women stood as candidates for the new federal and state parliaments, and large numbers were successful, making the proportion of women in state and federal parliaments the highest on the continent. The processes also began educating men to understand about sharing power at all levels, from the home to international governance. The outcome has been a constitution that declares South Africa to be a non-racist and non-sexist state, and institutionalized mechanisms to protect the gains made. (Ashworth, 1996, p. 17)

In India, Gupta documents how women's participation in local governance has gradually moved from mere presence in public spaces to a consolidation of their positions as legitimate actors in planning and decision-making processes. In the process, the definition of 'governance' and the perception that officials are primarily concerned with managing macro policies and directives from 'above' are changing to a more demand-oriented approach to development planning. According to Gupta, the women's initiatives in local development have created a dynamic process of negotiation through which to change and renegotiate their own 'participation' demanded by donor agencies:

> (Women's) involvement (in development programs) is generally in the form of implementers who will ensure efficient service delivery, rather than as potential planners and decision-makers who will redesign development programs and then run them. Many women's collectives, however, have accepted these terms of engagement. They have used their participation in government programs as an opportunity to build their capacities by learning about the program and understanding the administrative hierarchy that manages it. Once familiar with the officials and the program, women have provided constructive feedback on how programs can be modified to benefit them. In doing so women's collectives have expanded their own spaces for participation. This in turn will provide new learning opportunities and feed into the creation of new terms of engaging with the state and more meaningful participation in governance. (Gupta, 2001, pp. 203-4)

Even if there were participatory approaches, that does not, however, always ensure that is also an equitable approach for women with respect to men.[1] There are a lot of participatory exercises that are totally un-engendered. Proponents of decentralization argue that when local governments and NGOs have a larger role in choosing the use of public resources, these choices will respond more closely to local needs and preferences, an outcome that favors efforts to make government more efficient and democratic. However, decentralization does not guarantee more transparency, accountability, or pro-poor and gender-sensitive results. It can result in highly unequal local power structures bolstering the fiscal control of local elite and increasing the likelihood of corruption. One way to address the challenges of checks and balances on decentralized systems is through central auditing or control. Yet in many instances macro-level checks and balances on decentralized expenditures are not sufficient. Another solution is popular participation in budgetary processes by local communities. Budgets, either at the local or national levels, establish priorities for action, and are the means by which citizens' access to public goods, resources, and services is largely determined. If budgets fail to be responsive to the needs and demands of the poor and of women, resources will not be adequately directed to the achievement of equality and equity goals and for gender-responsive programs, such as the elimination of violence against women and the provision of adequate services to support women's unpaid work, and promote their equal opportunities. As a result of discrimination and gender inequality, many of women's contributions to national development may remain unrecognized, unpaid, and unaccounted for. The failure to acknowledge their contributions perpetuates and reinforces barriers to their equal rights to access goods and services. At the same time, women carry a hugely disproportionate role in reproduction, child-rearing, and family and health care, also undervalued and unrecognized. Gender-sensitive budgeting can make a critical contribution to remedying and addressing discrimination and inequalities, and to promoting more effective use of public resources. A discussion on gender-sensitive budgeting is included in the State Planning Organization's Report of the Commission on the

Institutionalization of Gender. It concludes that, even though in the 1990s many citizens in Turkey have become more aware of the national budget, its different categories, and the politics of the budgetary process, there is not yet much sensitivity on how the local government budgets are shaped by political processes and how those may affect different groups of people differently.[2]

Participation of the poor in decision-making does not guarantee gender equality either. Even when there is community participation in the budgetary process women, especially poor women, are not guaranteed to be there. The political and fiscal bodies at the local level have few women in decision-making positions. Clearly the equitable (in terms of urban-rural divide, race, class and gender), informed and gender-aware participation of stakeholders is an important aspect of fiscal decentralization. But this can only be achieved by building local and central checks and balances, social auditory processes, which as yet are not part of accepted practices.

For local governments to effectively collaborate with civil society organizations, they need to have some autonomy and access to resources in order to become viable partners. One of the outcomes of public sector reforms in many developing countries has been the decision of governments to undertake decentralization. This refers the restructuring of authority so that it is shared between governing institutions at the central, regional, and local levels. It is claimed that decentralization can encourage greater participation (both electoral and civil society participation) and can enhance local government responsiveness to local demands. It can foster a more efficient use of resources if projects are locally conceived.

There are a number of requirements for decentralization to fulfill the goal of greater democratization and good governance. Local authorities who claim a greater degree of autonomy, financial autonomy in particular, must be able to demonstrate transparency, accountability and the political will to deliver local services in a participatory manner. Civil society and non-governmental organizations formed by groups within civil society are expected to act as interest groups: to lobby, to mobilize people who otherwise do not have access to state power, and to gather them together in groups so that they can have some influence and participate in the governmental decision-making process. The political functions of civil society groups are to increase participation in political processes, provide voice and political empowerment to members and force governments to be more open and responsive.

Paradoxically the NGOs of civil society can expand their capacity only if the government expands its own governance capacity to regulate and enforce human rights protection. All over the world, since the invigoration of grassroots NGO development efforts, even 'nonpolitical' NGO efforts to help poor people have led to the deaths or harassment of activists at the hands of threatened interests, with the government being unable or unwilling to provide any effective protection. Literacy in their own language, expanded job opportunities, family planning information, preservation of community environmental resources, even preservation of minority cultures – all these goals of NGO activities have been seen as threatening to powerful interests at certain times and in certain countries, including the Philippines, Myanmar, Kenya, Nigeria, Guatemala. In Turkey, the laws on establishing NGOs are very restrictive, and many people have feared establishing or even joining NGOs for fear of police intervention. Organizations with extremist or separatist ideologies have been banned and their members taken in custody. Thus, strengthening NGOs, and their status as partners and collaborators with the government are still issues on the agenda; examples of successful collaboration are just beginning to appear.

Decentralization is most often practiced as the transfer of government decision-making and administrative authority to semi-independent local units who may still be legally and financially accountable to the central government. But there is usually a strong tension that arises between the center and the local government which is an issue of *control versus capacity*. The central government wants local government to accomplish a number of tasks but they do not really want to give away the authority to let them do it. A second tension arises from the issue of accountability: accountability exists at the local level but it is selective. We want accountability in good governance but who are the local elites accountable to? Who do the local authorities represent in terms of economic classes, traditional clans or ethnic groups? Local authorities are likely to be listening to certain constituencies already; they might have established patronage-based relationships in which both sides gain. Thus one major question that arises is: will decentralization of financial and decision-making authority strengthen local and traditional power structures or will they encourage participatory processes in general? This issue continues to occupy the national and political agenda in Turkey. In fact, the draft bill to rearrange the relationship between local, provincial and central governments is in the Parliament, but it has stirred some significant debate, and it is not yet clear what the outcome will be. A BBC Report on a public protest against the draft Bill for Decentralization attests to these tensions:

> Up to 80,000 people have demonstrated in Ankara against government plans to reform Turkey's administration. A bill is being considered by parliament to decentralize the administration and allow local government greater freedom in the hiring of staff. Opponents fear that this could lead to job cuts and politicization of the civil service. The Turkish capital has not seen a demonstration of this size since before the Iraq war. The demonstrators braved winter weather to make their views known. Turkey has a very centralized system of government. Few decisions, even of the most minor kind, escape the scrutiny of civil servants in Ankara. The governing AKP party wants to loosen the control of the capital over the far-flung provinces. Critics of decentralization plan believe that allowing local government greater flexibility over the hiring and firing of civil society could open the civil service to religious influence. (March 6, 2004)

Thus, it is obvious that the decentralization debate is colored and shaped by the underlying view that pits principles of secularism and their supporters versus the potential power of local elites who run local governments (perceived as synonymous with religious elites and political Islam) such that a centralized top-down administration that rules from Ankara is more suitable than any attempt to give more decision-making power to local elites. Local elections have, however, been gaining in importance in Turkey, especially in big metropolitan areas, and local governments have gained more power. İncioğlu (2002) argues that given the large concentration of voters in urban areas, political parties now consider local elections as crucial in expanding their popularity at the national level. Also, controlling such large municipalities means access to sources of political patronage to recruit new supporters. Such interest and the rising importance of local elections in Turkish politics may be attributed to the rapid growth of urbanization (İncioğlu, 2002).

Historically, the Turkish administrative system has been highly centralized, which reflected the relative weakness of local institutions. But the rapid urbanization process since the 1970s has been accompanied with the so-called municipal movement that sought greater local autonomy (Finkel, 1990). The local government reform carried out in 1984 created a two-tier system of municipal governance in the country's largest cities, namely Greater City Municipalities which significantly enhanced the political status and power of metropolitan mayors, and increased the financial resources of municipal administrations, as well as expanding the scope of their activities (Kalaycioğlu, 1989). Greater City Mayors had the opportunity to become influential in national politics, including the current Prime Minister Tayyib Erdoğan who served as the Mayor of Metropolitan Istanbul.

Experiences with Women's Participation in Local Governance

Local Agenda 21 and Women's Platforms

Another significant United Nations conference for bringing local governance and the participation on the global agenda is the 1992 Rio conference. This Conference led to a UNDP-supported program around the world, called Local Agenda 21, including in Turkey. There is no doubt that the implementation of Local Agenda 21 in Turkey has created some significant opportunities for women's participation. This program aims to strengthen local constituencies and encourage the establishment of city councils and other citizen groups who partake in local decision-making and collaborate with municipalities. Thus, Local Agenda 21 helped to establish local platforms for civil society members (especially for women and youth) and organizations in 50 cities where representatives of civil society have a platform to engage in dialogue with government officials. It is implemented by the International Union of Local Administrations, Eastern Mediterranean and Middle East (IULA-EMME). Among the project cities, over 15 partner cities established women's platforms.[3] These platforms gave many women an opportunity to make their voices heard, to learn about their rights, and to begin to establish various forms of collaboration with municipalities.

The 1996 UN Habitat Conference held in Istanbul was also very influential in the dissemination of global norms on local governance in Turkey. The Habitat

Conference's agenda stressed accountability and transparency for sustainable development, and the need for strengthening local governance and its partnership with civil society. The Habitat Conference was also vital in the promoting the view that local governments' partnerships with women's organizations are more likely to yield quick results. The National Report on Turkey, prepared for the Habitat Conference, emphasized the strengthening of women in urban settings by supporting women's participation in the public sphere, and supporting the establishment of counseling centers, women's shelters, and kindergartens:

> It is of utmost importance that local community centers where women can get together are established. In such centers, women can receive education and training. Their establishment should be modeled on a partnership with civil society organizations. Women are eager to participate in such ventures, and such participation is very likely to raise their quality of life, as well as the quality of life of the community in general. (in Ecevit, 2001, p. 237)

During the Habitat Conference the World Academy of Local Governance and Democracy (WALD) met in Istanbul, and their declaration emphasized the importance of women's participation in urban living and in urban governance. Research results showed that women in Turkey are less able to access services in cities and towns offered by local governments, especially those that have recently migrated from other regions, and remain alienated and cloistered within their homes (Ecevit, 2001).

The women's platforms that were established as a result of the Local Agenda 21 process deserve close attention as examples of emerging partnerships of local governments with women. *The Antalya Women's Platform* was established in 1994 with the participation of about 100 women and has worked as a 'women's lobby'. This platform was disbanded in 1997. In its place, a Women's Council was formed within the Antalya City Council, part of the Local Agenda 21 network with 374 members. At first, this Council was seen by female politicians as a place to attract supporters. According to Eroğlu et al (2002), the novelty of the Women's Council was that individual women could join independently. They did not need to represent or be attached to a particular organization. Thus, the group included women from diverse backgrounds: housewives, retirees, women who wore Islamic dress, literate or illiterate. The Women's Council then formed commissions on specific topics, such as gender-based violence, education and employment, health, environment and political participation. Its members participated in many public campaigns and conferences. One of the commissions, the Commission on Gender-Based Violence was particularly active in establishing a Counseling Center for Women, with the Antalya Municipality's support. The Municipality provided office space and financial support. The members of this Center hosted a national meeting on women's shelters in Antalya in 2001. They offered literacy programs, computer training, seminars on gender-based violence and have made site visits to shelters in Europe, including Denmark. The Antalya Women's Council members indicated in interviews that they have learned to work together under the umbrella of the City Council and have begun to appreciate the participatory mode of interaction and implement it more and more over time. The problems they experience included the differences of perspectives among members leading to lack of agreement and inaction, small number of active women who take leadership roles, and lack of regional collaborative projects.[4]

The Bursa Women's Platform (Bursa Independent Women's Initiative), another active group, established a Women's Communication and Support Center in Bursa in 1998, in partnership with the Bursa Greater City Municipality. Other women's platforms function as a loose network of women's groups and organizations, engaged in social welfare, lobbying, education and income-raising activities. The Eskişehir Women's Platform is led by the Eskişehir mayor's wife. This platform includes the representatives of different women's organizations such as the Association to Support Modern Life (Çağdaş Yaşamı Destekleme Vakfı) and the Turkish University Women's Union (Türk Üniversiteli Kadınlar Birliği). They are particularly interested in promoting literacy among girls and women through training and literacy seminars. *The Gaziantep Women's Platform* was established in 1994 and has participated in public events, given speeches, and has been particularly active in lobbying against honor crimes. Samsun Women's Council organizes women's handicrafts markets. Women's platforms in Diyarbakır and Adana have also been recently established.

A meeting to evaluate the Local Agenda Women's Platforms took place in Aliağa, İzmir on 19-20 February 2001.[5] The participants collectively reached the following conclusions:

Strengths and Achievements of Women's Platforms:

1. Built awareness of gender equality issues and empowerment of women.
2. Made gender issues more visible for the public.
3. Established new civil society organizations, including several women's cooperatives.
4. Organized income generation, skill building and educational workshops and activities.
5. Formed partnerships and instituted collaborative activities with public institutions.
6. Members learned negotiation strategies.
7. Began networking activities at national and international levels.

Constraints and Weaknesses:

1. Projects that support traditional gender roles.
2. Traditional customs and norms, customary laws that perpetuate gender inequality.
3. Lack of focus on men (gender roles can only be changed with the help of both men and women).

4. Low level of communication and sharing of experiences among and inside women's platforms; lack of a common language.
5. Low level of understanding and interpretation of global norms of gender equality and their application to local realities.
6. Need for greater professionalism and capacity among women's groups and civil society organizations.
7. Need for skills in project design and implementation and in fund raising; concerns for sustainability of activities/programs.
8. Lack of gender sensitivity and expertise among local decision-makers.
9. Difficulties in securing funds and dependence on external donors.

Capacity-Building for Women's Participation in Local Governance

There are now many short-term training, education, human resource development programs usually designed and delivered by women's NGOs or university centers, in municipality venues or with municipality sponsorship. One example is the programs offered by Marmara University's Center for Women's Employment and Income Generation. This center, in partnership with the Kadıköy Municipality, developed and delivered a training program on women's political participation. Some of the participants later were elected 'muhtar', or became members of Municipality Councils.[6] Another project with the same municipality was a Citizenship Education project delivered to about 8,000 women. This project was implemented with financial support from the Kadıköy Municipality; the instructors and guest speakers provided their services for free. (Ecevit, 2001) Gender training programs were offered to municipality employees, both women and men, in Bursa, Antalya and Antakya as part of a World Academy for Local Democracy (WALD) project that aimed to incorporate gender sensitivity in local governance. These training programs were developed with support from the World Bank-funded 'Women's Employment Project' implemented by the NWM. A training manual was developed by consultants by examining current gender training manuals developed by international organizations, such as Oxfam and adopting them to the Turkish context. The participants included both male and female employees and were well-received after initial skepticism. As one of the trainers noted:

> One of the constraints we encountered was that the participants initially thought this training was very irrelevant. They did not believe in gender sensitivity training, and they saw it as a waste of time and nonsensical. But after the training started, almost all of them were convinced of the importance and necessity of such training. We unfortunately could not do any follow-up activities or undertake any long-term evaluation. (Ataüz, 2000, p. 6)

These programs remained sporadic and were not extended to other municipalities, even though they were successful according to the evaluations of the participants. Ataüz thinks that such training programs must be expanded across the country, which requires the training of new trainers, and the financial support of the government, including the municipalities themselves (2000: p.7) Finally, programs to develop the capacity of women's NGOs, including partnerships with the public sector, also exist. For example, the Foundation to Support Women's Economic Work (KEDV) and the Social Services Administration (SHCEK) have implemented a project, funded by the European Union, to support Women's Leadership in Turkey's Local Development. Its objectives include increasing the capacity of women's NGOs, enabling the women to develop small projects, to cooperate with other sectors, and developing local, national and international communication networks (*Flying News*, 2003, p. 29). Another example is the NGO Capacity Development Training delivered by the British Council. (Uçan Süpürge, No. 9, July 2000)

Women's Shelters with Local Governments

As mentioned earlier, the women's movement in Turkey focused on violence against women and by the early 1990s, formal organizations, such as women's shelters, began to be established. In this context, women's organizations approached municipalities for assistance in establishing women's shelters. Unfortunately, the shelters that were established by women's NGOs together with municipalities have not survived in many cases. The first women's shelter in Turkey was opened by the Bakirköy Municipality in Istanbul in collaboration with a women's counseling center, and served more than 1,500 women. But it was closed when a new mayor was elected from a different political party. The Altındağ shelter set up in partnership with the Municipality and run by Women's Support Foundation, was closed after 7 years. In İzmir, the Bornova Municipality set up a Women's Counseling Center in 1990, and it is still functioning even though it was closed intermittently. Centers in Nazilli, Küçükçekmece, Aydın and Bursa were not able to sustain their operations. Currently, Esenyurt (Istanbul) municipality works with women's groups. Antakya Municipality established a women's counseling center after the election of a female mayor. At this time, the only women's shelters are under the Social Services Administration and according to the new SHCEK statute (April 2001), this organization has the right to permit (or not) any independent shelter's operations, and the right to monitor them. Ironically, the ostensible achievement of the women's movement to convince the state to classify women's shelters as part of the social services, and therefore to their institutionalization within the public sector, has resulted in the public sector's move to 'swallow them up'.

Limitations to Collaboration

The experiences so far show that formal and sustainable partnerships are yet to be developed. Public sector attitudes towards shelters or counseling centers have been either to appropriate them as their own, not recognizing the partner NGO, or to run them outright (which includes putting roadblocks in front of women's organizations to open independent shelters in the case of new SHCEK policy), or to refuse to support a shelter/center established under a different government. Projects supported by one set of elected leaders have been dropped by the next group due to political and ideological reasons and this has occurred in administrations across the political spectrum (Ecevit 2001). An example of the first instance is when the Altındağ Municipality called the Women's Shelter that was opened in partnership with the Women's Solidarity Foundation in Ankara, just 'Altındağ Women's Shelter', ignoring the Women's Solidarity Foundation's role and contribution. A Çanakkale Women's Organization tried to set up an independent shelter only to be told that it is against government policy. The Women and Youth Foundation (Çağdaş Kadın ve Gençlik Vakfı) opened a Women's Community Center in Mamak where the municipality rented them a building but the new local government asked them to leave and stopped paying for the utilities.

The notion of civil society organizations as 'partners' to government is a relatively new one for Turkey. NGOs have traditionally been shaped by the Turkish state, provided funds by the state, and given permission to operate by the state. Local governments do not necessarily view women's organizations as 'separate entities' or as 'equal partners' but rather may view them as extensions of themselves. For example, at the meeting on women's platforms discussed above, participants pointed out that municipalities tended to see the women's platforms as extensions of themselves. Some women may claim that the municipality is obliged to provide services, personnel, buildings, or transportation, putting themselves in the position of consumer of government services rather than 'partners'.[7] Women's organizations may also have a limited perspective on the range of possibilities for collaboration. For example, suggestions for potential avenues of collaboration with the government at a workshop on women's empowerment training only included two items: the provision of space by municipalities for training and education programs, or training of trainers within the public sector (Ankara Üniversitesi, Empowerment through Education Conference proceedings, 2000, p. 70). The State Planning Organization Report identifies problems of cooperation for both sides. Women's organizations are relatively inexperienced in working with governments, and the municipalities do not have a tradition of collaboration with civil society organizations.

Another limitation to collaboration is the lack of procedural and legal mechanisms for partnerships. Even though dialogue and consultation have begun between women's groups and municipalities, mechanisms and procedures for participation in decision-making are lacking. Those that have been established, such as women's commissions within the provincial government, are not effectively used due to lack of knowledge or interest. This concern is a general one for the Local Agenda 21 process as the most recent evaluation report indicates: (2001, p. 8)

A major issue pertains to the institutionalization of the Local Agenda 21 process. Project partners devote considerable time and effort towards developing a suitable model for institutionalizing the participatory platforms/City Councils, and other mechanisms and processes. The apparent and most frequently resorted model, namely the establishment of a foundation or an association by local stakeholders, is not favored in general for a number of reasons. They include the reluctance of the local stakeholders to register themselves under the umbrella of another organization while they have their own, as well as the difficulties in combining the forces of the Municipality, the Governorate and civil society organizations under the proposed model. Despite the flexible and commonly-endorsed *modus operandi* of the existing city-wide platforms, a number of bottlenecks have resulted from their lack of a legal entity [such as being able to receive funds directly from the respective municipalities, to receive donations from the private sector, and employing non-municipal staff in Local Agenda 21 offices].

The pending bill on local governance also contributes to the uncertainty for the future. Overall, it appears that appropriate legal/institutional arrangements to make sure that Local Agenda 21 is integrated into decision-making processes of local governance are of utmost priority. At the same time, city councils and women's platforms, arrangements that came into being as a result of the Local Agenda 21 process, have no doubt contributed to local initiatives for greater participation in local governance while municipalities are beginning to share and publicly discuss their project and programs and consider the preferences of City Councils (Local Agenda 21, 2001, p. 10). Meanwhile, women's platforms share these constraints and opportunities stemming from the Local Agenda 21 process, as well as those that pertain to civil society organizations in general and women's organizations in particular.

Finally, a major problem has been identified as the lack of sustainability of collaborative activities. Most women's organizations have turned to external donors for support of their programs. The UNDP, the Local Agenda 21 Program, The European Commission in Turkey, the British Council and Embassy, and other European donors have also provided opportunities for women's collaborative activities with local governments through their support but they are in the form of project support with a limited time frame.

A Partnership Case Study: Women for Women's Human Rights – New Ways and Social Services Administration (SHCEK)

The Women's Human Rights Education Program, implemented with the collaboration of a state agency, the Directorate of Social Services and Children's Protection (SHCEK) across Turkey in 24 provinces by 57 SHCEK experts is an example of a working partnership.[8] This does not mean that there are no constraints and problems that are experienced. But overall, it represents a successful case of long-term collaboration, started in 1990, and deserves careful investigation. This partnership gave the WWHR training program greater legitimacy and recognition, supported by the Social Services Administration and its Community Centers across the country. At the same time, the SHCEK workers gained expertise in women's human rights, and the delivery of participatory training programs, thus contributing to their professional development.

The ultimate goal of the training program is to prepare the participants for grassroots organization, policy advocacy and collective action, which includes dealing effectively with all levels of government. The experiences of the participants since 1998 provide us with important lessons about the conditions necessary for women's participation in local governance and the processes it involves. First, it showed that participants (or graduates of the program) go through a number of stages in their organizational efforts and experiences. At each level, they gain greater experience in how to approach government organizations. They go through a 'learning process' whereby they become more skilled in assessing their own needs and becoming policy advocates. The types of grassroots organizing (one could also see them as stages) include:

1.   Becoming resource people on an individual basis for the community.
2.   Forming informal groups that meet periodically.
3.   Organizing events together such as conferences, panels, workshops, campaigns, March 8 international women's day celebrations.
4.   Participating in on-going events.
5.   Establishing an ongoing activity group such as folklore, theater, project group.
6.   Establishing new organization such as association, cooperative or foundation.
7.   Approaching government institutions.

Many participants of the Women's Human Rights program shared what they learned by becoming resource people for their family and community first:

1.   I let a friend know that she could get a lawyer free of charge and she was able to start divorce proceedings.
2.   One of my relatives had not married in a civil marriage. I told him that his children would not be considered his lawful children and I could get a document to that effect. He got married in a civil ceremony soon afterwards.
3.   I was working for the Highway Administration and I was the only woman among 190 men. I almost felt like a man myself. I distributed the training booklets (on women's human rights).
4.   One day a male colleague who suffered from violence want me to talk to his wife,. My male colleagues suffer as well from this feudal order they are in; they feel obliged to implement the traditional rules.
5.   I invited my daughter's friends home and discuss women's rights issues with them.

Many participants started meeting informally at homes and at the Community Centers, and soon they were also involved in organizing events first at the community centers, and then organizing workshops, campaigns etc. (The examples given below are not exhaustive but meant to relay the type of activities).

Grassroots organizing and collaboration with other entities depend on a number of conditions to come together:

1.   Emergence of leaders among participants: it is very important that leaders emerge who are willing to take responsibility and initiative.
2.   Achieving consensus on concrete achievable objectives: members conduct needs assessment in their communities and come to a consensus on concrete and achievable objectives.
3.   Support from social workers and community centers: social workers who act as facilitators for the training programs continue to support the women in their efforts at organizing after the training.
4.   Family and spousal support.
5.   Collaboration with other women's organizations and their support: Established women's NGOs offer support by teaching how to prepare project proposals, seek funding or approach government organizations.
6.   The effective use of policy advocacy strategies – having the relevant evidence/facts/information to support demands and learning how to make allies and negotiate.

Below are personal accounts of the leaders of women's organizations who successfully negotiated with local government organizations.

Women are Pushing the Barred Doors in Diyarbakır (Açıkgöz, 2002):[9]

I am the first female child who went to school in my family. I finished primary school but I was not allowed to go to Middle School. My family got me married to my uncle's son. All my life I could not even walk out the door when I wanted. I discovered the Women's Human Rights Training Program after I had my sixth child. Then both my family life and social life changed. I started to talk about this training and our rights with every woman I knew. After a while, we started to gather together with my women relatives and neighbors to discuss women's human rights. We would tell our husbands and elders that we are meeting for coffee or tea; they would not know what we are up to. I saw that you have your own rights, as a woman, as a mother, and that you have the right to know about these rights. Yet, I realized this fact during the training.
    We are eight people in our household. There were eight mouths to be fed, and only my husband who had a job. While participating in the training, I decided I wanted to have a job too. And I was not the only one, many women in our training group were thinking like me. We came together around our common needs and formed a group. We met with friends working at KEDV (Foundation to Support Women's Economic Work), and figured we can start a candle production workshop with them.
    Formerly, I would not think it possible even to tell my husband that I had such a wish. Yet, once a person finds her own desire acceptable, she is able to express herself. I told my husband, I want to work, I will go out and work alongside other women and men and I will surely converse with them too. We started working as a group after the Women's Human Rights Training. Our main subject is protection of

women's economic rights. We made a comprehensive survey in our neighborhood. The results showed that there is no place for children to play or to receive education. Yet there is such a big need for it. We considered opening a kindergarten for the children. We had to start somewhere. First of all, our group should have a formal identity, an official status. We decided to become a cooperative. We conducted a market research to determine what we might produce, and we decided to make candles. With this aim our group prepared a project and we presented the project to the governorship. The governorship accepted our project. Now we are producing candles.

When we first started this job, we did not even have a studio, we were making the candles at home. Then we rented a small store. The Municipality paid for its rent for five months. Until the opening of our studio, no one would believe that we were actually going to work. Once the Governor showed up at our opening ceremony, congratulations and compliments started to flow in.

By the way, there have been many people who tried to hinder our work. There are many women's organizations but they do not have solidarity among themselves. Once you start working on an issue, everybody else starts doing the same thing. Why do they not take care of some other problem, if I am already taking care of this one?

We want to become a cooperative to have an identity. This is our short-term goal. Currently we are in the process of establishing it in consultation with our lawyer. In order to solve the marketing problem, we made contacts with wholesalers. The quality of training and the variety of our candles have improved. We have stands at hotels and meetings and take the orders of the local shops and supermarkets. Most importantly, we do everything ourselves. Be it the production, or the sales, we take care of it all. There is no middleman. Thus we named our studio 'Group of Trust'. We shut our doors to trouble.

We will conduct another market research. We have to find out the demands of the market besides candles, and see what else we can produce. We might also engage in the mosaic and screening wire production. We are currently determining the resource people and institutions that can support us in all this work. In the past, I was hardly able to leave the house, but now I am talking about making connections with the Ministry of Industry and Commerce, the Directorate of Cultural Affairs, the City Directorate and private firms.

As one can see from the above excerpt, the conditions that make for effective grassroots organizing, and forging collaborative relationships with government agencies, other NGOs and private firms were all present in the above case. Müseyyer Açıkgöz was one of the leaders that emerged. The group conducted a needs assessment and decided to work on opening a kindergarten and make candles. They enlisted support from another women's NGO. And they approached the mayor and the municipality with successful outcomes.

Women's Independent Grassroots Organization in Çanakkale (Sarışen, 2002)[10]

Once we completed the Women's Human Rights Training Program, we immediately moved to organize among ourselves. We decided to put into practice the things we learned during the training and implement our rights. As women we experience discrimination in our own lives, and see it happen to other women around us. We realized that it is necessary to be organized as a group in order to fight against this discrimination. Thus we decided to acquire a legal identity. We aim to ensure that Çanakkale women actively participate in the social, economic and political spheres. All the governmental and nongovernmental institutions in our city must function with a gender-sensitive perspective. We received the Women's Human Rights Training at the Community Center, but after a while, one has to break free from the Community Center and become independent. Otherwise, it is rather difficult to link the training with the larger women's movement. At the organizing stage, the idea of founding an association came up. We held long meetings among ourselves and with the other institutions in our city. Finally, in 1998, we founded the Çanakkale Kadının El Emeğini Değerlendirme Derneği (Association for Realizing Women's Handwork Labor in Çanakkale). We encountered opposition from the police at the establishment stage. The police told us that there already existed 'The Mothers' Association' in Çanakkale, and we should go and become members there. They created obstacles in approving our charter. But we were successful because we enlisted the support of a woman lawyer who had the professional legitimacy and clout to deal with the police and get the necessary approval.

In the beginning we had simply wanted to arrange for a market place where women could sell their handwork products. At first, we had no problems with the local government, but they merely saw us as 'a bunch of women'. That is, we were being belittled in the economic sphere as well, simply because we were women. Yet, everything changed once we formed our organization. Now they perceive us in a different light, with a different status. When we go with a demand to the Municipality or the Governorship, they all know that we will follow up on the issue, and that we will finish the job we started.

We founded an association concerning women's economic rights.[11] Yet, we work on various subjects. We aim to reach as many women as possible, and enable their active participation in public life. One of our main subjects is violence against women. In the background of all our activities, we aim to raise consciousness on this subject. We started out with economic rights in order to spread at the ground level. Our actual aim is to put an end to the violence against women.

Ever since the establishment of our association, we have held meetings Women for Women's Human Rights – New Ways. Their persistence in following up and carrying through issues, their support for putting things in perspective now and then, our participation in the Third Annual Meeting for Women's Shelters, and the other women's organizations and programs we encountered there have enabled us to think from a larger perspective. In this process, we aimed to go one step further each year. Last year we started to work on creating a Women's Shelter in Çanakkale. In as short a time as 6 months, we managed to get the space and everything necessary for the shelter. Yet we were stopped by bureaucratic obstacles of the SHCEK statutes (which now say that SHCEK is solely responsible and in charge of setting up women's shelters). While we were trying to find a solution, we channeled our work towards creating a Women's Center. Finally in 2002, we opened the Women's Center. Meanwhile, we are still selling our handwork products. Our market is located in a tourist area, so the women felt the need to learn a second language. In order to meet this need, we are offering English courses at the center.

Unfortunately, during our work, we have met people who have tried to discourage us. Certain institutions and even certain NGOs have tried to claim our work as theirs and sometimes hinder our work. For instance, another NGO in the region filed a complaint against us saying 'how can an association open such a center?', which bore no legal validity or meaning. Following the opening of the Women's Center, we were even taken to the Police Headquarters for interrogation.

On the whole, we have worked to have very good relationships with the Governorship, City Directorate of Social Services, the Municipality, the Bar, and other organizations. We have succeeded in placing our representatives on various commissions at the Governor's office (for example, the Children's Commission). This presence and participation have given us more confidence and political experience. This political experience and ability to deal with different levels of government has been crucial along with our persistence in the face of resistance or rejection. We have gotten recognition from the community by our public campaigns, information meetings and even police training sessions on violence against women and children. We have gradually become more and more accepted by the Çanakkale residents and the local government.

Women of Gazi Neighborhood in Istanbul are Organizing around their Own Needs (Han and Karaman, 2002)[12]

We participated in the Women's Human Rights Training Program in 2001-2. Women participating in the previous period had already organized themselves, and conducted field research to determine what prevented women's mobility in the neighborhood. They found out that the biggest obstacle was child care. We decided to open a kindergarten to solve this problem.

We prepared a survey. Through this survey we reached 131 women in neighborhoods. As we examined the survey results, we saw that 85% of the mothers we talked to were unable to work because they had no place to leave their children. Once we decided to open a kindergarten, we took training in pre-school education. When our group started working on this subject, the Community Center rented a small apartment for us. We found out the number of children, public spaces, and the unused lands in the Gazi neighborhood that can be allotted to us. After evaluating the surveys, we talked to the muhtars, the municipality, the school directors and the provincial district governor. We visited a kindergarten in İzmit, opened by women, and inquired about their experiences. Then we planned our next steps.

We went to the deed office, to find out about available land. We asked for detailed and specific information. By then we were well-informed about everything including the city blocks, map sections, lot numbers. Even the officials were surprised. They sent an engineer from the office of the cadastral and deed information while we did more research to see which lands are appropriate for us and which ones can actually be allotted to us. We visited the provincial district governor and introduced our group and activities. As we talked with him, we told him that as women, we have certain demands for our neighborhood. Then we visited the Mayor, and we asked him why we are not receiving any services in this neighborhood. We said that given this area and the population that lives here, there should be at least 4 kindergartens.

After we presented this information and our demands, the Mayor promised to allocate land to us. We asked for a big building on the land, because we want to be able to create not only a kindergarten, but also a large space where women can work and socialize. We might offer occupational training courses for women once we move to a permanent residence. We want to engage in production. To start with, we will conduct a market research. We will open a workshop studio and sell our products. Currently our plan is to sign a protocol with the Department of Social Services (SHCEK) for building the kindergarten. Once we have legal status, we will take over the land in our name. The Municipality will construct the building, but they will not interfere with its inner structure, nor with its teachers. We, the women, will run this place. The first step is to acquire an official status, and we are planning to set up a cooperative.

The above experiences demonstrate the process that leads women towards organizing themselves at the grassroots, defining their goal, setting up a formal organization and engaging with various government agencies. The lessons learned include the importance of clear and concise objectives based on needs assessment, participatory procedures among themselves, doing one's homework and approaching officials with relevant facts and information, putting the demands on the table, finding supportive allies, and being persistent. It is also clear successful organization efforts were aided by the empowerment training they received. Women's human rights education empowered these women and encouraged them to take the initiatives they did, under the protective umbrella of community centers and supportive social workers.

What Conditions Promote More Effective Collaboration and Partnerships?

The five activity domains where partnerships between NGOs and local governments may be forged are service delivery, human resource development, resource mobilization, research and innovation, and public information, education and advocacy (Levinger and McLeod, 2000). In the Turkish case, we see examples of collaborative activities in service delivery, education and advocacy, and human resource development where governments usually provide buildings, land, personnel, pays rent, utilities, or salaries, while the NGO delivers programs on human resource development, training, education and advocacy or services. According to studies done in Latin America on NGO-government collaboration, complementarity is a key concept. These may be the types of resources, knowledge, methods and stakeholders that each side brings to the partnership. Such partnerships may be effective if each side brings resources that the other sides lack. According to Levinger and McLeod (2000), the necessary principles for an effective partnership are common goals, mutual trust and complementary characteristics of the partners.

These principles hold true in the Turkish case as well. Several municipalities including ones in Istanbul, İzmir, Bursa, Mersin, Antalya, and Ankara have collaborated with women's NGOs to set up schools, counseling centers, kindergartens and women's shelters. According to Ecevit (2001), the successful cases of collaboration shared the following common characteristics:

1. Clear and shared goals.
2. Participatory procedures.

3.   Flexibility.
4.   Clear assessment of the nature and extent of voluntary labor involved.
4.   Training programs for volunteers.
6.   Problem-solving approaches and the use of feedback mechanisms.

Thus, common and shared goals are important but also participatory and problem-solving approaches, flexibility, and a clear understanding and definition of voluntary labor are emphasized.

According to Levinger and McLeod (2002), the benefits of government-NGO partnerships are as follows:

1.   State-NGO partnership can produce a complementary effect: different resources, knowledge, methods and allies will complement each other.
2.   NGOs may have access to regions and issues outside the reach of the state.
3.   Sustainability may be achieved.
4.   A well-planned collaboration between the partners may lead to more comprehensive, economic and successful results.
5.   The partners may learn from each other.
6.   The risks may be reduced; different partners will minimize threats coming to the program from the outside and increase the possibility of dealing with such situations.
7.   Even though different experiences and perspectives may lead to some conflicts, they also provide space for some creativity.

The partnership of the WWHR and SHCEK was such that they complemented each other and learned from each other. The Women for Women Rights/New Ways developed a Women's Human Rights Training Program, trained social workers from SHCEK who then delivered the training. SHCEK officials and representatives of WWHR signed a protocol to implement this training program in 1998 and it has been on going ever since. The protocol states that the training of the trainers (the social workers) will be undertaken by WWHR and that the social workers will be provided with all relevant teaching materials. The WWHR would monitor the implementation through interviews, communication on an ongoing basis with the trainers and periodic reports filed by them. According to the protocol, social workers who take the training begin a training session in 3 months or less, and offer at least two training sessions per year. They are asked to work with WWHR, make necessary changes in collaboration with WWHR as needed. The protocol further stipulates that WWHR and SHCEK together will select potential trainers and that SHCEK will pay travel and local expenses for the social workers to participate in training sessions provided by WWHR. The training sessions, evaluation meetings and any other meeting during the implementation of the program are organized collaboratively as well.

The *complementarity* factor was an important element of success. SHCEK offered access to the community centers across the country and access to trainees, while benefiting from WWHR's expertise, resources, and the training it offered to social workers who delivered the training. Community Centers already represent a built-in potential group of women who are eligible for the Human Rights Training Program. There are already qualified social workers who work at these centers and act as group facilitators. Community Centers are seen as safe places by the women and their families. This makes it easier for them to participate in training programs. From SHCEK's perspective, the social workers received training in facilitation of training, as well as in the substantive field of women's human rights, which they then were able to apply to other aspects of their profession. And the partners learned from each other. As the social workers interviewed noted, they were able to transfer what they learned in terms of both substance and teaching and communication strategies to other areas of their work. Most social workers also express appreciation of their training as facilitators and the opportunity to be involved. It helped them gain professional skills as better facilitators, as well as substantive skills in this area. They reported that they valued the program highly and considered it an asset to their own professional development as well as to the empowerment of the participants. They indicated that they have used and applied what they learned in other training programs and aspects of their profession. Some claimed that they had to grapple with their own gender identity and examine their personal relationships and become more conscious of gender-based discrimination themselves. Having social workers deliver the program as group facilitators means that a trained group of government workers are delivering a Human Rights Training Program for women, a discourse hitherto not part of the official government policy, across the country, giving it legitimacy and sustainability. Furthermore, there was also space for creativity, as both participants and social workers had the opportunity to discuss and examine their own lives in terms of women's human rights, a first of its kind in Turkey. The community centers have followed a more participatory approach unlike most other bureaucratic institutions in Turkey. Their primary objectives are improving the living conditions, finding participatory solutions, developing a sense of community and sharing. In this pursuit, women have been a key target group. In this respect, the objectives of WWHR and Community Centers overlap. The participants have widely publicized the centers, and recruited more women to join them. Therefore, not only do women learn to use a public institution, but also the community centers find their true owners. All these outcomes have confirmed that SHCEK and WWHR are in a complementary partnership.

This was a partnership built on mutuality of goals, and complementarity but it did face some important issues as well, the most important one being that of sustainability. The funding for the program comes from external donors, and the only way to make this sustainable is if it is institutionalized within SHCEK permanently, but this, of course, would require a redefinition of the existing 'partnership' and the role of WWHR. Another issue is the importance of personal relations in Turkey; the program was strongly supported by the Director with whom the protocol was initially signed, but directors and employees that work with SHCEK may come and go, and not all staff members share the same enthusiasm and commitment that WWHR naturally holds for its own program. The structures of WWHR and SHCEK are very different from each other. There are complementarities, but there are also potential for disagreements. SHCEK functions as part of the state bureaucracy, while the foundation is an independent non-hierarchical institution. The WWHR-New Ways is highly committed to the program, very efficient in follow-up and monitoring, while a state agency obviously has a wide variety of programs to implement with limited resources and functions more slowly.

Conclusions

Norms of local democracy and participation as defined at global conferences are obviously not automatically implementable. Without sufficient incentives, there would be little reason on the part of decision-makers to pay attention to them. Impediments in the Turkish case include the centralized nature of the administration and the viewing of potential decentralization through the prism of contestation between secular and religious norms among the elites. Since there is no automatic implementation, the existence of mediators committed to these norms would act as a significant catalyst. In the Turkish case, we see that the Local Agenda 21, and the support of donors such as the UNDP, and European Commission in Turkey, along with bilateral European donors, have supported women's participation in local governance. But the process of implementation of norms is a political process – and decision-makers tend to follow a logic of cost benefit calculations. The question then is: are women's groups becoming politically savvy to negotiate with the local government, and are decision-makers on the local government feeling obliged to accommodate them or justify their behavior if not in compliance with norms?

There are still very few women representatives on local governments. Women in Turkey gained the right to elect and be elected (in local elections in 1930 and national elections in 1934) and they have equal political rights with men. However, in actuality, the participation of women in political life and their contribution to policy-making and implementation is still minimal even today. Without the meaningful participation of women in political life, it is not possible to say that there is political commitment to gender equality. Without political commitment to gender equality, good governance is compromised. In 1999, the percentage of women MPs in the National Parliament was 4.3%, 24 out of 550 members. There are no women ministers in the cabinet at this time. In local governments, (provincial councils), the percentage of elected women is 1.05%. There are no women governors at this time but there are a very small number of women mayors and 'kaymakam'.[13] Out of 806 (kaymakams), only 3 are women. Regarding political parties, two parties have begun to use a quota system: DYP (10%) and CHP (25%) in their internal procedures. Women's branches of political parties can now be legally established; yet, most women's branches have functioned as auxiliary organizations doing fundraising and propaganda work for male candidates, rather than helping to establish a national gender equality policy.

The experiences of women as they approach local governments reveal some interesting contradictions where state agencies both encourage women's political activism but also continue to see them as either 'more votes' or as extensions of themselves. For example, the women's platforms set up within the Local Agenda 21 network complained that the municipalities see them as extensions of themselves. Of course, the top-down state tradition historically has only provided space for state-sanctioned 'civil society institution'. One of the obstacles to grassroots organizing is the repression of civil society organizations after the 1980 military coup. Associations can only be set up with permission from the police and police can at any time inspect an association's activities. Thus, women who wanted to organize have searched creatively for various forms of formal organization that would allow them greater flexibility, such as limited companies, cooperatives or foundations. It is not surprising for women to turn to government workers at Community Centers for help in their own organizational efforts. The SHCEK workers are seen as a bridge between the people and the state, and community centers as one of the few places where women can come without fear. Perhaps women's organizations have found natural bureaucratic allies in Social Services Administration and its Community Centers, and the National Women's Machinery. But experiences also show that even their relationships with women's organizations may take an autocratic turn. The existing cases of effective partnerships do, however, conform with the experiences around the world: it is a learning process on both sides, where complementarities must be emphasized; risks must be taken; a learning process must mutually be embarked upon, and each side's contributions must be acknowledged.

Notes

[1] The following comes from communication with Dr. Simel Esim.
[2] Devlet Planlama Teşkilatı (State Planning Organization), Kurumsallaşma ve Kadın Alt Komisyonu Raporu, (Institutionalization and Gender Subcommission Report) Toplumsal Cinsiyete Duyarlı Bütçeleme ve Bütçe Analizleri (Gender Sensitive Budgeting and Budget Analysis).
[3] *Local Agenda 21*, Annual Project Report, 'Implementation of Local Agenda 21 in Turkey: January 2000-December 2000', p. 5.
[4] Personal communication with the members of the Antalya Women's Council, February 2001.
[5] The author was present at that meeting and conclusions come from her notes.
[6] 'Muhtar' is an elected official of the smallest administrative district.
[7] Personal communication with women at the Tuzluçayir Community Center run by the Women and Youth Foundation.
[8] The Women's Human Rights Education Program is discussed in detail in Chapter 4.
[9] Excerpts from the speech by Museyyer Açıkgöz, from Diyarbakır at the Meeting for Grassroots Organizing, organized by WWHR/New Ways in Istanbul, June 2002.
[10] Excerpts from Gülay Sarışen's speech at the Meeting for Grassroots Organizing 2002. Sarışen is the founding member and director of the Çanakkale Kadının El Emeğini

Değerlendirme Derneği (Association for Realizing the Handwork Labor of Women in Çanakkale).
[11] I suspect also that an association on women's handicrafts seemed much less contentious than an association fighting gender-based violence in the Turkish context.
[12] Excerpts from speeches of Güler Han and Nurcan Karaman at the Meeting for Grassroots Organizing, organized by WWHR-New Ways in Istanbul, June 2002.
[13] Kaymakam is the official charged with governing a provincial district.

Conclusions

A women's human rights regime has emerged and is on the global agenda. There are now global norms, legal instruments and monitoring mechanisms in place. All member states who signed and ratified CEDAW are asked to 'recognize women's human rights, and fundamental freedoms in the political, economic, social, cultural, civil or any other field and to overcome any distinction, exclusion or restriction made on the basis of sex' (CEDAW, Article 1). Turkey is one of those member states. Has Turkey engaged with women's human rights as embodied in CEDAW and other global documents, and if so how? To what extent has Turkey been accountable to this regime? The immediate response is that accountability has increased over time, as evidenced by the removal of reservations to the Convention, a new Civil Code, and more recently a new Penal Code that aims to remove discrimination against women. The activities of a national women's machinery, as well as the country reports to the CEDAW committee are also manifestations of accountability.

It was suggested in the introduction that a constructivist perspective is helpful in moving us beyond the level of political and bureaucratic responses, not devaluing their importance, but for the purpose of revealing the complexities of ongoing debates on gender norms and women's human rights in Turkey. Employing such a perspective reveals some fascinating and significant insights. In order to understand how global women's human rights norms can become meaningful in Turkey, we need to see where competing gender norms and identities come from, and what institutional contexts they are rooted in. Furthermore, it is necessary to examine how global material and discursive changes have opened opportunity spaces for new definitions and new interpretations for the women's movement as active agents. Finally, we must investigate how particular global norms, in our case, women's empowerment, violence against women, and political participation in local governance, are defined in local contexts. Such an investigation points us to the following conclusions.

In Turkey, the engagement with global women's human rights norms can best understood when viewed through the prisms of several dualisms that permeate politics and are central in the formation of identities. In fact, any effort to understand a country's response to global women's rights would be futile without an investigation of contested values as they permeate different institutions. As we investigate how global norms on women's rights are interpreted and rendered meaningful within different institutions in Turkey, it is critical to question the four major so-called dualisms as they relate to gender roles and relations: secularism versus Islam, individual versus collective identities, private versus public spheres and individual rights versus state control. All these dualisms are seen in tension with each other, whereas a major conclusion of this book is that these are no longer dualisms, in opposition to each other, but are engaged in a dynamic exchange. Furthermore, these dualisms are interpreted differently by different institutions: legal, judicial, bureaucratic, religious, family and kinship, and markets. For example. while the legal institutions side with individual rights of women, the judicial and bureaucratic institutions may place women in the private sphere, and in their familial, collective identities. While the state has traditionally claimed secular values, many organizations in society and some political parties promote Islamic values. Yet, a party with Islamist roots is now espousing 'secular' human rights values, and major legal reforms that promote human rights and women's human rights have taken place under the AK party government. These dualisms are beginning to break down and the opportunity for increased dialogue among women is visible. These opportunities are increasing as more women's groups are engaging in lobbying and advocacy activity, with universal norms and Turkey's international and EU commitments as negotiating tools. Such activity is becoming more and more possible as material conditions, by creating dissonances, are also providing opportunity spaces for change.

In Turkey, women's rights have historically been viewed through the prism of the secularism versus Islam debate. Linked to this, and even more fundamentally important is that the woman question became a core issue of the Modernization and Westernization project that the new Republic of Turkey undertook in the 1920s. Until the 1980s, the state has continued to hold on to the claim that Atatürk's reforms have taken care of women's rights, thus turning a near blind eye to persistent violations (right to education, right to freedom of movement, right to be free from violence and the like). The rise of the women's movement in the early 1980s was paradoxically aided by a space created by the closing of political parties, the crushing of the leftist student movements and the ensuing military coup. The women's movement was first viewed as non-threatening attempts of urban women, reexamining and questioning the apparent contradictions in their 'socially constructed roles' as women. Many women who were active in leftist student movements in the 1970s now focused on women's rights. These women, drawing also from feminist movements in the West, began to see the gaps between the much touted legal rights they had, and their actual positions in the family based on patriarchal norms. The laws still proclaimed the man as the head of the family who decided where the family would live, whether the wife could work outside the home, or travel outside the country. The violence against women, including harassment on the streets, became the focus of a successful campaign. Thus, the 1980s opened up an opportunity space for women in Turkey which they used to shape a women's movement centrally focused on violence against women. It is important to note that the women's movement in Turkey had already begun to focus on violence against women in the 1980s, while it took until the 1990s for global norms to be established in this area.

In the early 1990s, as politics became increasingly colored by the secularism versus Islam debates, so did gender issues and women's roles. While the Ministry of Labor and İmren Aykut, the Minister of Labor and Social Welfare, responded to

Turkey's international obligations primarily to demonstrate yet again Turkey's Westernist and modernist orientation, these attempts got mired in the divided politics within the ruling ANAP party. Conservatives refused to allow a new bureaucracy strictly focused on women's well-being and empowerment as individuals, unless they got another unit focused on 'The Family'. The liberal wing's draft bill tried to appease the conservatives by including the wording that 'the new national women's machinery will be directed according to the national viewpoint', a flag that decries conservative Islamist perspective, infuriating the secular women's groups, as well as leftist political parties. So the response to global obligations, to set up a national women's mechanism, created another opportunity space to place women's rights issues firmly and irrevocably on the national agenda and galvanized women's groups and organizations to become actively involved.

By the late 1990s, the broader political and economic context in Turkey had changed extensively. The globalization process has contributed to the rise of women's human rights norms. The rise of global women's networks and donor assistance for gender equality such as that of the United Nations Development Programme (UNDP), other United Nations agencies, the European Commission in Turkey and other bilateral donors have played significant roles in their support of the National Women's Machinery. The NWM in turn has collaborated with women's organizations, supported the creation of gender expertise, supported women's organizations, women's studies centers at universities and strengthened women's links with international and regional forums. But the post Cold War international system has also brought fragmentation and redefinition of ethnic, religious and gender identities. Kandiyoti and Saktanber (2002) speak to the fragmentation of norms in Turkish culture, and the shifting identities including gender identities. According to some feminist social scientists, such dissonance may open up space and opportunity, especially if they come together with material conditions that provide an opening (Sassen, 1998; Bayes and Kelly, 2001). This is what happened in Turkey.

The material conditions, and most recently the EU membership application process, have created some significant space for attention to women's human rights. The women's movement has risen to this challenge, by the double strategy of education as a mechanism for change, along with legal reforms. (Berktay et al, 2004) The women's movement has also acquired policy advocacy skills to succeed at global forums as seen at the Beijing Plus Five Conference, as well as to influence the policy process at all levels; not just problem definition and agenda building, but also at law-making and implementation. Women's organizations demonstrated new ways of collaborating with government institutions. The weakest link, however, is still implementation: as there more generally tends to be a gap between legislative reforms and implementation as the public administration literature informs us. The legal system now espouses human rights and women's human rights. But the justice system will need to adapt to the new legal reforms over time. Legislative reforms involve different stakeholders than implementation. The stakeholders include the members of Parliament, representatives of the legal

institutions at the national level and of international organizations, women's
networks and lobbyists, the media; while implementers of legal reforms are local
courts, police, and the local political and economic elite who tend to uphold
traditional norms and are more resistant to change. Family and kinship systems in
different parts of the country live by their own gender norms. Different ethnic
groups such as the Alevis or the Kurds have their own norms on gender
relationships. Religion is represented by a diverse set of organizations and tarikats
(Sufi organizations). But all these institutions are interrelated and changes in the
legal system will surely create changes in other institutions, beginning with the
bureaucracy. Changes that legislate against honor crimes, for example, have been
followed by instructions from the Religious Affairs Directorate to all imams
around the country to announce honor crimes as sinful in Islam. Changes in
legislation to punish violence against women are being echoed in public campaigns
and training programs addressed to both women and men. Thus, global processes,
and especially the EU membership process has disrupted and begun to change
local institutions.

The rise of Islamist debates and the mobilization of women by the Refah
Party in the 1990s revealed new dynamics and new questions. Women in low
income areas had found a legitimate justification (sanctified by husbands and
fathers) to leave their homes and become political activists. But the Refah Party
government mobilized women only to reject them as actual 'politicians' when time
came to choose their candidates for office. Meanwhile, the emergence of women
university students in public spaces, who wanted to wear Islamic dress and define
themselves in terms of Islamic rather than secular values, created new questions
and new perspectives on women's rights. Thus, competing gender norms and
identities emerged. But were they really dissonant and contradictory or are there
avenues for complementarity? This research reveals that while political elites still
viewed women in instrumental terms, the secularist and Islamist women had begun
to learn from each other and started adopting each other's strategies and terms.
Secularist women became much more involved in grassroots organization and
political activism, while Islamist women have begun to demand their rights, both at
home and in the public, going as far the European Court of Human Rights for the
right to wear their scarves at universities. This brings us to the conclusion that the
supposed dualism between secularism/Westernism and Islam may be a false
dichotomy.

As Navaro-Yashin notes (2002, p. 9): 'I argue that there is no inherent
conflict or necessary difference between Turkey and Europe, Islam and the West.
It is not possible, in the context at hand (Turkey) to distinguish native from
Western points of view because there is no space where they have not been
integrally and historically engaged with one another'. She further notes that
'westernization' as a category of historical analysis is a positivist notion that
assumes an original distinction and incommensurability between a constructed East
and West. The very President of Turkey, Turgut Özal, who led the country into the
liberal capitalist world economy and integration with the West in the 1980s was
also known to belong to an important Sufi organization, the Nakhshibendis.

Islamist groups have claimed modernity, they have embraced capitalist practices, but incorporated the element of 'social relatedness' and 'trust' into the way they do business (Yavuz, 2003). The political party in power, the AK party with its Islamist roots, has enacted more legal reforms on human rights, in an effort to satisfy the Copenhagen Criteria, than any other government before it. As the European Commission concluded, Turkey has satisfied the Copenhagen Criteria. Abdullah Gül, the Foreign Affairs Minister, at a recent conference of Islamic countries, reiterated the importance of gender equality and women's rights. The Prime Minister's wife, Emine Erdoğan, specifically asked to visit women's shelters while she was on an official visit to the United States, thus making a political statement. The Family Research Organization leaning towards an Islamist view has just completed a study on gender-based violence. The various women's empowerment programs bring together women from many diverse backgrounds and ideological persuasions. In short, there is room for greater dialogue and exploration of women's human rights once the dualism of secularism versus Islam is transcended to reveal the multiplicity and complementarity of views. As this study shows, secularist and Islamist women learned from each other and began to employ each other's tactics. As Islamist women became more aware of their individual rights, many secular women engaged with the grassroots and began a dialogue with women from diverse backgrounds. This reveals another false dichotomy that women's individual rights are seen synonymous with secularism and modernity, and women as part of the 'family' as connected with Islamist values. This even led to the establishment of two distinct bureaucracies: one for women, and one for the family! The belief that women's equality and individual human rights is a Western notion again makes women hostage to the West versus Islam debate. Human Rights are universal values, that are not under the monopoly of any country or any civilization. As Tripp (2002: 416) says, 'International human rights and respect for civil and political liberties are not the prerogative of Westerners. Today international rights norms are being shaped by people the world over'.

Perhaps the dualism of individual rights versus state control is just as important for women as the secularism versus Islam debate. Up to the point of passing legal reforms to abide by the Copenhagen Criteria, the state was not in the business of protecting individual rights but on the contrary, of limiting individual rights for the maintenance of secularism and of the unity of the Republic. The limitations on political participation and on the establishment of civil society organizations meant that women's efforts to organize and approach state institutions required a great deal of courage and effort. Women (and men) had traditionally perceived of the state as a top-down institution, thus were afraid of demanding accountability. Women had generally been confined to the private sphere (making it difficult to step into the public sphere) and they identified themselves in their familial roles (making it difficult to see themselves as individuals with rights). These dualisms still persist but are much more complex and dynamic, rather than black and white. The very state that exerts top-down control also began to provide women's human rights education programs in its very bureaucracies (Social Services Administration) and by its bureaucrats (social workers). Collaboration between the state and women's NGOs started as evidenced by the partnership between the Women for Women's Human Rights–New Ways and SHCEK elaborated in Chapter 4. In local governments, similar processes are visible in the establishment of women's platforms in partnership with municipalities as elaborated in Chapter 6.

How can women step comfortably into public spaces, when they are seen as part of the 'private sphere' while men are presumed to belong in the public spaces? Some women have found the solution in stepping out into the public space but dressed in hijab. Islamist women have also become defenders of women's rights and collaborate with secular women. Take Hidayet Tüksal, a headscarved teacher of religion, who is urging women to seek education and insist on their rights. Tüksal has started a joint education project with secular feminists and the Religious Affairs Directorate, that involves training 3,000 state-employed female preachers and Koran instructors to propagate women's education, also publicizing recent changes in the penal code (*Economist,* 4 November 2004).

The dualism that is most difficult to break down is individual versus collective identities. How will women's individual rights be protected in a country where traditionally women's identity (including chastity and honor) is integrally linked to that of the family and the community? The fear to accord women their rights as individuals must be first investigated in the deep underlying identities that shape what 'masculinity' and 'femininity' mean. The link of masculine identity to the control of women's sexual behavior and men's honor linked to women's chastity are not limited to any specific religion. We know, for example, that honor crimes occurred in Greece, or that until 1978 when the law was changed, men did not receive a jail sentence for murdering their wives in crimes of passion in Spain![1] Gender identities define one's attitudes and beliefs towards 'sexuality'. Sexuality is of utmost importance because it reflects human beings' deepest desires and needs. Male identity tends to be strongly tied to the ability to control and 'protect' females so that women 'belong' to a man and the man's family, rather than to herself. This 'belonging' bestows the right on the male to do as he pleases with 'his woman'. Just recently, a famous singer in Turkey, Ibrahim Tatlises, has announced that he is the only one who can decide (not, Asena, a famous dancer and his partner) whether the relationship is over. He claimed that she is his 'honor' (namus) and beat her in public in front of the police who watched. However, now this issue has been claimed by those against masculine domination and it has become a matter of public debate. Asena has filed a legal suit, whereas in the past many people would have turned away saying that a man has a right to do whatever he wants with his 'woman'. Losing the control and 'sovereignty' over females and especially their sexual behavior means that a man has lost face, in some cases lost his honor, and he has lost his masculine identity! The bottom line is there is no way to speak about women's human rights, and gender equality when gender relations are based on relations of domination and submission. This obviously is not just peculiar to Turkey but the point is it is very prevalent in Turkey and without understanding the deeper dynamics of gender relations and sexuality, I strongly believe that no global norms on women's rights will make inroads into people's everyday lives. As Bourdieu (2001, p. 20) writes: 'A political sociology of the sexual act would show that, as is always the case in a relation of domination, the practices and representations of the two sexes are in no way symmetrical. Not only because, even in contemporary European and American societies, young men and women have very different points of view on the love relation, which men most often conceive in terms of conquest, but also because the sexual act itself is seen by men as a form of domination, appropriation, 'possession'. Bourdieu (2001) continues to say that if the sexual relation appears as a social relation of domination, this is because it is constructed through the fundamental principle between the active male and the passive female, which then is reflected in political, economic and social relationships as well.

When we turn to Turkey, we see that the legal system had reflected this principle of domination where men are legally entitled to decide on behalf of women intervening in women's civil, political, economic and social rights, even women's right to live! It has been reflected in the 'buying and selling of women in return for bride price or exchange of brides' in especially eastern and southeastern regions. It is reflected in the reduced sentences when men are 'severely provoked' in cases of female sexual misbehavior, and when sexual assaults against women are classified as crimes against public decency rather than crimes against an individual (until October 2004). If sexuality was not seen through the lenses of 'domination and submission', then male claims of sovereignty over women would surely not be so strong and oppressive. Without an education on sexuality where masculine and feminine identities are debated and renegotiated, any change towards greater respect for women's human rights is bound to be very limited. Sexuality is part and parcel of every individual. Sexuality permeates every facet of private and public life-rituals, rites, etc. The basis of gender-based norms and socialization is very well instituted and stems from a society's expression and/or understanding of sexuality. As Ortaş (2004) has insightfully written about gender relations in Turkey:

> If we go back a few years, we realize that the 20-year-olds today were born during the Sept. 12th period (military rule), education was almost put on hold, where reading books, thinking independently, debating issues were put on hold; keeping books in one's hold could lead to a charge of guilt. Students' social activities were prohibited. In this environment, many young people grew up claiming personal freedom as the highest value, while opposing others' claims for the same freedom. Thus, a young man just recently killed a young woman who did not return his affection! In some areas of our country, women are traded in return for money (there are even currently popular TV shows, where brides are bought for the 'aga'). This and even polygamy is seen as natural and part of traditions and customs. On the other hand, if girls, let alone have sex with a man, look at a man, this sometimes is leading to their victimization and murder!

Ortaş (2004) continues to say that the history of sexuality has grown along with the growth of societies. The institution of marriage was shaped and supported by religions, as well as economic and political power relationships. According to him, under the victimization of women lie centuries-old sexual taboos, and beliefs that chastity is between a woman's legs, defined by the patriarchal culture. Thus, the men, especially the macho men, must be educated about these norms on 'chastity and honor'. As the reader will remember, the empowerment training programs for women, discussed in Chapter 4, even though clearly very valuable, were limited because of resistance from families, and even female members of families. Many of the participants of these programs stress the importance of educating men. Men and women must learn about each other's sexualities and bodies because there is a great of misinformation and ignorance. Meanwhile, it is well-known that pornographic materials are most popular among immigrant Turks compared to other immigrant groups in Europe. Ortaş claims rightly that Turkish society must solve its own problems with sexuality through widespread education programs on sexuality and gender identities, which will then lead a generation of young people who no longer discriminate on the basis of gender and who understand that 'chastity' is found in one's head, and not in one's sexual organs.

Our beliefs and assumptions of our own sexuality and gender identities are the hardest and most resistant to change, once formed. Unfortunately these beliefs have placed women in an inferior position, not just in Turkey but in many cultures. A natural extension of the belief system that places women under masculine domination also legitimizes violence against women. If women try to break out of this cycle, or show disobedience, the use of force, as a potential or real threat helps to keep them in their place. Earlier this year, the Spanish Roman Catholic Bishops Conference foolishly declared that violence against women was the 'bitter fruit' of the sexual liberation of the 1960s (Schipper, 2004). But as Schipper has found out as a result of her collection of thousands of proverbs about women, some as much as 4,000 years old, all over the world and throughout centuries, proverbs present beating as a 'natural' way to overcome male fear and to force women – especially wives – into subservience and virtue. Violence is often recommended as the way for men to prove their manliness, for example in the Arabic proverb: 'The man who can't slaughter his sheep, or can't beat his wife (when she deserves it) is better dead than alive'. Schipper (2004) has found that many proverbs reflect considerable male anxiety: 'Never marry a woman with bigger feet than your own' is the way they put it in Malawi, meaning, of course, never to take a wife who is smarter or more successful or more talented than you are. This same warning is apparently echoed in many variants in numerous cultures and reflects this obsessive fear of a scenario in which a man would be a woman's inferior.

It is clear that masculine superiority has been perpetuated in Turkey in cultural, religious, economic and political institutions. Discriminatory and even harmful practices to women, such as honor crimes, virginity tests, have been defended in the name of traditions, customs and other cultural identities. But Tripp argues that such practices defended in the name of customs and traditions, are also often seeking to protect certain political and/or economic interests. An evidence of that in Turkey is the resistance to equal sharing of property in marriage more than any other item of the new Civil Code. Tripp (2002, p. 414) notes that cultural preservation and identity concerns are, of course, real, but they are also often tied to broader political and economic context that affects their sustainability: 'This means, ultimately, that practices which hurt women have also to be addressed as a political problem primarily by actors within that society itself'.

In Turkey, incentive structures are changing as a global regime on women's human rights emerged and EU criteria pressure the government towards greater attention women's human rights. The processes of globalization are creating new cultural identities, practices and patterns which create dissonance but also greater space and opportunity, and openness to transformation or reinvention. Women's diverse voices are becoming louder, and as they demand greater rights and resources. As at the global level, the Turkish engagement with women's human rights is being reshaped by the struggle between the forces that want to stop masculine domination and those that stand opposed to such a change. Women's human rights can ultimately only be attained as both feminine and masculine identities are reshaped, not as distinct from each other and fixed but as interconnected. As Murata (1992) notes, in Islam women and men do not embody mutually exclusive or opposite attributes; rather they incorporate both masculine and feminine attributes. Each manifests the whole. A Tibetan proverb echoes the same idea: 'A hundred male and a hundred female qualities make a perfect human being' (Schipper, 2004).

Notes

[1] Article 428 of the Spanish Criminal Code until 1978 (Ley No 22/1978) was the following: The husband who, surprising his wife committing adultery, kills on sight any or both of the adulteress/adulterer, or causes them gross physical damage will be condemned to the penalty of exile (forced to move to another province). If the physical damage is of any other kind, no penalty will be imposed. The same penalties will apply to fathers who catch by surprise their daughters younger than 23 and their corrupters if the daughters still live in their parents' homes.

Bibliography

Abbott, Pamela, and Wallace, Claire (1991), *An Introduction to Sociology: Feminist Perspectives*, Routledge, London.

Acar, Feride (2000), *Turkey, The First CEDAW Impact Study*, Centre for Feminist Research, York University and the International Women's Rights Project, Toronto.

Acuner, Selma (March 2000), *Women's National Machinery in Turkey*, Flying News, Ankara, Turkey.

Afshar, Haleh (1998), 'Disempowerment and the Politics of Civil Liberties for Iranian Women' in Haleh Afshar (ed.), *Women and Empowerment, Illustrations from the Third World*, Macmillan Press, London.

Alvarez, Sonia (2000), 'Translating the Global Effects of Transnational Organizing in Local Feminist Discourses and Practices in Latin America', *Meridians: Feminism, Race, Transnationalism* Vol. 1, pp. 29-67.

Alvarez, Sonia (1990), *Engendering Democracy in Brazil*, Princeton University Press, Princeton.

Amnesty International (February 2004), EUR 44/001/2004, 'Memo to the Turkish Prime Minister on the Occasion of the visit to Turkey of a delegation led by Irene Khan, Secretary General of the Amnesty International'.

An-Naim, Abdullah (1995), 'The Dichotomy between Religious and Secular Discourse in Islamic Societies', in Mahnaz Afkhami (ed.), *Faith and Freedom: Women's Human Rights in the Muslim World*, Syracuse University Press, Syracuse.

Arat, Yesim (1997), 'The Project of Modernity and Women in Turkey', in Sibel Bozdogan and Resat Kasaba (eds.), *Rethinking Modernity and National Identity in Turkey*, University of Washington Press, Seattle.

Ashworth, Georgina (1996), *Gendered Governance: An Agenda for Change*, Gender in Development Monograph Series, No. 3, UNDP, New York.

Baden, Sally, and Goetz, Anne Marie (1997), 'Who needs sex when you can have gender?': Conflicting Discourses on Gender at Beijing, *Feminist Review*, Vol. 56, pp. 3-25.

Baines, Erin (1999), 'Gender Construction and the Protection Mandate of the UNHCR: Responses from the Guatemalan Women' in M. Meyer and E. Prügl (eds.), *Gender Politics in Global Governance*, Rowman & Littlefield, Lanham.

Bangura, Yusuf (1996), *The Concept of Policy Dialogue and Gendered Development: Understanding its Institutional and Ideological Constraints*, UNRISD, Geneva.

Barlas, Asma (2002), *Believing Women in Islam: Unreading Patriarchal Interpretations of the Qur'an*, University of Texas, Austin.

Barnett, Michael and Finnemore, Martha (1999), 'The Politics, Power and Pathologies of International Organizations, *International Organization*, Vol. 53, pp. 699-732.

Bayes, Jane, and Kelly, Rita Mae (2001), 'Political Spaces, Gender and NAFTA' in R.M Kelly, J. Bayes, M. Hawkesworth, B. Young (eds.), *Gender, Globalization and Democratization*, Rowman & Littlefield, Lanham.

BBC Report (6 March 2004) 'Protest against Decentralization'.

Beijing Plus Five NGO Report of Turkey (5-6 Feburary 2000), Prepared by Beijing Plus 5 Coordination Unit, Ucan Süpürge, Ankara, Turkey.

Bekman, Sevda (1998*), An Evaluation of the Mother-Child Education Program*, Mother-Child Education Foundation, Pub. 13, Istanbul.

Bend, Jill (1988), 'Off our Backs: Dossier 4, Turkey – The Fight Against Power', *Women Living Under Muslim Law*, August/September.

Berktay, Fatmagul, Keresticioglu, Inci Ozkan, Ucan Cubukcu, Sevgi, Terzi, Ozlem and Kivilcim Forsam, Zeynep (2004), *The Position of Women in Turkey and in the European Union: Achievement, Problems, Prospects*, Ka-Der Press, Istanbul.

Berktay, Fatmagül (1991), 'Has Anything Changed in the Outlook of the Turkish Left on Women?' in Sirin Tekeli (ed) *Women in Modern Turkish Society*, Zed Books, London.

Blondet, Cecilia (2002), 'The 'Devil's Deal': Women's Political Participation and Authoritarianism in Peru', in Molyneux and Razavi (eds.), *Gender Justice, Development and Rights*, Oxford University Press, Oxford.

Blumberg, Rae L. (1995), 'Engendering Wealth and Well-Being in an Era of Economic Transformation' in Blumberg, Rakowski and others (eds.), *Engendering Wealth and Well-Being*, Westview Press, Boulder.

Bourdieu, Pierre (2001), *Masculine Domination*, Stanford University Press, Stanford.

Breitmeir Helmut (1997), "International Organizations and the Creation of Environmental Regimes", in Oran Young, ed. *Global Governance: Drawing Insights from the Environmental Experience*, MIT Press, Cambridge.

Bratton, Michael (1989), 'Beyond the State: Civil Society and Associational Life in Africa', *World Politics*, Vol. 41, pp. 407-30.

Breitmer, Helmut (1997), 'International Organizations and the Creation of Environmental Regimes', in Oran Young (ed.), *Global Governance: Drawing Insights from the Environmental Experience*, Cambridge, MIT Press.

Bunch, Charlotte, Rielly Niamph (1994), 'Demanding Accountability: The Global Campaign and Vienna Tribunal for Women's Human Rights', Center for Women's Global Leadership and UNIFEM, New York.

Byrne, B. and Koch Laier, J. with Baden, S., and Marcus, R. (1998), 'National Machineries for Women in Development', *BRIDGE Report No. 36*, Institute of Development Studies, Sussex.

Bystiydzienski, Jill (ed) (1992), *Women Transforming Politics: Worldwide Strategies for Empowerment*, Indiana University Press, Bloomington.

CEDAW, Second and Third Periodic Report of Turkey (1994 and 1997), CEDAW/C/TUR/2-3.

CEDAW, Fourth and Fifth Combined Periodic Report of Turkey (2002 and 2003).

Chen, Martha (1996), 'Engendering World Conferences: The International Women's Movement and the UN' in Thomas Weiss and Leon Gordenker (eds.), *NGOs, the UN and Global Governance*, Lynne Rienner, Boulder.

Cook, Rebecca (1997), 'Women' in Christopher Joyner (ed.), *UN and International Law*, Cambridge University Press, Cambridge.

Couturier, Kelly, (27 January 1998), 'Suicide Attempts Fuel Virginity Test Debate', *Washington Post*.

Dateline, 15 October 1990.

Dateline, 17 November 1990.

Dawson, Elsa (1998), 'Assessing the Impact: NGOs and Empowerment' in Haleh Afshar (ed.), *Women and Empowerment, Illustrations from the Third World*, MacMillan, London.

De Nevers , Renee (1999), Regimes as Mechanisms of Global Governance', *Project on World Security*, Rockefeller Brothers Fund, New York.

Deutz, Andrew (1993), 'Gender and International Human Rights', *The Fletcher Forum of World Affairs*, Vol 17, pp. 33-51.

Development Assistance Committee (1998), *DAC Source Book on Concepts and Approaches Linked to Gender Equality*, OECD, Paris.

Dore, Elizabeth (ed.) (1997), *Gender Politics in Latin America*, New York, Monthly Review Press.

Economist (4 November 2004), 'The paradox of devout Muslim feminists'.

Economist (19 February 2004), 'Thou shalt not kill'.

Ehlstain, J. Beth (1974) 'Moral Women and Immoral Man: A Consideration of the Public-Private Split and Its Political Ramifications', *Politics and Society* 4 (4), pp. 460-61.

Ertürk, Yakin, 'Turkey's Modern Paradoxes in Identity Politics, Women's Agency and Universal Rights' (forthcoming)

Ertürk, Yakin (2003a), 'Violence in the Name of Honor within the Context of International Regimes', 4-5 November 2003, Stockholm.

Ertürk, Yakin (2003b), *Integration of the Human Rights of Women and the Gender Perspective: Violence against Women, Report of the Special Rapporteur on violence against women*, Commission on Human Rights, Economic and Social Council of the UN, E/CN.4/2004/66, December.

Ertürk, Yakin (1997), 'Identity Politics: Implications for Gender Analysis, Policy and Training', *Instraw News*, No. 27, pp. 9-15.

Esim Simel, and Cindoğlu Dilek (1999), 'Women's Organizations in 1990s Turkey: Predicaments and Prospects', *Middle Eastern Studies*, Vol. 35, pp. 178-188.

European Union (2003), *Regular Report on Turkey's Progress Towards Accession*.

Fazlioglu, Aygül (2003), *Catom (Multipurpose Community Center): A Model for Empowering Women in Southeastern Anatolia*, State Planning Organization, Ankara, Turkey

Finkel, Andrew (1990), 'Municipal Politics and the State in Contemporary Turkey', in Andrew Finkel and Nukhet Sirman (eds.), *Turkish State, Turkish Society*, Routledge, London.

Finnemore, Martha (1996), *National Interests in International Society*, Cornell University Press, Ithaca.

Flying News Women's Communication Bulletin (2003), Special Issue in English.

Flying News Women's Communication Bulletin (2000), *Women & Women's Movement in Turkey*, Special Issue in English, Ankara, Turkey.

Foucault, Michel (1988), *Politics, Philosophy, Culture – Interviews and Other Writings 1977-1984*, Routledge, London.

French, Michel (1994) 'Power/Sex', in H. L. Radtke and H.J. Stam (eds.), *Power/Gender, Social Relations in Theory and Practice*, Sage Publications, London.

Galey, Margaret (1984), 'International Enforcement of Women's Rights,' *Human Rights Quarterly* Vol. 6.

Giddens, Anthony (1984), *The Constitution of Society: Outline of the Theory of Structuration*, University of California Press, Berkeley.

Göçek, Fatma Müge, and Blaghi, Shiva (eds.) (1994), *Reconstructing Gender in the Middle East: Tradition, Identity and Power*, Columbia University Press, New York.

Goetz, Anne Marie (2001), 'The World Bank and Women's Movements' in Robert O'Brien, Anne Marie Goetz, Jan Aart Scholte, Marc Williams (eds.), *Contesting Global Governance*, Cambridge University Press, Cambridge.

Goetz, Anne Marie (ed.) (1997), *Getting Institutions Right for Women in Development*, Zed Press, London.

Goetz, Anne Marie (1995), *The Politics of Integrating Gender into State Development Processes: Trends, Opportunities and Constraints in Bangladesh, Chile, Jamaica, Mali, Morocco and Uganda*, UNRISD, Geneva.

Göle, Nilüfer (1999), *The Forbidden Modern: Civilization and Veiling*, University of Michigan Press, Ann Arbor.

Gülçür, Leyla (2000), 'An Overview of the Women's Movement in Turkey', *Flying News Women's Communication Bulletin*, Special Issue in English, pp. 13-14.

Gupta, Suranjana (2001), 'Transforming Governance Agendas: Insights from Grassroots Women's Initiatives in Local Governance in Two Districts of India', in Rita Mae Kelly et al (eds.), *Gender, Globalization and Democratization*, Rowman & Littlefield, Lanham.

Haas, Ernst (1990), *When Knowledge is Power*, University of California Press, Berkeley.

Haas, Peter M. (ed.) (1992), *Knowledge, Power and International Policy Coordination*, International Organization Vol. 46.

Halliday, Fred (1991), 'Hidden from International Relations: Women and the International Arena' in Grant and Newland (eds.), *Gender and International Relations*, Indiana University Press, Bloomington.

Hanochi, Seiko (2001), 'Japan and the Global Sex Industry', in R.M. Kelly et al (eds.), *Gender, Globalization and Democratization,* Rowman & Littlefield, Lanham.

Hansenclever, Andreas, Mayer, Peter and Rittberger, Volker (1996), 'Interests, Power, Knowledge: The Study of International Regimes', *Mershon International Studies Review,* Vol. 40, pp. 177-228.

Hartman, Betsy (Summer 1997), 'Cairo consensus sparks new hopes, old worries,' *Forum for Applied Research and Public Policy,* vol. 12, no. 2.

Heinen Jaqueline, and Porter, Stephane (2002) in Maxine Molyneux and Shahra Razavi (eds) *Gender Justice, Development, and Rights,* Oxford, Oxford University Press.

Hijab, Nadia WS/Future/1999/EP.5, 8 November 1999, *Women, Development and Human Rights,* United Nations Workshop on Beijing Plus Five.

The Humanist (7 September 2004), 'Turkey divided over adultery Laws: Feminists outraged at plans to criminalize adultery'.

İlkkaracan, Pinar, (2002), 'Eliminating Violence Against Women: Turkish Initiatives and Repercussions', unpublished paper.

Ilkkaracan, Pinar, 'Translating the B+5 Agreements into National and Local Policies and Programs', speech given at the 28th Annual Conference of the Global Health Council, 29 May-1 June 2001, Washington D.C.

Incioğlu, Nihal (2002), 'Local Elections and Electoral Behavior', in Sabri Sayari and Yilmaz Esmer (eds.), *Politics, Parties and Elections in Turkey,* Lynne Rienner, Boulder.

International Labor Organization (ILO) (1994), *Women and Work: Selected ILO Policy Documents,* ILO, Geneva.

Jaquette, Jane (1995), 'Losing the Battle, Winning the War: International Politics, Women's Issues and the 1980s mid-decade Conference', in Anne Winslow (ed.), *Women, Politics and the United Nations,* Greenwood Press, Westport.

Jehan, Rounaq (1995), *The Elusive Agenda: Mainstreaming Women in Development,* Zed Press, London.

Joachim, Jutta. (1999), 'Shaping the Human Rights Agenda', in M. Meyer and E. Prugl, (eds.), *Gender and Politics in Global Governance,* Rowman & Littlefield, Lanham.

Kabeer, Naila (2000) 'From Feminist Insights to an Analytical Framework' in N. Kabeer and R. Subrahmanian (eds.), *Institutions, Relations and Outcomes – A Framework and Case Studies for Gender-aware Planning,* Zed Books. London.

Kabeer, Naila (1994), *Reversed Realities – Gender Hierarchies in Development Thought,* Verso, New York.

Kalaycioglu, Ersin (1989), 'Division of Responsibility', in Metin Heper (ed.), *Local Government in Turkey: Governing Greater Istanbul,* Routledge, London.

Kandiyoti, Deniz and Saktanber, Ayse (eds.) (2002), *Fragments of Culture: The Everyday of Modern Turkey,* Rutgers University Press, New Brunswick.

Kardam, Filiz (2000) 'Experiences of the Women's Movement', *Flying News Women's Communication Bulletin, Women & Women's Movement in Turkey,* Special Issue in English, Ankara, Turkey.

Kardam, Nüket (2004), 'The Emerging Global Gender Equality Regime from Neoliberal and Constructivist Perspectives in International Relations', *International Feminist Journal of Politics* 6:1 March 2004, pp. 85-109.

Kardam, Nüket (2003), *Women's Human Rights Training Program 1995-2003,* Evaluation Report, Women for Women's Human Rights– New Ways, Istanbul, Turkey.

Kardam, Nüket, and Acuner, Selma (2003), 'National Women's Machineries: Structures and Spaces', in Shirin Rai (ed.), *Mainstreaming Gender, Democratizing the State?,* Manchester University Press, Manchester.

Kardam, Nüket, and Ertürk, Yakin (1999), 'Towards Expanded Accountability? Women's Organizations and the State in Turkey', *International Journal of Organization Theory and Behavior* Vol. 2, pp. 167-197.

Kardam, Nüket (1991), *Bringing Women In: Women's Issues in International Development Programs,* Lynne Rienner, Boulder.

Keck, Margaret, and Sikkink, Kathryn (1998), *Activists beyond Borders: Advocacy Networks in International Politics,* Cornell University Press, Ithaca.

Kelly, Rita Mae, Bayes, Jane, Hawkesworth, Mary and Young, Brigitte (eds.) (2001), *Gender, Globalization and Democratization,* Rowman and Littlefield, Lanham.

Keohane, Robert (1991) 'International Relations Theory: Contributions of a Feminist Standpoint' in R. Grant and K. Newland (eds.), *Gender and International Relations,* Indiana University Press, Bloomington.

Keohane, Robert (1984), *After Hegemony,* Princeton University Press, Princeton.

Korten, David (1990) *Getting to the 21st Century: Voluntary Action and the Global Agenda,* Kumarian Press, Connecticut.

Krasner, Stephen (ed.) (1983), *International Regimes,* Cornell University Press, Ithaca.

Kratochwil, Frederick, and Ruggie, John (eds.) (1994) 'International Organizations: A State of the Art on an Art of the State', *International Organization: A Reader,* HarperCollins College Publishers, New York.

Levinger, Beryl, and McLeod, Jean (2000) *Togetherness: How Governments, Corporations and NGOs Partner to Support Sustainable Development in Latin America,* Inter-American Foundation.

Local Agenda 21 (2001), *Annual Project Report,* Istanbul, Turkey.

Macaulay, F., (1998) 'Localities of Power: Gender, Parties and Democracy in Chile and Brazil' in Haleh Afshar (ed.), *Women and Empowerment, Illustrations from the Third World,* Macmillan Press, London.

Maguire, Patricia (1984), *Women in Development: An Alternative Analysis,* Center for International Education, University of Massachusetts, Amherst.

Migdal, Joel (1988), *Strong Societies and Weak States,* Princeton University Press, Princeton.

Miller, Carol, and Razavi, Shahra (eds.) (1998), *Missionaries and Mandarins:*

Feminist Engagement with Development Institutions, UNRISD, Geneva.

Mohamad, Maznah (2002), 'The Politics of Gender, Ethnicity and Democratization in Malaysia: Shifting Interests and Identities' in Maxine Molyneux and Shahra Razavi (eds), *Gender Justice, Development, and Rights,* Oxford University Press, Oxford.

Molyneux, Maxine, and Razavi, Shahra eds. (2002) *Gender Justice, Development, and Rights,* Oxford University Press, Oxford.

Molyneux, Maxine (2000) 'Twentieth-Century State Formations in Latin America' in E. Dore and M. Molyneux (eds.), *Hidden Histories of Gender and State in Latin America,* Duke University Press, London.

Molyneux, Maxine (1981), 'Women in Socialist Societies: Theory and Practice', in *Of Marriage and the Market: Women's Subordination in International Perspective,* Kate Young, Carol Wolkowitz and Roslyn McCullagh (eds.), CSE Books, London.

Moser, Caroline O. N. (1993), *Gender Planning and Development,* Routledge, London.

Murata, Sachiko (1992), *The Tao of Islam: The Sourcebook on Gender Relationships in Islam,* State University of New York Press, New York.

Murphy, Clare, (23 September 2004), *Spotlight on Turkish women's rights,* BBC News.

Murthy, Ranjani, (2000) 'Gender Training Experiences with Indian NGOs' in N. Kabeer & R. Subrahmanian (eds), *Institutions, Relations and Outcomes – A Framework and Case-Studies for Gender-aware Planning,* Zed Books, London.

Mohamad, Maznah (2002), 'The Politics of Gender, Ethnicity and Democratization in Malaysia: Shifting Interests and Identities' in Molyneux and Razavi (eds.), *Gender Justice, Development and Rights,* Oxford: Oxford University Press.

Murata, Sachiko (1992) *The Tao of Islam: A Sourcebook on Gender Relationships in Islamic Thought* Albany: State University of New York Press.

Naciri, Rabea (1998) 'Engaging the State: The Women's Movement and Political Discourse in Morocco' in Carol Miller and Shahra Razavi, (eds.), *Missionaries and Mandarins: Feminist Engagement with Development Institutions,* Intermediate Technology Publications, London.

Navaro-Yashin, Yael (2002), *Faces of the State: Secularism and Public Life in Turkey,* Princeton University Press, Princeton.

Osirim, Mary J. (2001) 'Making Good on Commitments to Grassroots Women: NGOs and Empowerment for Women in Contemporary Zimbabwe', *Women's Studies International Forum* Vol. 24, No. 2, pp. 167-180.

Özdalga, Elisabeth (1998), *The Veiling Issue, Official Secularism and Popular Islam in Modern Turkey,* Curzon Press, Surrey.

Paidar, Parvin (2002), 'Encounters between Feminism, Democracy and Reformism in Contemporary Iran', in Molyneux and Razavi (eds.), *Gender Justice, Development and Rights,* Oxford University Press, Oxford.

Pervizat, Leyla (Fall 2003) 'In the Name of Honor', *Human Rights Dialogue.*

Purushothaman, Sangeetha (1998) *The Empowerment of Women in India,* Sage

Publications, London.

Platform for Action and the Beijing Declaration (1995), *Fourth World Conference on Women,* United Nations, New York.

Prügl, Elizabeth (1996), 'Gender in International Organizations and Global Governance: A Critical Review of the Literature' in *International Studies Notes* Vol. 21, No. 1, pp. 15-24.

Rai, Shirin (ed.) (2003), *Democratizing the State: National Machineries for Women,* University of Manchester Press, Manchester.

Razavi, Shahra, (1999), 'Reply to Jacque Baudot', *UNRISD News 21* Autumn/Winter.

Razavi, Shahra, and Miller, Carol (1998), *Missionaries and Mandarins: Feminist Engagement with Development Institutions,* Intermediate Technology Publications, London.

Reuters (7 September 2004), 'Turkish Premier Defends Plans to Outlaw Adultery', Ankara, Turkey.

Rosenau, James (1995) 'Governance in the Twenty-first Century' *Global Governance* Vol. 1 Winter.

Rosenau, James (1992), 'Governance, Order and Change in World Politics' in James Rosenau and Ernst-Otto Czempiel (eds.), *Governance without Government: Order and Change in World Politics,* Cambridge University Press, Cambridge.

Rowlands, J. (1998) 'A Word of the Times, But What Does it Mean? Empowerment in the Discourse and Practice of Development' in Haleh Afshar (ed.), *Women & Empowerment, Illustrations from the Third World,* Macmillan Press, London.

Ruggie, John Gerard (1998), *Constructing the World Polity: Essays in International Institutionalization,* Routledge, London.

Sassen, Saskia (1998), *Globalization and its Discontents,* The New Press, New York.

Sawer, Marilyn (1995), *Femocrats and Ecorats: Women's Policy Machinery in Australia, Canada and New Zealand,* UNRISD, Geneva.

Schalkwyk, Johanna, and Woroniuk, Beth (March 1997), *Source Book: Prepared in Conjuction with the Draft Principles for Development Cooperation on Equality Between Women and Men,* Prepared for the Expert Group on Women in Development OECD-DAC, Paris.

Schild, Veronica (2002), 'Engendering the New Social Citizenship in Chile: NGOs and Social Provisioning under Neo-Liberalism', Maxine Molyneux and Shahra Razavi (eds.), *Gender Justice, Development and Rights,* Oxford University Press, Oxford.

Schipper, Mineke (20 April 2004), *A Thousand Proverbs Later, It's Still a Brutality* Los Angeles Times.

Shadow NGO Report on Turkey's Fourth and Fifth combined Periodic Report to the Committee on CEDAW (July 2004), prepared by Women for Women's Human Rights–New Ways, Turkey.

Silverman, E. L. (1994), Women in Women's Organisations: Power or Pouvoir', in

H.L. Radtke and H.J. Stam (eds.), *Power/Gender, Social Relations in Theory and Practice*, Sage Publications, London.

Sirman, Nükhet (1989) 'Feminism in Turkey: A Short History', *New Perspectives on Turkey* Vol. 3, No. 1, pp. 1-34.

Skran, Claudena (1995), *Refugees in Inter-War Europe,* Clarendon Press, Oxford.

Stephenson, Carolyn (1995). 'Women's International non-governmental organizations at the United Nations', in Anne Winslow, (ed.), *Women, Politics and the United Nations,* Greenwood Press, Westport.

Subramanian, Ramya (2002), 'Engendering Education: Prospects for a Rights-Based Approach to Female Education Deprivation in India', in Molyneux and Razavi (eds.), *Gender Justice, Development and Rights,* Oxford University Press, Oxford.

Tinker, Irene (1999), *'NGOs: An Alternative Power Base for Women'* in M. Meyer and E.Prugl (eds.), *Gender Politics in Global Governance,* Rowman & Littlefield, Lanham.

Tinker, Irene (ed.) (1990), *Persistent Inequalities: Women and World Development,* Oxford University Press, Oxford.

Tomasevski, Katerina (1993), *Women and Human Rights,* Zed Books, London.

Tripp, Aili Mari (2002), 'Women's Rights and Cultural Diversity', in Maxine Molyneux and Shahra Razavi (eds.), *Gender Justice, Development and Rights,* Oxford University Press, Oxford.

Ucarer, Emek (1999), 'Trafficking in Women: Alternate Migration or Modern Slave Trade?' in M. Meyer and E. Prugl (eds.), *Gender Politics in Global Governance,* Rohman & Littlefield, Lanham.

United Nations Children Fund (UNICEF) (2003) *A Gender Review in Education,* Ankara, Turkey, www.unicef.org/turkey

United Nations (2001) From Beijing to Beijing Plus Five, New York.

UN International Institute for Research and Training for the Advancement of Women (INSTRAW) (1999) *Engendering the Political Agenda: A South African Case Study,* Gender Research Project, University of the Witwatersrand, South Africa.

United Nations (1996) *Platform for Action and the Beijing Declaration, Fourth World Conference on women, Beijing, China, 4-15 September 1995,* Department of Public Information, New York.

United Nations Development Programme (UNDP) (1995), *Human Development Report,* Oxford University Press, Oxford.

Wadud, Amina (1999), *Quran and Woman: Rereading the Sacred Text from a Woman's Perspective,* Oxford University Press, Oxford.

Waylen, Georgina (1997), 'Women's Movements, The State and Democratization in Chile: The Establishment of SERNAM', in Anne Marie Goetz, (ed.), *Getting Institutions Right for Women in Development,* Zed Press, London.

Weiss, Thomas (2000), 'Governance, Good Governance and Global Governance: Conceptual and Actual Challenges', *Third World Quarterly,* Vol. 21, No. 5.

Wendt, Alexander (1987) 'The Agent-Structure Problem in International Relations Theory', *International Organization* Vol. 41, Summer, pp. 335-370.

Women for Women's Human Rights-New Ways (2002), *The New Legal Status of Women in Turkey*, Istanbul.

Whitworth, Sandra (1994), *Feminism and International Relations: Towards a Political Economy Gender in Interstate and Non-Governmental Institutions*, New York, St. Martin's Press, New York.

World Bank (2001), *Engendering Development: Through Gender Equality in Rights, Resources and Voice*, Oxford University Press, Oxford.

World Bank (1999), *Entering the 21st Century – World Development Report 1999/2000*, Oxford University Press, Oxford.

Yavuz, Hakan (2003) *Islamic Political Identity in Turkey*, Oxford University Press, Oxford.

Young, Oran (1991), 'Political Leadership and Regime Formation: On the Development of Institutions in International Society', *International Organization* Vol. 45, pp. 281-308.

Young, Oran (1989), 'The Politics of International Regime Formation', *International Organization*, Vol. 43, pp. 349-376.

Works in Turkish

Acar, Feride (1990), 'Türkiyede İslamcı Hareket ve Kadın, in Şirin Tekeli (ed.), *Kadın Bakiş Açısından 1980ler Türkiyesinde Kadın*, İletisim Yayınları, İstanbul.

Acuner, Selma (2002a), '90lı Yıllar ve Resmi Düzeyde Kurumsallaşmanın Doğuş Aşamaları, in Aksu Bora and Asena Günal (eds.), *90larda Türkiyede Feminizm*, İletişim, Istanbul.

Acuner, Selma (2002b), 'AB ve Türkiye Ulusal Programı: Kadın-Erkek Eşitliği Arasında Fırsat Eşitliği Politika Hedefleri', *Uçan Haber*, Sayı 1, pp. 4-6.

Acuner, Selma (1999) Gender Equality and the Process of Institutionalization, (in Turkish) doctoral dissertation, Ankara University, 1999.

Aile Araştırma Kurumu (1989), *Türk Aile Yapısı*, Ankara.

Akkaya, Fatma Demirci (2003), 'Eskişehir Kadın Platformu', *Uçan Süpürge*, Sayi 18, Nisan/Mayis.

Akşin, Sina (ed.), (1995), *Çağdaş Türkiye 1908-1980, Türkiye Tarihi*, Cem Yayınevi, Istanbul.

Ankara Üniversitesi, (2000), *Eğitim Yoluyla Güçlenme: Kadın Eğitimi Toplantısı, 7-8 Şubat, 2000)*, Kadın Sorunlari Araştırma ve Uygulama Merkezi, Ankara.

Arat, Yeşim (1998) ,'Türkiye'de Modernleşme Projesi ve Kadınlar' in S. Bozdoğan ve R. Kasaba (eds.), *Türkiye'de Modernleşme ve Ulusal Kimlik*, Istanbul, Tarih Vakfı Yurt Yayinlari, Istanbul.

Arıkan, Atabek et al (ed.) (1996), *Ve Hep Birlikte Koştuk – İlerici Kadınlar Derneği – 1975-1980*, Açı Yay, Istanbul.

Ataüz, Akin (2000), in *Eğitim Yoluyla Güçlenme, Kadın Eğitimi Toplantısı, 7-8 Şubat 2000,* Ankara Üniversitesi Kadın Sorunlari Araştırma ve Uygulama Merkezi, Ankara.

Avrupa Birliği ve Eşitlik (EU and Gender Equality) (2000), İstihdamda Eşit Fırsatlar, Avrupa Komisyonu Türkiye Temsilciliği, Ankara.

Bağır Herkes Duysun:Dayağa Karşı Dayanışma Kampanyası (1988), Kadın Çevresi Yayınları, Gümüş Basımevi, Istanbul.

Bilgi Üniversitesi, (2003) İnsan Hakları Merkezi, Sosyal ve Krimonolojik Araştırmalar Çalışma Raporu, *Kadına Yönelik Şiddet Konulu Araştırma Raporu,* Istanbul.

Bora, Aksu ve Asena Günal (eds) (2002), *90larda Türkiye'de Feminism,* İletişim Yayınları, Istanbul.

Cağatay, Nilüfer and Soysal, Yasemin (1990), 'Uluslaşma Süreci ve Feminizm Üzerine Karşılastırılmalı Düşünceler', in Şirin Tekeli (ed.), *Kadın Bakış Açısından 1980ler Turkiyesinde Kadın,* İletisim Yayınları, Istanbul.

Çağdaş Kadın ve Gençlik Vakfı (2001), *Bir Eğitim Yolculuğu* , Ankara.

Çağdaş Kadın ve Gençlik Vakfı (2000), *Dizlerim Titriyordu, Bir Eğitim Yolculuğu,* Ankara.

Collins, P. H. (1995), 'Siyah Feminist Düşüncenin Toplumsal Yapısı' in S. Çakır & N. Akgökçe (eds.), *Farklı Feminizmler Açısından Kadın Araştırmalarındaı Yöntem,* Sel Yayinlari, Istanbul.

Cumhuriyet, (10 July 2003), 'Ev Kadinlari Daha Maço'.

Devlet Planlama Teşkilatı (DPT) (2000) Kurumsallaşma ve Kadın Alt Komisyonu Raporu.

Devlet Planlama Teşkilatı, (DPT) (2000) Kadına Yönelik Şiddet Alt Komisyonu Raporu.

Ecevit, Yıldız (2001) "Yerel yönetimler ve kadın örgütleri", in Aynur Ilyasoğlu and Necla Akgökçe, (eds.), *Yerli bir Feminisme Doğru,* Sel Yayincilik, Istanbul.

Kadın Sorunları Araştırma ve Uygulama Merkezi (7-8 February, 2000) *Eğitim Yoluyla Güçlenme,* Kadın Eğitimi Toplantısı, Ankara Üniversitesi, Ankara.

Eraslan, Sibel (2002), 'Uğultular...Silüetler' in Bora and Günal (eds.), *90larda Türkiye'de Feminism,* İletişim Yayınları, Istanbul.

Eroğlu, Nilgün, Doğan, Süheyla, Yılmaz, Kamile, Akay, Perihan and Öner, Ayla (2002) '1990 sonrası Antalya Kadın Hareketi Tarihi' in Bora and Günal (eds.) *90larda Türkiyede Feminizm,* İletişim Yayınları, Istanbul.

Eşitlik için Anayasa Değişikliği Paketi, 8 March 2002.

Freire, P. (1991) *Ezilenlerin Pedagojisi* (trans. from English by D. Hattatoğlu), Ayrıntı Yay, Istanbul.

Gülçür, Leyla (1996), "Aile İçinde Kadına Uygulanan Şiddet: Ankara Araştırması" in İlkkaracan, Gülçür and Arın (eds.), *Sıcak Yuva Masalı: Aile İçi Şiddet ve Cinsel Taciz,* Metis Yayinlari, Istanbul.

Gürsoy, Elif (November 2002), Bekaret Denetiminin Kadın Sağlığına Etkisi ve Konuya Sağlık Ekibinin yaklaşımı, Uçan Süpürge, *Uçan Haber,* Sayi 16.

Hürriyet (31 March 2004), 'Özkaya: Töre Cinayetlerine İndirim Yapılmamalı'.

Hürriyet (20 October 2004), 'Aile Içi Şiddete Son Küçükköy'den başladı'.

Işık, Nazik (2002) '1990larda Kadına Yönelik Aile İçi Şiddetle Mücadele Hareketi içinde Oluşmuş bazı Gözlem ve Düşünceler' in Bora and Günal (eds.), *90larda Türkiyede Feminizm*, İletişim Yayınları, Istanbul.

Istanbul Bilgi Üniversitesi, Kadın Hakları Arastırma Merkezi (2003), *Sosyal ve Kriminolojik Araştırmalar Çalışma Grubu, Kadına Yönelik Şiddet Raporu.*

İlkkaracan, Pınar, Leyla Gülçür, and Arın, Canan (1996) *Sıcak Yuva Masalı: Aile içi Şiddet ve Cinsel Taciz*, Metis Yayinlari, Istanbul.

Ka-Der Brosürü (2003) *Mevcut Siyaset Anlayışını Değistirmek, Yasamımızı Etkileyen Kararlara Katılabilmek, Eşitlik ve Adaleti Sağlayabilmek için, Adaylarımızı Kendimiz Belirleyelim, Sorunlarımızın Çözümü için Çalışacak Kadınları Destekleyelim*, Ka-Der Subesi, Ankara.

Kadının Statüsü ve Sorunları Genel Müdürlüğü (1996) *Eylem Platformu ve Pekin Deklarasyonu*, Ankara.

Kadinin Insan Haklari Projesi-New Ways, Pekin Artı 5: Birlesmis Milletlerde Kadının İnsan Hakları ve Türkiyenin Taahhütleri, (2001), Istanbul.

Kahraman, Bülent (1 March 2004), 'Kadınları Öldürelim', *Radikal.*

KAMER'in Hikayesi (Story of KA-MER) (unpublished material)

Kandiyoti, Deniz (1997), *Cariyeler, Bacılar, Yurttaşlar*, Metis Yayınları, Istanbul.

Kandiyoti, Deniz (1998,) 'Modernin Cinsiyeti: Türk Modernleşmesi Araştırmalarında Eksik Boyutlar' in S. Bozdoğan ve R. Kasaba (eds.), *Türkiye'de Modernleşme ve Ulusal Kimlik*, Tarih Vakfı Yurt Yayinlari, Istanbul.

Karataş, K. (ed.) (1999), *Çağdaşlaşma Sürecinde Toplum Merkezlerinin Yeri ve İşlevleri*, Çağdaş Kadın ve Gençlik Vakfı, Ankara.

Kardam Filiz ve Yıldız Ecevit (2002), '1990larin sonunda bir kadın iletişim kuruluşu: Uçan Süpürge', in Bora and Günal (eds.), *90larda Türkiyede Feminizm*, İletişim Yayınları, Istanbul.

Korap, Elif (23 November 2003), 'Çıkınca büyükler bir iki tokat atar, bu konu kapanır', *Milliyet.*

Kümbetoğlu, Belkıs (2002), 'Kadınlara İlişkin Projeler', in Bora and Günal (eds.), *90larda Türkiyede Feminizm*, İletişim Yayınları, Istanbul.

Mies, Maria (1995), 'Feminist Araştırmalar için Bir Metodolojiye Doğru' in S. Çakır & N. Akgökçe (eds.) *Farklı Feminizmler Açısından Kadın Araştırmalarındaı Yöntem*, Sel Yayınları, Istanbul.

Mert, Nuray (15 February 2001), *Radikal.*

Milliyet (23 November 2003).

Ortaş, İbrahim (2004), 'Namus Cinayetleri ve Eğitim Sorunu: Cinsel Sağlık Eğitimi dersi üniversitelerimizde okutulmalı mı?', Çukurova Üniversitesi, Adana.

Özvarış, Ş. Bahar (2001), *Sağlık Eğitimi ve Sağlığı Geliştirme*, Hacettepe Halk Sağlığı Vakfı, Ankara.

Pelek, Semra (20 November 2003), 'Evlilikte Irza Geçmeyi Suç Sayamazsın', *Milliyet.*

Pusch, B. (2000), 'Kamusallığa Doğru: Türkiye'de İslamcı ve Sünni Muhafazakâr Kadın Sivil Toplum Kuruluşlarının Yükselişi' in *Türkiye'de Sivil Toplum ve Milliyetçilik*, İletişim Yayınları, Istanbul.

Radikal (1 March 2004), 'Güldünya göz göregöre soldu'.

*Radikal (*21 October 2004).

Sabah (12 July 2003).

Sevindi, Nevval (1998), 'Refahlı Kadınlar', in Zeynep Göğüş (ed.), *Kadınlar Olmadan Asla*, Sabah Kitapları, Istanbul.

Stanley, L., and Wise, S. (1995), 'Feminist Araştırma Sürecinde Metod, Metodoloji ve Epistemoloji' in S. Çakır & N. Akgökçe (eds.) *Farklı Feminizmler Açısından Kadın Araştırmalarındaı Yöntem*, Sel Yayınları, Istanbul.

T.C. Başbakanlık Kadının Statüsü ve Sorunları Genel Müdürlüğü, *Ulusal Eylem Planı*, August 1998, Ankara.

T.C. Basbakanlık Kadının Statüsü ve Sorunlari Genel Müdürlüğü (1997), *Birleşmiş Milletler Kadınlara Karşı Ayrımcılığın Önlenmesi Komitesine (CEDAW) Sunulan 2. ve 3. Birleştirilmiş Dönemsel Ülke Raporu,*, Takav Yayıncılık, Ankara.

T.C. Basbakanlik Aile Araştırma Kurumu (1990), *Türkiye Aile Yıllığı*, Ankara

Tekeli, Şirin. (1991), 'Tek Parti Döneminde Kadın Hareketi de Bastırıldı' in L. Cinemre ve R. Çakır (eds.), *Sol Kemalizme Bakıyor*, Metis Yayınları, Istanbul.

Tekeli, Şirin (1989), '1980lerde Kadın Hareketinin Tarihi', *Birikim*, Vol. 3, pp. 34-41.

Temelkuran, Ece (1 March 2004), 'Kadınları Baştan Öldürelim', *Milliyet.*

Timisi, Nilüfer ve Gevrek, Meltem Agduk (2002), '1980ler Türkiyesinde Feminist Hareket: Ankara Çevresi', in Aksu Bora and Asena Günal (eds.), *90larda Türkiyede Feminizm*, İletişim Yayınları, Istanbul.

TODAİE, (1998), *Yüzyılın Sonunda Kadınlar ve Gelecek (Conference Proceedings)*, Ankara, pp. 449-521.

Turan, Serafettin (1999), 'Etkin bir Egitim, Kultur ve Sosyal Dayanisma Kurumu Olarak Halkevleri', in . Rona (ed.), *Bilanço 1923-1998: Türkiye Cumhuriyetinin 75 Yılına Toplu Bakış*, Tarih Vakfı Yayınları, Istanbul.

Türk Resmi Gazetesi (20 April, 1990), No. 20498, pp. 2-3.

Türk Resmi Gazetesi (28 October, 1990), No. 20679, p. 2-3.

Türker, Yıldırım (1 March 2004), 'Kadınlık Sınavı', *Radikal.*

Uçan Süpürge, *Uçan Haber*, (Feb/March 2003), 'Törenin Kanatlarii Altında', No. 17, pp. 38-39, Ankara.

Yazıcıoğlu, Yıldız (21 April 2004), 'Güldünya Katliamında Kadın Tahriki Var', *Milliyet.*

Yerasimos, S. (2000), 'Sivil Toplum Avrupa ve Turkiye', in *Turkiye'de Sivil Toplum ve Milliyetcilik*, İletişim Yayınları, Istanbul.

Yıldırım, Aysel (1998), *Sıradan Şiddet*, Boyut Kitapları, Istanbul

Yücekök, A., Turan. I., and Alkan, M.O. (1988), *Tanzimattan Günümüze Istanbul'da Sivil Toplum Kuruluşları,* Türkiye Ekonomik ve Toplumsal Tarih Vakfı, Istanbul.

Index

Abadan-Unat, - 47
Acar, Feride 26, 59, 64, 65, 70-1, 72, 79
accountability 136, 138, 139, 143, 144, 146, 163, 167
Açıkgöz, Müseyyer 153-4
activism *see* grassroots activism
Acuner, Selma 47, 48, 49, 51, 78, 123
adultery 4, 67-8, 121-2, 131, 171n1
Afghanistan 114
African Charter on Human and People's Rights 9
agency 31, 32
AK Party *see* Justice and Development Party
AKDER *see* Association of Women's Rights against Discrimination
Alvarez, Sonia 17, 19-20, 21, 24, 36, 39, 43
Amnesty International 6n7, 129, 130, 131
An-Naim, Abdullah 33
ANAP *see* Motherland Party
Ankara University Women's Studies Center (KASAUM) 89, 128
Antalya Women's Council 146-7
Arat, Yesim 39-40
armed conflict 11, 110
Arnaz, Zuhal 90, 92
Ashworth, Georgina 138, 141
Association to Support Modern Life 47, 51, 76, 77, 147
Association of Women's Rights against Discrimination (AKDER) 74
Atatürk, Mustafa Kemal 26, 38-9, 46, 50, 74, 86, 88, 164
Ataüz, Akin 148
Australia 13, 24-5, 43, 70
Aykut, İmren 47, 48, 50-2, 54, 56-7, 164-5
Azerbaijan 13
AÇEV *see* Mother Child Education Foundation

Baden, Sally 15

Bahamas 13
Baktır, Gültekin 51
Bangladesh 25, 70
Barbados 13
Bardakoğlu, Ali 125, 131
de Beauvoir, Simone 44
behavioral approach 12-13
Beijing Conference (1995) 7, 14, 19, 21, 25, 56
  conservative opposition to gender equality 15
  empowerment 83, 89
  NGO influence 17-18
  training programs 89
Beijing Declaration 10, 56
Beijing Platform for Action (PfA) 10, 26, 33, 56, 79
  civil society organizations 141
  critical areas for action 11
  European Union 4
  violence against women 109, 110
Beijing Plus Five Conference (New York, 2000) 7, 71-2, 79, 110-11, 123, 131
Belize 13
Berktay, Fatmagül 34
Bolivia 13
Bora, Aksu 112
Bourdieu, Pierre 169
Bratton, Michael 118
Brazil 13, 43
bride price 169
British Council 149, 151
budgeting 142-3
Bunch, Charlotte 109
burqas 114
Bursa Women's Platform 147

Cairo Conference (1994) 15, 18, 19, 21, 108, 141
Canada 13, 24-5, 35, 43, 70
capacity-building 86, 148-9
capitalism 42, 46, 48, 49, 54
  globalization 139

Islamist groups 167
liberal 77
ÇATOMs (Multipurpose Community
  Centers) 63
CEDAW *see* Convention on the
  Elimination of Discrimination Against
  Women
chastity 2, 49, 122, 129, 133, 168, 170
Chen, Martha 16, 17
Chile 13, 36, 43
CHP *see* Republican People's Party
Çiçek, Cemil 49, 52, 57
Civil Code 38, 65-8, 71, 79, 80
  marriage 4, 27, 41, 66, 170
  violence against women 121-2, 127
civil rights 14, 21, 108
  men's control over 169
  neo-liberalism 35
  training programs 99
  women's exclusion from public sphere
  34
civil society 50, 51, 68-77, 108
  activism 102
  collaboration with government 56, 58,
  63, 150
  'good governance' 136, 138, 139, 140
  local governance 64, 140-1, 143, 145
  repression of organizations 161
  training 86, 87
  women's platforms 147
  see also women's organizations
cognitive approach 13-15
Cold War 21, 108
collective action 84, 86, 88, 93, 100-1,
  103, 152
collective identity 3, 28, 49, 54, 134
  Family Protection Law 121
  individual identity dualism 163, 164,
  168
  training programs and women's
  empowerment 91, 100, 103
  violence against women 117
Colombia 13
Commission on the Status of Women
  (CSW) 11, 16, 20, 109, 111
Committee on the Elimination of
  Discrimination Against Women
  reports to 12, 23, 26, 56, 59, 71, 163
  violence against women 65, 109, 110,
  120
  see also Convention on the

Elimination of Discrimination Against
  Women
community centers 63, 128
  government workers 161
  Women's Human Rights Education
  Program 100-1, 105, 150, 151-2, 155,
  157, 158-9
consensus 13, 14, 15
conservatism
  Islamist 77, 165
  legal reforms 66
  neo-liberal approach 35
  opposition to gender equality 15
  opposition to National Women's
  Machinery 47, 48, 49-50, 52, 54, 57
constructivism 2, 30-3, 163
Contemporary Women and Youth
  Foundation 89-93, 150
Convention Concerning Equal
  Remuneration of Men and Women
  Workers for Work of Equal Value 9
Convention on Consent to Marriage,
  Minimum Age for Marriage and
  Registration of Marriages 9
Convention on the Elimination of
  Discrimination Against Women
  (CEDAW) 1, 2, 4, 59, 79, 163
  definition of discrimination 10
  empowerment 101
  enforcement 23
  government obligations 12, 56
  liberalism 33, 34
  monitoring 11, 30
  National Women's Machinery 47, 48
  NGOs 70-1
  opposition to 36
  Optional Protocol 12, 27, 74
  ratification of 7, 9, 12, 22, 25
  reservations to 64-5, 66
  special measures 27, 67
  Turkey's ratification of 25-6, 64, 77
  US refusal to ratify 35
  violence against women 108-9, 111,
  119
  see also Committee on the Elimination
  of Discrimination Against Women
Convention on the Nationality of
  Married Women 9
Convention on the Prohibition of
  Discrimination in Employment and
  Occupation and Workers with Family

Responsibilities 9
Convention on the Rights of the Child 24
Convention for the Suppression of
    Traffic in Persons and the Exploitation
    of the Prostitution of Others 9
Cook, Rebecca 10, 19, 23
Coomaraswamy, Radhika 111
Copenhagen Conference (1980) 7, 19
Copenhagen Criteria 2, 4, 27, 67, 79,
    140, 167
Costa Rica 13
counseling centers 127, 128, 146, 149,
    157
crimes against humanity 11, 110
Criminal Code 27, 112, 120, 121, 124-5,
    134
CSW *see* Commission on the Status of
    Women
cultural rights 14, 21, 108
culture
    cultural values 2
    the family 66
    masculine privilege 36
    multiculturalist arguments 36-7
    norms 31
    Turkish 52
custom (tore) 119, 123, 125, 129, 133,
    147
    see also tradition

decentralization 140, 141, 142, 143, 144,
    160
Declaration on the Elimination of
    Violence against Women 18-19, 109,
    111
democracy 34, 37, 44
    Copenhagen Criteria 79, 140
    'good governance' 137, 140
    local 160
    secular 3
democratization 4, 14, 16, 21, 35, 108,
    143
development agencies 1, 11
development issues
    global gender equality regime 14, 15,
    18
    women in development approach 48,
    54, 83
    see also human development
DGWSP *see* Directorate General for
    Women's Status and Problems

dignity 21, 108, 109
Directorate General of Social Services
    and Child Protection (SHCEK)
    community centers 98, 157, 161
    shelters 63, 127-8, 149, 155
    WWHR partnership with 151-3, 158-
    60, 168
Directorate General for Women's Status
    and Problems (DGWSP) 4, 46, 52-3,
    56-62, 78, 89
    see also National Women's Machinery
discrimination
    cultural values 2
    definition of 10
    gender-sensitive budgeting 142
    'good governance' 138
    humanitarian principles 22-3
    international conventions 9
    National Development Plans 62
    positive 15, 27, 67, 80, 101
    private domain 34
    public campaign against 45, 64
    training programs 155
    Turkish legal reforms 26-7
    UN accomplishments 19
divorce 4, 13, 38, 41, 77, 100, 119, 127
donor funding 16, 19-21, 24, 63
    local governance programs 151, 160
    National Women's Machinery 58, 59-
    60, 61, 62, 78, 165
    neo-imperialism 36
    NGOs 72-3, 87
    WWHR/SHCEK partnership 159
dress 38, 39, 46, 73-4, 76, 77, 166
    see also hijab
DYP *see* True Path Party

Ecevit, Yıldız 44, 157-8
Economic Commission on Latin
    America and the Caribbean (ECLAC)
    20
economic issues 11, 15
    'good governance' 136, 137, 139
    liberalization 25, 43, 48, 49
    women in development approach 48,
    54
economic rights 14, 15, 21, 108
    men's control over 169
    social justice approach 35
    training programs 99, 153-4, 155
Ecuador 13

education 15, 27, 38, 165, 168
  Beijing Platform for Action 11
  empowerment 5, 90, 102
  gender/women's studies 59, 60
  human rights 4, 72, 167
  Islamist women's organizations 74, 75
  men 95, 105-6, 170
  Mother Child Education Foundation 93-5
  National Development Plans 62, 63
  NWM commission 59
  right to 18, 100
  secularist activism 76, 77
  sexuality 169, 170
  violence against women 113, 116, 127
  women in development approach 48
  Women's Human Rights Education Program 98-101
  see also literacy; training
employment *see* work
empowerment 1, 5, 14, 82-107, 150, 157
  Contemporary Women and Youth Foundation 89-93
  European Union 79, 80
  gender equality regime 10
  Ka-Mer Women's Center 82, 95-8
  Mother Child Education Foundation 93-5
  strategies of 85-6
  WWHR Women's Human Rights Education Program 98-101, 105
England 34
Enlightenment principles 33, 37, 38
environment 11, 18
equality 2, 4, 37-8
  government obligations 56
  International Labor Organization 32
  Kemalist state 38, 40
  liberalism 33, 34
  see also gender equality
equality of opportunity 34, 142
  EU laws 79
  positive discrimination 27, 67
Eraslan, Sibel 73, 74-5
Erbakan, - 52
Erdoğan, Emine 132, 167
Erdoğan, Tayyib 67-8, 145
Eroğlu, Nilgün 146
Ertürk, Yakin 43, 58, 110, 111, 133
Eskişehir Women's Platform 147
EU *see* European Union

European Commission 72, 79, 151, 160, 165, 167
European Convention for the Protection of Human Rights and Fundamental Freedoms 1, 9, 68
European Court of Human Rights 4, 74, 79, 166
European Union (EU)
  adultery 68, 122
  family protection legislation 121
  Turkey's accession to 4, 27, 79-80, 140, 165, 171
  women's commissions 20
  Women's Leadership project 149

family
  Commission on the Turkish Family Structure 52-3
  conservatives 49, 52, 54
  inferior role of women 103-4
  patriarchal norms 34, 41
  traditional values 40, 52
  women's empowerment 92, 94-5, 99-100, 104, 105, 170
  see also Family Protection Law; marriage
family planning 15, 59, 63
Family Protection Law 27, 65, 113, 121, 131
  EU accession 80
  implementation of 127, 128, 130
  lack of knowledge about 130
Family Research Organization 26, 53, 57, 78, 132, 167
femininity 134, 168
feminism 32, 38, 70, 165
  conservative critique of 49
  empowerment 85, 89
  Kemalist 39, 46, 54
  liberal 33-4, 44, 45, 48, 50, 54
  limitations of feminist organizations 104
  NGOs 15, 17, 20, 71
  power 83-4
  'project' 72
  radical 44, 45, 51, 54
  social construction of gender 31
  socialist 44, 45, 51, 54, 75, 113
  'state' 40, 46
  training 87, 88, 99
  Turkish women's movement 41-3, 45,

52, 53-4, 164
violence against women 65, 108, 113
Western 44, 54
women's networks 17, 18, 19
Filori, Jean-Christophe 68
Finnemore, Martha 14
Flying Broom (Uçan Süpürge) 70, 71, 125, 131
forced pregnancy 11, 110
Ford Foundation 20, 21
formal approach 9-12
Foucault, Michel 83-4
Foundation to Support Women's Economic Work (KEDV) 149, 153
Freire, Paulo 85

GAP Administration 63
Gaziantep Women's Platform 147
Gender Commission 62
gender equality 1, 2, 5
    community participation 143
    constitutional reforms 67-8
    constructivist perspective 33
    donor funding 20-1, 24, 165
    empowerment 83
    EU accession 79-80
    global regime 7-29
    global women's networks 16, 17, 18
    'good governance' 137, 138, 160
    Islamic discourse 33
    Kemalist state 38, 40, 41
    monitoring and compliance 30
    National Development Plans 62
    political instability 62
    state accountability 78
    strategic gender needs 84
    training programs 88
    Turkey's implementation of global norms 25-8
    UN role 16, 19
    Western/Islamist dichotomy 37
    women's platforms 147
gender identity 3, 5, 38, 165, 168, 170
gender justice 34, 35-6
gender mainstreaming
    government hostility towards 22
    government obligations 56, 79
    National Development Plans 63
    peace and security issues 11
gender studies 59, 60
genital mutilation 110

girl child 11
globalization 87, 138, 139, 165, 171
Goetz, Anne Marie 15, 24, 43, 58, 61
Göle, Nilüfer 37, 38
governance
    global 31
    'good' 136-40, 143, 160
    local 5, 6n7, 63-4, 136-62
    national 63
Grameen Bank 85
grassroots activism 141, 152-3
    empowerment 83, 85, 99, 101
    secularist women 76, 78, 166
    Welfare Party 75-6, 78
Greece 118, 168
'guesthouses' 63, 127-8
    see also shelters
Gül, Abdullah 4, 167
Gülçür, Leyla 116
Güner, Halime 125, 131
Gupta, Suranjana 141-2
Gürsoy, Elif 130

Habitat Conference (Istanbul, 1996) 140, 145-6
health 11, 18, 59, 63, 89
hijab 3, 46, 57, 73-4, 168
    see also dress
Hijab, Nadia 23-4
honor 3, 41, 49, 114, 116-18, 129-30, 132, 170
honor crimes 110-11, 123-4, 127, 129-30, 170
    denouncement by imams 125, 131, 166
    gender identity 168
    honor killings 27, 45, 117-18, 123, 125, 132, 134
    legal reform 4, 67, 119, 125
    psychological interpretation of 133
    public panel on 126
    women's platforms 147
    see also rape; violence against women
human development 35, 108, 136, 137
human rights 1-4, 14-15, 16, 21, 163-4, 171
    Beijing Platform for Action 11
    compartmentalization of 72, 108
    constructivist approach 32
    global women's networks 18
    'good governance' 137, 138, 140

honor killings 134
institutionalization of 56-81
Islamic discourse 33
liberalism 33-4, 35
training programs 90, 96, 98-101, 151-7, 158-60
universal values 167
Vienna Conference 18-19
violence against women 108, 109, 111
women's organizations 72
see also civil rights; cultural rights; economic rights; legal rights; political rights; social rights
Human Rights Committee 23
Human Rights Watch 131
humanitarianism 22-3, 137

ICC *see* International Criminal Court
identity
cultural 31, 170, 171
female 76, 134, 171
gender 3, 5, 38, 165, 168, 170
male 132, 168, 171
see also collective identity
identity politics 43
İlkkaracan, Pinar 71-2, 112, 116, 120-1
ILO *see* International Labor Organization
İmam Hatip schools 74
IMF *see* International Monetary Fund
İncioglu, Nihal 145
India 86, 141-2
individual freedoms 2, 33, 38
INSTRAW *see* International Research and Training Institute for the Advancement of Women
Inter-American Convention on the Prevention, Punishment, and Eradication of Violence against Women 1, 9-10
International Criminal Court (ICC) 11, 110
International Labor Organization (ILO) 9, 12, 32
international law 1, 7, 9, 11, 74
International Monetary Fund (IMF) 35
International Research and Training Institute for the Advancement of Women (INSTRAW) 20
Iran 36
Işik, Nazil 113

Islam 26, 33, 44, 171
conservatism 49, 77, 165
elites 36
Family Protection Law 121
honor crimes 111, 118, 166
Justice and Development Party 2, 4
Kemalist feminist opposition to 39, 54
political 39, 45-6, 54, 88, 139-40, 144
secularism dualism 163, 164, 166, 167
training programs 88
Welfare Party 75-6, 166
Western values conflict with 3, 37
women's organizations 46, 73-6, 78
see also Qur'an
Istanbul Conference (1996) 145-6
Istanbul University 51, 77

Japan 13
Jehan, Rounaq 25, 70
Joachim, Jutta 21, 108
Justice and Development Party (AK Party) 2, 27, 164, 167
adultery 67, 68, 122, 131
decentralization 144
Islamic values 3, 4
violence against women 125, 131

Ka-Der (Association for the Support and Training of Women Candidates) 70
Ka-Mer Women's Center 82, 95-8, 126
Kabeer, Naila 84, 85, 103
Kandiyoti, Deniz 165
Karaevli, Binnur 28
Kardam, Filiz 5, 44, 45, 82, 105
KASAUM *see* Ankara University Women's Studies Center
Keçeciler, Mehmet 52
Keck, Margaret 17-18, 19, 21, 109
KEDV *see* Foundation to Support Women's Economic Work
Kemalist state 38-40, 41, 86, 88
Keohane, Robert 9, 22
Khan, Irene 131
kindergartens 101, 146, 154, 156, 157
Krasner, Stephen 8, 23
Kratochwil, Frederick 13
Kümbetoğlu, Belkıs 58, 70
Kurdish nationalists 43

LACAP (Project for Leader Women) 104

Latin America 13, 17, 25, 36, 70, 157
leftist groups 41, 42, 50, 76, 87, 164
    see also socialist feminism
legal rights 14, 84, 88, 89, 90, 127, 164
legislation 4, 64-8
    Bill for Decentralization 144
    Civil Code 38, 65-8, 71, 79, 80
        marriage 4, 27, 41, 66, 170
        violence against women 121-2, 127
    Criminal Code 27, 112, 120, 121, 124-
    5, 134
    Family Protection Law 27, 65, 113,
    121, 131
    EU accession 80
        implementation of 127, 128, 130
        lack of knowledge about 130
    implementation problems 125-8, 165-
    6
    Penal Code 4, 27, 41, 64-5, 67, 119,
    122-5, 131
        violence against women 119-28
lesbians 15
Levinger, Beryl 157, 158
liberalism 32, 33-5, 48
literacy 6n7, 59, 63, 69
    female adult literacy rate 102
    legal 101
    training programs 88, 90, 93, 97
    women's platforms 147
Local Agenda 21 64, 127, 140-1, 145-8,
    150-1, 160, 161

McLeod, Jean 157, 158
mainstreaming *see* gender
    mainstreaming
Malaysia 13, 36, 121
Marmara University 77, 148
marriage 4, 13, 41, 82, 169
    forced 123, 124, 125, 131
    legal reforms 27, 65, 66, 170
    rape within 27, 67, 115, 119, 124, 125
    see also family
Marxism 87
masculinity 2, 114, 132-3, 168
media 11, 112-13
Mexico Conference (1975) 7, 15, 19, 56
Michel, A. 44
Migdal, Joel 41, 118
misogyny 133
Mitchell, J. 44
modernity 34, 37, 44, 46, 167

modernization 37, 38, 39-40, 41, 86, 87,
    164
monitoring 1-2, 11-12, 24
Mor Çati (Purple Roof) Women's
    Foundation 69, 126
Mother Child Education Foundation
    (AÇEV) 63, 93-5
Motherland Party (ANAP) 45-6, 47, 48-
    9, 61, 120, 165
multiculturalism 36-7
Murata, Sachiko 171
murder *see* honor crimes

Nairobi Conference (1985) 7, 14, 19, 51,
    109
Nairobi Forward Looking Strategies
    (1985) 10-11, 47, 48, 56
Namibia 13
National Development Plans 62-3
'national viewpoint' 49-51, 52, 53, 165
national women's machineries 7-8, 13,
    56
National Women's Machinery (NWM)
    4-5, 25, 26, 56-62, 63, 78
    establishment of 46-53, 54, 165
    legal reforms 67
    partnerships with women's
        organizations 161, 165
    training programs 89
    violence against women 113, 121,
        127, 128, 131
    'Women's Employment Project' 148
    see also Directorate General for
    Women's Status and Problems
nationalism 39, 43
Navaro-Yashin, Yael 76-7, 166
neo-liberalism 15, 30-1, 35, 36, 60
neo-utilitarianism 32
networks
    feminist empowerment programs 88,
    89
    global 7, 8, 14, 16-19, 21, 24, 137
    policy advocacy 5
New York Conference (2000) 7, 71-2,
    79, 110-11, 123, 131
New Zealand 25, 70
non-governmental organizations (NGOs)
    1, 69-73
    capacity-building 149
    collaboration with government 60,
    150, 157, 158, 168

competition between 104-5
criticism of women's organizations 96, 155-6
education programs 4
feminist 15, 17, 20
gender equality norms 16
global governance 136
legal reforms 66, 67
local governance 142, 143, 153
National Women's Machinery 59, 61, 63, 78
policy advocacy 17-18
professionalization of 87
representatives 5
rural development projects 86
threat to powerful interests 143-4
training programs 82, 89, 90, 101, 104, 148
UN consultation with 7, 21, 108
violence against women 120, 123, 131
see also civil society; women's organizations
norms
construction of 30-1, 138
contestation of 46, 58, 138
ethnic groups 166
fragmentation of 165
global 1-3, 7, 16, 25, 28, 33, 36, 148, 163
'good governance' 138
local participation 160
regimes 8, 9, 10-11, 12
role of international organizations 20
sexuality 169
socially constructed 2, 103
state compliance 22, 23
Turkey 2, 28, 30-55
violence against women 108-11, 113-19, 129-30
Western 36, 37
see also values
NWM *see* National Women's Machinery

Oakley, A. 44
OAS *see* Organization of American States
Okin, Moller 36
ÖNDER (alumni of İmam Hatip schools) 74
Organization of American States (OAS) 20, 25, 70

Ortas, İbrahim 169-70
Ottoman Empire 3, 37, 68
Oxfam 148
Özal, Turgut 42, 48, 49, 54, 166

Parents Mutual Help and Support Organization 73
participatory learning 89, 90, 91, 103
patriarchy 34, 41, 54
Penal Code 4, 27, 41, 64-5, 67, 119, 122-5, 131
Peru 36
Pervizat, Leyla 118, 132, 134
PfA *see* Beijing Platform for Action
Philippines 13
Poland 36
policy advocacy 4, 5, 16-19, 20
National Women's Machinery 58, 61
training programs 101, 102, 152, 153
Turkish women's groups 44, 54, 58, 69, 78-9, 80, 165
violence against women 119-21, 129
political issues 24-5, 43
gender equality 15, 62
lack of female representation 160
local governance 63-4, 136-62
National Women's Machinery 47-53
obstacles to implementation of gender equality 2
participation of women 44, 89, 99
shelters 149, 150
social constructivism 32
political rights 14, 21, 108, 160
Kemalist values 88
men's control over 169
neo-liberalism 35
women's exclusion from public sphere 34
polygamy 13, 38, 41, 77, 118, 169
population control 14, 18
positive discrimination 15, 27, 67, 80, 101
poverty 11, 95, 104
neo-liberalism 36
Turkish reforms 27, 48
power 83-5
power relations 10, 31, 33, 66-7, 84, 134
principles 8, 9, 10, 12
Progressive Women's Association 42
Project for Leader Women (LACAP) 104

prostitution 11, 12, 27, 110
'provocation' 4, 117, 119, 123-4, 169
Prügl, Elizabeth 31
public/private distinction 33-4, 40, 42-3,
    163, 167, 168
  constructivist perspective 32
  training programs 91-2, 103, 104
  violence against women 14, 108
Purple Roof (Mor Çati) Women's
    Foundation 69, 126

Qur'an 33, 45, 49, 118, 133

rape 4, 18-19, 45, 109, 110, 127
  Amnesty International report 6n7
  honor killings 117-18
  marital 27, 67, 115, 119, 124, 125
  police training 13
  Rome Statute 11
  systematic 14, 110
  Turkish legal reform 27, 64-5, 67, 112,
    125, 131
  virginity of victim 117, 124
  see also violence against women
Razavi, Shahra 16
realism 32
refugees 22
regimes 7-8
  behavioral approach 12-13
  cognitive approach 13-15
  constructivist approach 30
  definition of 8
  formal approach 9-12
  maintenance of 22-5
Reilly, Niamph 109
relatedness 3, 28, 167
religion 2, 15, 166
  discourse in Islamic societies 33
  the family 66
  masculine privilege 36
  radical groups 43
  see also Islam; secularism
reproductive rights 15, 18, 88, 89, 99
Republican People's Party (CHP) 27, 38,
    68, 160
reputational effects 22, 25
Research Association of Women's
    Social Life 115
Revolutionary Women's Organization 42
Rio Conference (1992) 18, 21, 64, 108,
    140, 145

Rome Statute 11, 110
Rosenau, James 31
Rowlands, Jo 82-3, 84
Ruggie, John 13, 30-2
rule of law 79, 136, 137, 138, 140
rules 8, 9, 10, 31, 32

el Saadawi, Nawal 44
Saktanber, Ayse 165
Samsun Women's Council 147
Sarışen, Gülay 154-6
Sassen, Saskia 74
Sawer, Marilyn 24-5, 43, 70
Saygın, Işilay 120, 121, 122
Schipper, Mineke 170
secularism 2, 3, 26, 74, 77-8, 140
  activist women 76-7, 166
  decentralization 144
  discourse in Islamic societies 33
  feminism 54
  Islam dualism 163, 164, 166, 167
  Kemalist state 38, 46
  training programs 88
  Westernization 38, 53
  see also religion
Segal, L. 44
self-confidence 92-3, 94, 99
Self-Education Process (SSP) 86
Self-Employed Women's Association
    (SEWA) 85
Sevindi, Nevval 75, 76
SEWA *see* Self-Employed Women's
    Association
sexual assault 110, 116, 125, 169
  see also rape
sexual harassment 27, 45, 46, 67, 110,
    119
  Declaration on the Elimination of
    Violence against Women 18, 109
  on the streets 112, 133, 164
  workplace 125, 127
sexual rights 15
sexual slavery 11, 18-19, 109, 110
sexuality 2, 41, 49, 114, 117, 132-3, 168-
    70
Sharia 38
SHCEK *see* Directorate General of
    Social Services and Child Protection
shelters 63-4, 69, 126-8, 130, 146, 149-
    50, 155, 157
Sikkink, Kathryn 17-18, 19, 21, 109

Sirman, Nükhet 44
social constructivism 32
social harmony 3, 28
social justice 25, 34, 35, 60
social movements 35
social rights 14, 21, 108
  men's control over 169
  social justice approach 35
social workers 98, 101, 105, 153, 157, 158-9
socialism 42, 87, 113
socialist feminism 44, 45, 51, 54, 75, 113
South Africa 141
Soviet Union, former 36, 136
Spain 118, 168
Special Rapporteur on Violence against Women 19, 109, 111
SSP *see* Self-Education Process
state behavior 12-13
state intervention 35, 36, 50
State Planing Organization 54, 56, 57, 63, 142-3, 150
state sovereignty 23, 137
strategic gender needs 84, 85, 88, 104
structure 31, 32

Tanzania 25, 70
'Tanzimat Reforms' 37
Tatlises, Ibrahim 168
Tekeli, Şirin 40, 43
Temelkuran, Ece 105-6
Third World 38-9, 85, 118, 136
Tinker, Irene 18
Tomasevski, Katerina 23
tradition 2, 31
  the family 66
  masculine privilege 36
  violence against women 119, 170
  see also custom
training
  Beijing Platform for Action 11
  capacity-building 86, 148
  CEDAW 71
  Contemporary Women and Youth Foundation 89-93
  empowerment 82, 85, 86, 87-8, 89-106, 150
  gender sensitivity 59, 60, 88, 148
  Ka-Mer Women's Center 82, 95-8
  Kemalism 86-7
  Mother Child Education Foundation 93-5
  National Women's Machinery 59, 60, 63
  police 13, 59, 128, 132, 156
  WWHR Women's Human Rights Education Program 98-101, 105, 151-7, 158-60
  see also education
Tripp, Aili Mari 31, 66-7, 167, 170-1
True Path Party (DYP) 120, 160
Tüksal, Hidayet 168
Tunisia 13
Türker, Yıldırım 119, 133, 134
Turkey
  construction and contestation of gender norms 30-55
  dualisms 37, 163-4, 167-8
  empowerment 86-106
  gender equality/human rights norms 2-5, 25-8, 163, 165, 171
  'good governance' 139-40
  government initiatives 13
  institutionalization of women's human rights 56-81
  Kemalist state 38-40, 41
  local governance 141-61
  NGOs 144
  secularism/Islam debate 164-5, 166-7
  sexuality 168-70
  violence against women 110, 111-34, 170
  women's activism 40-6
Turkish University Women's Union 147
Turkish Women Lawyers' Association 51, 69
Turkish Women's Federation 38
Turkish Women's Union 51, 68

Uçan Süpürge (Flying Broom) 70, 71, 125, 131
Uganda 31, 36, 43
UNDAW *see* United Nations Division for the Advancement of Women
UNDP *see* United Nations Development Programme
UNICEF *see* United Nations Children's Fund
UNIFEM *see* United Nations Development Fund for Women
United Nations (UN) 16, 19-21, 23, 25, 70

Charter of the 20
Commission on the Status of Women
    11, 16, 20, 109, 111
conferences 7, 18, 19, 108
Decade for Women 13, 108
Declaration on the Elimination of
    Violence against Women 18-19, 109,
    111
Economic Commission on Latin
    America and the Caribbean 20
liberalism 35
lobbying 119
non-interference 137
peace and security 11, 110
Special Rapporteur on Violence
    against Women 19, 109, 111
Subcommission on the Prevention of
    Discrimination and Protection of
    Minorities 11-12
United Nations Children's Fund
    (UNICEF) 24, 102
United Nations Conference on
    Environment and Development (Rio,
    1992) 18, 21, 64, 108, 140, 145
United Nations Conference on
    Population and Development (Cairo,
    1994) 15, 18, 19, 21, 108, 141
United Nations Development Fund for
    Women (UNIFEM) 19-20, 73
United Nations Development
    Programme (UNDP) 1, 20, 128, 165
    local governance 64, 137, 141, 151,
    160
    National Women's Machinery 59-60
United Nations Division for the
    Advancement of Women (UNDAW)
    6n2, 11, 20
United States 13, 35
universal rights 2, 14, 33, 36, 38
urbanization 48-9, 145
utilitarianism 32

values 2, 14-15
    family 52
    Islamic 3, 32, 37, 164, 167
    religious elites 43
    secularism 38, 164
    traditional 40
    universal 167
    Western 3, 32, 52, 53
    see also norms

Vienna Conference (1993) 14, 18-19, 21,
    25, 108, 109
violence against women 4, 5, 13, 108-35,
    170
    Amnesty International report 6n7
    Beijing Platform for Action 11
    definition of 10, 109-10
    Family Protection Law 65, 113
    Ford Foundation funding 20
    global norms 108-11
    global women's networks 14, 16
    Inter-American Convention 1, 9-10
    Ka-Mer Women's Center 95, 96, 97
    National Development Plans 63
    policy reform 27, 119-28
    public agenda 111-13
    public/private distinction 32
    social norms supporting 113-19, 129-
    30
    strategic gender needs 84, 88
    training programs 89, 99, 155, 156
    Turkish public campaigns against 45,
    64, 69, 112-13, 119, 131-2, 164, 166
    Vienna Conference 18-19, 109
    see also honor crimes; rape; shelters
virginity tests 27, 67, 122-3, 125, 131,
    170

WALD *see* World Academy of Local
    Governance and Democracy
war crimes 11, 110
WEDO *see* Women's Environment and
    Development Organization
Weiss, Thomas 136, 137
Welfare Party (Refah Partisi) 3, 75-6, 78,
    120, 121, 126, 166
Westernization 37, 38, 39, 53, 87, 164,
    166
Whitworth, Sandra 32
women in development (WID) approach
    48, 54, 83
Women for Women's Human Rights-
    New Ways (WWHR) 63, 66, 70, 71-2
    partnership with SHCEK 98, 151-3,
    158-60, 168
    training and empowerment 98-101,
    151-7
    violence against women 120-1
Women's Environment and
    Development Organization (WEDO)
    18

Women's Human Rights Education
  Program 98-101, 105, 151-7, 158-60
Women's International Democratic
  Federation 16
women's organizations 40-6, 53-4, 68-
  77, 78-9, 164
  Islamist 46, 73-6
  legal reforms 64, 65, 66, 67, 80
  local governance 146-7, 150, 151,
  153-7, 160, 161
  National Women's Machinery 50, 51-
  2, 53, 54, 58-9, 61, 165
  training programs and empowerment
  83, 86-101, 102-5
  violence against women 120-1, 123,
  126-8, 129, 131
  see also civil society; non-
  governmental organizations
Women's Solidarity Foundation 63-4,
  69, 120, 126, 128, 149, 150
women's studies 59, 60
work 9, 13, 40, 48
  husband's permission 41, 65, 121

National Development Plans 62, 63
NWM commission 59
right to 100
'Women's Employment in Turkey'
  project 60
World Academy of Local Governance
  and Democracy (WALD) 146, 148
World Bank 15, 20, 35, 60, 73, 137, 148
World Conference on Human Rights
  (Vienna, 1993) 14, 18-19, 21, 25, 108,
  109
WWHR *see* Women for Women's
  Human Rights-New Ways

Yıldırım, Aysel 116
Yılmaz, Seda 94
Yirmibeşoğlu, - 129
Young, Oran 17, 23

Zacher, Mark 12
Zambia 13
Zimbabwe 13

For Product Safety Concerns and Information please contact our EU
representative GPSR@taylorandfrancis.com
Taylor & Francis Verlag GmbH, Kaufingerstraße 24, 80331 München, Germany